IMPLEMENTING ORGANIZATIONAL CHANGE

THEORY INTO PRACTICE

Bert Spector

Northeastern University

Prentice Hall

Pearson Education International

Acquisitions Editor: Jennifer M. Collins
Editorial Director: Sally Yagan
Product Development Manager: Ashley Santora
Editorial Assistant: Elizabeth Davis
Editorial Project Manager: Claudia Fernandes
Marketing Manager: Nikki Jones
Marketing Assistant: Ian Gold
Permissions Project Manager: Charles Morris
Senior Managing Editor: Judy Leale
Production Project Manager: Renata Butera
Senior Operations Specialist: Arnold Vila
Operations Specialist: Renata Butera

Creative Director: Jayne Conte
Cover Designer: Lisbeth Axell
Cover Illustration/Photo: Getty Images, Inc.
Author photo: Craig Bailey/NU Photography
Composition: GGS Higher Education
Resources, A Division of Premedia Global, Inc.
Full-Service Project Management:
Yasmeen Neelofar
Printer/Binder: Bind-Rite, Robbinsville/
Command Web
Typeface: 10/12 Times Roman

Credits and acknowledgments borrowed from other sources and reproduced, with permission, in this textbook appear on appropriate pages.

Pearson Education Ltd., London
Pearson Education Singapore, Pte. Ltd
Pearson Education, Canada, Inc.
Pearson Education–Japan
Pearson Education Australia PTY, Limited

Pearson Education North Asia, Ltd., Hong Kong
Pearson Educación de Mexico, S.A. de C.V.
Pearson Education Malaysia, Pte. Ltd
Pearson Education Upper Saddle River, New Jersey

Prentice Hall
is an imprint of

10 9 8 7 6 5 4 3 2

ISBN-13: 978-0-13-701306-7
ISBN-10:   0-13-701306-X

CONTENTS

PREFACE

Organizational change comes in an almost endless variety of types and approaches. Just consider these examples:

- To open new growth and revenue opportunities for the Internet-based social network company, Facebook, the CEO announces a new business model.
- To respond to shifting demands of multinational customers, the CEO of IBM attempts to achieve seamless global responsiveness in an organization long noted for its highly decentralized multinational operations.
- To respond to competition from national chains and Internet sellers, the president of the small, independent Concord Bookshop seeks greater fiscal discipline in his operation.
- To encourage ongoing innovation, the cofounders of Internet search engine Google move to create greater tolerance for mistakes.
- To respond to sluggish performance, the newly hired "superstar CEO" attempts to infuse Hewlett-Packard with enthusiasm, innovation, and discipline.
- To respond to declining performance and intensifying competition, the CEO of General Motors announces the cutting of dividends, a reduction in white-collar benefits and executive pay, the intention to sell its highly profitable General Motors Acceptance Corporation, and the elimination of 30,000 jobs.
- To improve the efficiency of software development, a small company adopts Agile, a new approach based on multiple releases in short time frames.

From multinational colossuses to small businesses, employees at all levels seek to respond to the competitive dynamics that impact their organization's performance.

Volatile swings in national and international economies, new competitive environments, shifting customer expectations, increasing pressure from financial markets, emerging governmental regulation and deregulation, not to mention dramatic and unexpected geopolitical dynamics all demand responsiveness from today's organizations. Renewed strategies, designed to achieve and maintain a strong competitive position demand that organizations abandon the status quo. Instead of being an occasional event, organizational change is now a way of life.

Implementing organizational change has, as a result, emerged as a core competency for corporate executives. In fact, any leader today will discover just how vital leading change is. If you're not leading change, as the saying goes, you're not leading.

Knowing that change is vital, however, and successfully navigating an organization through a change effort are quite different matters. Despite good intentions, enthusiastic support, and the availability of resources, change efforts often fall short of the expectations and promises of their champions. Frequently, the flaw can be found in the misconceptulization of the implementation process. How change is conceived and how it is implemented—that is where the barriers usually reside.

THEORETICAL ORIENTATION

The purpose of *Implementing Organizational Change—Theory into Practice* is to understand and analyze effective change implementation. In order to achieve that objective, *Implementing Organizational Change* focuses on change that can be understood as *strategically aligned alterations in patterns of employee behavior*. While recognizing the multiplicity of change efforts that span the corporate landscape, the two core concepts of that definition allow us to pay special attention to change that is strategic and behavioral. That definition shapes the core perspectives of the book, which examines change that is *strategic*, *purposeful*, and *behavioral*. Let's look briefly at each one:

1. *Strategic*—the goal of change management is to help an organization support strategic renewal in order to achieve and maintain outstanding performance in the face of a dynamic environment. A *strategic* perspective focuses on aligning behaviors with renewed strategy and the requirements of outstanding performance.
2. *Purposeful*—change can occur *to* an organization or *by* an organization, most often some combination of the two. A *purposeful* perspective focuses on explicit interventions into the organization that are designed to respond to a dynamic competitive environment.
3. *Behavioral*—although change can occur in many forms, it is the alteration in employee behaviors—how employees enact their roles, responsibilities, and relationships—that allows organizations to implement their new strategies and achieve outstanding performance. A *behavioral* perspective focuses on the process of motivating employees at all levels of the organization to alter their patterns of behavior in ways that are sustainable, adaptive to shifts in the external environment, and will contribute to outstanding performance.

Wanting to achieve strategic behavioral change is relatively easy—implementing change is difficult. For that reason, the thread of *effective implementation* runs through the entire text. This is a book not just about *what* to change, but also *how* to change.

Implementing Organizational Change is informed primarily by the research and practice offered by the field of Organizational Development (OD). Leading writers have combined rigorous social science research with action learning to create an awareness of organizations as systems, suggesting that change efforts must be aware of the need to achieve and sustain a state of "fit" between various organization divisions and components. In terms of change processes, OD suggests that when individuals are involved in defining problems and solutions, they will be more motivated to achieve the desired outcomes.

Although richly informed by that field, *Implementing Organizational Change* is not intended to be an OD text. Instead, the book offers a view that integrates key OD insights with major perspectives from three additional fields:

1. *Strategic renewal*—This field recognizes that highly dynamic environments require more than occasional incremental improvements in the firm's operations; new strategic directions and approaches require new ways of thinking and acting.
2. *Strategic human resource management*—This field recognizes the requirement to align human capabilities with an organization's strategy for achieving and maintaining outstanding performance.

Organizational development (OD)	Views organizations as open systems; sees alignment and responsiveness as necessary components of outstanding performance; emphasizes potential for collaborative effort, individual contribution, and growth.
Strategic renewal	Dynamic competitive environments often require new directions supported by new systems, structures, and processes.
Strategic human resource management (SHRM)	Emphasizes the requirement to align human resource policies and practices—both individually and systemically—with the strategic goals of the organization and the requirements of outstanding performance.
Leadership	Focuses on the behavior of leaders at all levels of the organization who mobilize adaptive behavior among employees and orchestrate effective change interventions.
Others	Organizational learning, managerial accounting, conflict management, ethics, communications, information systems, supply chain management, and organizational innovation.

EXHIBIT P-1   Academic Underpinnings of *Implementing Organizational Change—Theory into Practice.*

3. *Leadership*—This field recognizes the role of leaders at all levels of the organization working both individually and collaboratively to mobilize adaptive behavior on the part of employees in order to drive change.

Those contributions, summarized in Exhibit P-1, will be supplemented by additional insights from fields such as organizational learning, managerial accounting, conflict management, ethics, communications, information systems, supply chain management, and organizational innovation.

BOOK ORGANIZATION

In order to present theories and practice of change, *Implementing Organizational Change* is divided into three sections:

- *Section 1*—"Theories of Effective Change Implementation" (Chapters 1, 2) analyzes the forces leading to strategic renewal and organizational change, as well as the theories that form the basis for effective implementation. The section concludes with a theory of effective change implementation that combines the insights of previous works.
- *Section 2*—"Implementing Change" (Chapters 3–6) guides the reader through the theory and practice of specific methods and approaches to implementing organizational change.
- *Section 3*—"A Broader View" (Chapters 7, 8) steps back from the specifics of change implementation to examine two larger organizational elements—culture and leadership—that exert a profound impact on attempts to implement change.

TEXT FEATURES

Because *Implementing Organizational Change* is intended for both practitioners and students of change management, the text includes a multiplicity of learning features.

- All chapters open with a bulleted list of key learning objectives. In addition, "Theory into Practice" highlights the applied, practical applications of the theories being presented.
- A short opening case study illustrates the core concepts and challenges analyzed in the chapter. These real-world examples of change implementation are referred to throughout the chapter to emphasize learning points.
- Key vocabulary items are highlighted in the text in order to help the reader develop a vocabulary of change.
- Each chapter includes a conclusion summarizing key points of the chapter and introduces key theme of the following chapter.
- Discussion questions guide readers back through key points of the chapter.
- Finally, a longer concluding case (written by the author exclusively for the text) can be used to apply and debate key points of each chapter.

The goal of each chapter is to integrate the various learning features with a presentation and analysis of influential and important theories, as well as examples of organizational change efforts. Organizations ranging from large multinationals such as IBM, General Electric, SAP, and British Petroleum to smaller domestic companies such as Grand Union, the Concord Bookshop, and even nontraditional organizations such as the Rolling Stones, will help the reader apply change theories to real-world experiences.

ACKNOWLEDGMENTS

This second edition stands on the content of the first edition. For that reason, I thank all those who contributed so much insight to the original writing. The students, professors, and managers who responded to the first edition and offered both encouragement and suggestions for this revision are also warmly acknowledged. Most especially, I would like to thank:

- Northeastern University's MBA, Executive MBA, and Hi Tech MBA students.
- INSEAD executive participants in the Achieving Outstanding Performance program.
- Participants in the FBI Emerging Executive Program.

I continue to be influenced by terrific professionals at Northeastern, INSEAD, and beyond. For this second edition, I am pleased to acknowledge Harry Lane, Nicholas Athanassiou, and Dennis Shaughnessy at Northeastern, Deigan Morris, Ludo Van der Heyden, and José Santos at INSEAD, Bernard Burnes at the University of Manchester Business School, and Albert Mills at the Sobey School of Business, Saint Mary's University.

Both my original editor, David Parker, and my current editor, Jennifer Collins, have been indispensable. Renata Butera guided the manuscript and, more importantly, the author through the production maze.

As always, my most important thanks go to my family: Kayte Elizabeth Kelleher Spector, Tess Aileen Kelleher Spector, and Maureen Kelleher, to whom the book is gratefully dedicated.

CHAPTER 1

Organizational Change

When executives and students of management talk about organizational change, they mean many different things. Introducing a new enterprise resource planning system in order to coordinate and standardize internal processes is an organizational change. So is shutting down a factory, selling off a noncore business, or laying off employees. How about introducing a new business model to meet innovative competitors, adopting a new pay-for-performance system to motivate individual effort or a stock option plan to encourage a shared sense of ownership in the company? Entering global markets, integrating acquired companies, and outsourcing nonstrategic activities—these, too, are examples of organizational change.

In order to understand and analyze the dynamics of change, and particularly the requirements of effective change implementation, it is important to sort out and distinguish the various approaches an organization can take. This chapter will explore multiple paths to change, paying special attention to behavioral change. In particular, this chapter will:

- Identify the role of strategic renewal in propelling change
- Focus on the behavioral aspect of organizational change
- Analyze the dynamics of motivating employees to alter their behaviors
- Differentiate the three faces of change
- Understand the source of both employee resistance to and support for change

We will start by looking at an attempt by the president of a small but prestigious local bookstore to improve financial performance in the face of competition from national chains as well as from Internet giant Amazon.

TALES OF WOE AT CONCORD BOOKSHOP*

It's like a family quarrel that nobody wants and nobody knows how to stop.

---

*David Mehegan, "Tales of Woe at Concord Bookshop," *Boston Globe*, December 23, 2003, p. E1. Copyright © 2003 Bell & Howell Information and Learning Company. All rights reserved.

The Concord Bookshop, a 64-year-old independent store regarded as one of the best in New England, is beset by a bitter clash between owners and staff. The conflict puts pressure on the store at a time when independent booksellers are reeling from competition from chains and the Internet.**

Eight of Concord Bookshop's employees, including the trio of top managers, have quit or given their notice. The staffers' years of service add up to 73. The three managers, including [the] general manager . . . have worked at the store for a total of 34 years. Meanwhile, a group of outraged local authors . . . has fired off a letter to the owners supporting the staff.

The precipitating event was a surprise announcement last month by the owners— a group of three families represented by a board led by President Morgan "Kim" Smith of Concord—that a new general manager will be hired. No one was laid off, and no one's salary was cut. Yet many of the staff were outraged at the de facto demotions, as well as by what they saw as the owners' immovable stance . . .

"We asked for a meeting with the whole board," says [a departing staff member]. "We presented our concerns, and they thanked us for our input and said, 'We're going to do it our way, and if you don't like it, each of you will have to make up your mind as to how to proceed.' Something in me died, the fragile alchemy that made it such a great place to work had died. They had made their plans, we were expendable employees, and we could take it or leave it.". . .

"We're heartbroken about it," says David Donald, professor of history emeritus at Harvard University . . . "These are people we deal with all the time. It's a wonderful store, beautifully arranged. They are knowledgeable and are glad to look things up." Adds Joanne Arnaud, director of the Boston Literacy Fund and a Concord resident who also signed the letter: "What makes the Concord Bookshop different is the people and their institutional memory and their memory for a customer. I can say, 'I'm looking for a book for someone who liked the last book by Nicholas Basbanes. Can you help me?' They are so warm and welcoming."

The clash appears to be rooted in finances. Smith declined to give numbers but portrayed the store's financial situation as dire.

"Things have never been worse," he says. "We are offering something important to the town of Concord, which is wonderful, but it isn't profitable." Smith praises the three managers but says, "The owners felt the three-way management was not working out."

The managers say finances aren't so bad. They . . . issued a written comment: "In explaining to us the change in management structure, the owners told us they wanted to take the store in a different direction. We hold different opinions regarding the financial health of the store. We are very proud of what we have been able to accomplish these past five years."

There's no disagreement, though, that profit margins are tighter than ever, and that the past few years have been rough on independent bookstores, especially in the age of Barnes & Noble, Borders, and Amazon.com. Smith believes some of the store's

---

**Concord, a prosperous suburb of Boston, Massachusetts, is the site of the opening battle of the American Revolutionary War. Its rich literary history dates back to the nineteenth century when it was the home of the transcendental writers, notably, Ralph Waldo Emerson and Henry David Thoreau.

programs should be reexamined, such as regular weeknight author appearances and signings, which require paying staff to keep the store open.

"Increasingly, people are buying their books elsewhere and bringing them to signings," Smith says. "We had 70 people at the Tracy Kidder signing, but we sold only 10 books. I discovered a guy coming in with five copies of the book that he bought [elsewhere]. We want to preserve the store, but we need to make the finances work."

There's no dispute, either, on Concord's national reputation in the trade. "It is one of the jewels of New England," says . . . [the] executive director of the New England Booksellers Association. . . "They are the kind of store that's on everyone's A list. Publishers are interested in what Concord buys. They ask, 'How is Concord doing with the book?' They are exemplars for reaching out to the community and in cultivating authors". . .

The conflict illustrates the special place a bookstore can have in a small community, especially one such as Concord, with its numerous authors and links to such literary giants as Emerson and Thoreau. The store is regarded as a community resource, not just a business.

"This is Concord vs. Concord," says Martha Holland, who is quitting after 18 years. "There were a hundred points where it could have been smoothed over. How it got so out of hand, I don't understand. The owners have every right to run their business as they see fit. But if the staff goes, it's just a bunch of bookshelves and carpets."

STRATEGIC RESPONSIVENESS

Morgan Smith's attempt to bring financial discipline to the Concord Bookshop seemed quite sensible in the face of new competitive realities. Owners, employees, customers, and suppliers all agreed on the desirability of maintaining the store's viability. Yet Smith's approach to **change implementation**—the actions taken by organizational leaders in order to support strategic renewal and achieve outstanding performance—led to resistance, conflict, and resentment. Recognizing the need for change is a vital first step. Successful implementation, however, is required to translate that recognition into an effective strategic response.

We live in a period of rapid and dramatic change: significant alterations in customer expectations and demands, new technologies, competitors with innovative business models, shifts in workforce demographics and values, new societal demands and constraints. Organizations need to respond to external dynamics in order to create and maintain outstanding performance.

Building a Vocabulary of Change
Change implementation actions taken by organizational leaders in order to support strategic renewal and maintain outstanding performance in a dynamic environment.

Theory into Practice

Strategic responsiveness to a dynamic external environment demands organizational change.

In response to those dynamics, organizational leaders often decide to engage in a process of strategic renewal. **Strategic renewal** refers to an alteration of an organization's strategy with the intent of regaining sustainable competitive advantage.[1]

Company	Altered Strategy
Enron	Move from energy production to energy trading
GE	Move from commodity business to high value-added products and services
IBM	Move from product to service/consulting company
Marks and Spencer	Move from a department store appealing to traditional, conservative adult British shoppers to a store appealing to young, trendy shoppers
Renault	Move from French-based to internationally focused automobile company
Walgreens	Move from store-based chain in order to capture growing Internet business
Facebook	Move from restricted, college campus-only social network to become a "universal utility" open to everyone

EXHIBIT 1-1   Strategic Responsiveness in Sample Companies.

Exhibit 1-1 provides examples of organizations whose leaders made a purposeful decision to renew their strategies. Some attempts have been more effective than others. Strategic renewal at IBM and Walgreens proved successful, while efforts to transform Enron's strategy collapsed in failure. At different points in the text, we will explore and analyze the efforts of these companies to implement new strategies effectively.

> **Building a Vocabulary of Change**
> *Strategic renewal* a change in an organization's strategy through a process of creating new products, services, capabilities, and knowledge bases.

Strategic renewal requires organizational change (see Exhibit 1-2). Strategic renewal demands "wide-scale invention, reinvention, and redesign of business processes and organizational structures."[2] IBM pulled off strategic renewal as it moved from a product to a service/consulting company. Harley-Davidson managed a different but equally significant strategic renewal by redefining its relationship with its customers.

EXHIBIT 1-2   Strategic Renewal and Organizational Change.

Theory into Practice

To implement a renewed strategy, organizational leaders need to engage in a change process.

For strategic renewal to be effective, organizations need to do more than announce a new strategy. Leaders need to align internal processes, structures, and systems with the demands of that new strategy. New **organizational capabilities**— talents and skills possessed by employees—need to be built. Underlying all those shifts is the requirement to engage in discontinuous change: large-scale, long-term reorientation of most or all of the central aspects of organizational life. The goal is to create lasting alterations in patterns of employee behavior in order to support strategic renewal.

Building a Vocabulary of Change
Organizational capabilities the collective talents and skills of a firm's employees.

Strategic Renewal through a New Business Model

Apple Computer seemed well positioned to achieve a breakthrough into the corporate/business market. With the extraordinary popularity of its iPod and iPhone offerings, young customers were flocking to Apple products as never before. But successful penetration into the business market would require more than loyal customers and brand familiarity. Apple's business mode would need to change. The company's long-standing highly secretive culture (Steve Jobs enjoyed launching new products with high security prior to his grand announcements) would need to change. In the corporate world, customers expect to be treated as long-term partners, actually having a say in the development of new products.[3]

In order to extend its popularity among young, tech-savvy consumers into the corporate marketplace, Apple would need to alter its business model. **Business model** innovation has become an increasingly common avenue for corporate growth. At its most basic level, a business model is the organization's approach to generating revenue and making a profit. More specifically, business models involve the configuration of and the nature of the linkage between operations.[4]

Building a Vocabulary of Change
Business model the way in which an organization generates profitable revenues.

Start-up companies often gain a competitive advantage over long-standing market leaders by offering novel business models. Consider the following examples:

- Starbucks offered high-priced coffee specialty drinks in a relaxed environment.
- Amazon sold books online.
- Southwest Airlines provided an air service that competed with bus service and driving.
- Dell built computers to customer specifications.
- Zara placed low-cost high-fashion items on shelves with incredible speed.
- YouTube revolutionized the creation and distribution of video.
- Facebook integrated web-based interconnectivity with traditional school-based yearbooks.

All of those companies had the advantage of building the innovative business model from scratch, "greenfield" as it is often called. They could harmonize their internal processes and employee competencies and behaviors with the requirements of their model. They did not face the challenge of nurturing a new business model within an existing, long-standing approach to generating revenue.

Theory into Practice

It is possible to gain competitive advantage through the creation of a new business model, but changing your existing business model will create special change challenges.

Altering an existing business model, especially one that has been successful in the past, has proved much more challenging than a greenfield effort.[5] Some organizations have been successful:

- Under Louis Gerstner, IBM transformed its business model for generating profits from the sales of hardware to generating profits from services and software.
- Lufthansa's Jergen Weber moved the company from a centralized collection of functional stovepipes to a number of free-standing service offerings, including cargo handling, on-plane catering, and service maintenance.
- Carlos Ghosn changed the failing business model of Nissan by simultaneously centralizing product design and globalizing the company's supply chain.

Not all attempts to alter a company's business model lead to success, of course. Michael Armstrong's effort to move AT&T from a long-distance phone company to a full-service provider of a wide array of offerings—cable, long-distance, local, wireless, etc. —proved disastrous.[6] Most notoriously of all, Jeffrey Skilling's alteration of Enron's business model—from energy provider to energy futures trader—disintegrated over the company's inability to build sustainable profitability (and its leaders' willingness to hide that fact from the public, investors, and employees).[7]

Corporate leaders believe that business model innovation will be *the* major source of growth over the next decade.[8] To achieve that desired growth, however, they will need to become effective change leaders. Because business model innovation alters the nature of linkages among employees, it disrupts existing patterns of behavior while demanding new competencies and skills. The failure of a company to engage in organizational change undermines a company's capacity to innovate in their business model.[9] All business model innovation—that is, moving from the status quo to a new model—requires organizational change.

Theory into Practice

Adaptation of a new business model within a corporation will require organizational change.

Building a Vocabulary of Change

Behavioral change alterations in employee behavior in order to enable the organization to meet the demands of its strategy while achieving and sustaining outstanding performance.

BEHAVIORAL CHANGE

Effective strategic renewal requires **behavioral change** that directly targets patterns of employee actions and interactions in order to meet the company's strategy and to achieve and sustain outstanding performance.

Theory into Practice

If change interventions are to achieve significant and sustainable impact on performance, they must focus on altering patterns of employee behavior.

Building a Vocabulary of Change
Behavior the enactment of roles, responsibilities, and relationships by employees within an organization.

Effective implementation depends on an alteration in patterns of employee behavior. **Behavior** refers to the actions employees take to enact their roles and responsibilities within the organization. Behaviors involve what employees do and how they do it, how much effort they bring to their roles, and how persistent they are in achieving desired outcomes. Behavior also involves the enactment of relationships: how employees interact with others (peers, subordinates, superiors, customers, suppliers, the host community, and so forth). It is this enactment of roles, responsibilities, and relationships that constitutes employee behavior in organizations. The collective enactment of those roles, responsibilities, and relationships—that is, the *patterns* of employee behavior within organizations—constitutes the target of behavioral change efforts.

Behavioral change seeks more than a short-term alteration. New behaviors that are adopted for a short period of time and then dropped as employees return to old approaches will undermine strategic renewal. In order to support strategic renewal and outstanding performance, new behaviors need to be *sustainable* and *adaptive* to shifts in the external environment.

The reason sustainability of new behaviors matters can be stated simply: the ways in which employees behave significantly impact the organization's performance. Beyond products and market position, beyond plants and technology, employee behaviors affect the bottom-line performance of the organization.[10]

Theory into Practice

Organizational change seeks to create long-term, sustainable alterations in employee behaviors.

Just how does that happen? How is it that patterns of employee behavior impact a company's bottom-line performance? The key to understanding the relationship of behaviors to performance can be found in the idea of motivation.

Motivation, in this case, refers to the degree to which employees are committed to the achievement of outstanding performance both for themselves and for their company. Employee motivation pays off in bottom-line performance. High motivation creates in employees the capability and willingness to work together to solve problems. Quality improves, customer responsiveness increases, and adaptation occurs.

Chapter 4 will examine in detail efforts to redesign organizations to capture the benefits of enhanced employee involvement and commitment. For now, we can suggest that behaviors count. The competitive advantage delivered by behavioral change can be long term and sustainable. The manner in which work is organized, information is shared, decisions are made, coordination occurs, and problems are solved are all performance differentiators.[11] Furthermore, that performance edge is sustainable for decades, leading to significant and often staggering competitive advantage.[12]

Theory into Practice

The way employees behave impacts the bottom-line performance of the company.

Sources of Behavior

Effective change implementation needs to start with an appreciation of the source of an individual's behavior. What is it that leads an individual to behave in a certain way? Individual psychology is important, of course: who the individual is, what values he or she brings to the workplace, even how that individual thinks and learns. But individual psychology can be difficult to assess and slow to change. A leader seeking leverage over employee behavior can start by focusing not on individual psychology but on the organizational context in which employees work.

Theory into Practice

Behavior comes from both the individual and the organizational context in which the individual works.

Building a Vocabulary of Change
Organizational context the setting and circumstances in which employees work.

Organizational context—the setting and circumstances in which employees work—exerts a powerful impact on behavior. Companies as diverse as Google, Nordstrom, MySpace, and Southwest Airlines endeavor to promote an organizational context that shapes individual behavior. They call upon organizational culture and values, the behaviors of leaders, as well as rules and procedures to define a context that shapes how employees enact their roles, responsibilities, and relationships.

To appreciate the power of organizational context to shape behaviors, we can examine a specific example of an employee mistake. Sheryl Sandberg, an advertising manager at Google, made a mistake that cost the company millions of dollars. "Bad decision," she admitted, "moved too quickly, no controls in place, wasted some money."[13] Sandberg quickly informed Google cofounder Larry Page.

Employees make mistakes, even occasionally big ones such as Sandberg's. Leaders have an important opportunity to shape organizational context by the manner in which they respond to those errors. Quick and harsh repercussions—firing, for example, or demotion—will have one kind of impact on the organizational context in which employees work. That response may be justified and reasonable, but it may also work to stifle future risk-taking behaviors. Or perhaps employees will be less willing to admit mistakes, slowing down an organization's response time.

The boss may also respond in a less harsh and punishing manner. Listen to the reaction of Google cofounder Larry Page, to Sandberg's admission:

> I'm so glad you made this mistake, because I want to run a company where we are moving too quickly and doing too much, not being too cautious and doing too little. If we don't have any of these mistakes, we're not taking enough risk.

The point is not that Page's response is the only "correct" or reasonable response to the admission of a mistake. Leaders have to determine what type of organizational context they seek to create. That context will need to be aligned with the company's strategy and purpose.

Page and Google cofounder Sergey Brin believe that mistakes can provide fuel for improvements, even innovation. "We're willing to tolerate ambiguity and chaos," says senior vice president Shona Brown, "because that's where the room is for innovation." Google's leaders want a context that tolerates risk in order to generate innovation.

EMPLOYEE PARTICIPATION AND RESISTANCE TO CHANGE

Not all employees greet change with equal enthusiasm. It is useful, therefore, to examine the sources of employee **resistance** to change and the ways in which managers can overcome resistance. Resistance refers to action, overt or covert, exerted on behalf of maintaining the status quo.[14]

Why Employees Resist Change

You're either for this change or you're against it. That refrain may be familiar; it is not, however, accurate. Employee response to change runs across a broad spectrum, ranging from "commitment" at one end to "aggressive resistance" on the other (see Exhibit 1-3).[15] Each of these reactions to change helps shape the behavior of individuals and, ultimately, the success of a change effort.

Theory into Practice

Employees do not naturally resist change, but they often resist change because of the way change is implemented.

Theory into Practice

Try to understand the reasons behind employee resistance to change.

Most attention on employee resistance has focused on why individuals resist change; which is to say, why employees fail to "get on board." There are a number of underlying causes for individual resistance:[16]

- Individuals may be *satisfied with the status quo*. Because their needs are being met, they may view any potential change as negative.
- Individuals may view change as a *threat*, fearing it will adversely affect them in some significant way.
- Individuals may understand that change brings both benefits and costs, but feel that the *costs far outweigh the benefits*.

Commitment	Involves a strong emotional attachment to the goals of the organization and the aims of the change effort
Involvement	Involves a willingness to participate in the behaviors being called for by the change effort
Support	Involves speaking on behalf of the change effort without taking any other explicit actions to promote the effort
Apathy	Represents a neutral zone in which individuals know about the change effort and engage in no behavior either to support or oppose it
Passive resistance	A mild form of opposition that involves a willingness to voice reservation or even threatening to resign if the change goes through
Active resistance	Involves behaviors that block or impede change, usually by behaving in ways that contradict the goals of the change effort
Aggressive resistance	Involves purposeful sabotage and subversion of the change effort

EXHIBIT 1-3   Continuum of Individual Response to Change.
Based on Leon Coetsee, "From Resistance to Commitment"; *Public Affairs Quaterly* (Summer 1999), pp. 204–222.

- Individuals may view change as potentially positive, but may still resist because they believe that the organization's management is *mishandling the change process.*
- Individuals may believe in the change effort, but still believe that the change is *not likely to succeed.*

Managers can see employee resistance in negative terms: It is a "bad thing" that represents an irrational response to a dynamic competitive environment. In this way, employee resistance can be dismissed as invalid or disobedient.[17] Resistance to change, in this view, is a force to be overcome.

There is another way of thinking about resistance to change, however; one that may actually improve the effectiveness of implementation.

Theory into Practice

Employee resistance is not just a negative force to be overcome; it also presents an opportunity to learn.

How Managers Can Inadvertently Fuel Resistance During Implementation

It is tempting to believe that a certain type of individual is likely to resist change. Perhaps you've heard, or even thought, ideas such as: *Older workers are more likely to resist change than are younger workers. Middle managers are more likely to resist change than lower-level workers or upper-level executives. Men are more likely to resist change than women.* And so on.

Don't take these explanations at face value. Study after study of employee resistance to change in organizations refutes these and other individualistic contentions. Individual differences may account for *some* variance in employee acceptance of or resistance to change. But the overwhelming determinant of employee reaction to change comes from how the process is managed and the degree to which employees are allowed to participate in the process.[18]

Managers can inadvertently *create* resistance by the manner in which they pursue change. Here's a checklist of employee resistance and possible sources of that resistance:

- *Employees resist because they remain satisfied with the status quo.* Perhaps management has not included employees in the diagnosis and learning process.
- *Employees resist because they view change as a threat.* Perhaps management has not offered employees the opportunity to acquire the new skills that will be required in the renewed organization.
- *Employees resist because they see the cost of change outweighing the benefits.* Perhaps management has not articulated the goals of the change adequately to allow a true assessment of the costs and benefits.
- *Employees resist because they believe that management is mishandling the process.* Perhaps employees have not been given a voice in the process itself.
- *Employees resist because they believe that the change effort is not likely to succeed.* Perhaps management needs to articulate why this change process is more likely to be effective than past efforts.

By looking at the aforementioned reasons for employee resistance, we can see how many can be understood in part as a natural and expected outcome of implementation.

Theory into Practice

Participation in the change process is the best way to build support and overcome resistance to change; but remember—it's no guarantee.

In treating employee resistance as a negative force to be overcome, managers shut down the possibility that they can learn from resistance. When employee voice has been excluded from the change process, there is likely to be valuable data missing from the diagnostic and action planning phases of the effort. Employees may ask whether management really understands what customers expect from their products or services or what barriers the organization has erected to outstanding performance.

Even when employees question whether management has selected an appropriate strategic response, it is useful, perhaps even indispensable, for managers to learn about employee hesitations and concerns. Instead of treating resistance as a force to be overcome, managers may decide to treat resistance as an opportunity to learn from employees and improve the change process.

Not all resistance to change offers an equal opportunity to learn, of course. Some resistance will have to be addressed and overcome. We will explore specific techniques and approaches management can consider to avoid creating resistance. For now, let us understand employee resistance as a form of expression that is not always a bad thing and that needs to be considered and understood by change leaders.

Employee Participation Builds Support for Change

Building a Vocabulary of Change
Participation the process of allowing employees a voice in work-related decisions.

Just as there are ways in which a change implementation process may inadvertently fuel resistance to change, there are also techniques for purposefully building support for change. **Participation** in the process of defining problems and designing solutions will help build commitment to the new directions that result from that process.[19] By diagnosing problems, understanding their importance, and being part of the process of formulating solutions, people develop a psychological sense of "ownership" over the outcome. That ownership now creates in employees the heightened motivation to implement change in order to achieve desired goals.[20]

Change imposed from "above"—top executives telling employees that they must alter their behaviors in order to implement a new strategy or perform better under the old strategy—is likely to engender resistance. The employees resisting change at the Concord Bookshop complained that the board had dismissed employee suggestions to respond to the crisis by saying, "We're going to do it our way." Their felt loss of voice in the strategic response of the bookstore to new competitive realities contributed to high levels of resistance.

People don't resist change, the saying goes, they resist *being* changed.

The difficult challenge for managers, then, becomes how and when to engage employees in the process of diagnosis, problem solving, and planning for change. General Motors (GM) can offer some historical perspective on both approaches; change that is imposed from above, and change in which employees participate in designing the solution.

In the 1970s, soaring fuel prices and gas shortages made the U.S. consumer much more aware of the fuel *in*efficiencies of domestic automobiles. At the same time, Japanese car manufacturers such as Toyota, Honda, and Nissan captured significant market share by offering small, reliable, and fuel-efficient alternatives. GM, with its fleet of gas-guzzlers built for an era of expanding interstate highways and cheap gas, was especially vulnerable.

When Roger Smith became chairman of GM in 1980, the company was hemorrhaging money and market share. Layoffs, factory closures, and the shedding of non-auto-related businesses followed. Smith had more in mind than trimming costs, however. To lead strategic renewal, he called on a massive multibillion-dollar investment in state-of-the-art robotics and assembly technology. Out of that effort came the Chevrolet Vega, a small, fuel-efficient model produced at the company's newly retooled Lordstown, Ohio, plant.

The Vega represented GM's intent to face down the rising tide of imports. State-of-the-art robotics and automation would help GM keep the costs of producing the Vega low. Employees at the Lordstown plant, however, resisted the changes that had been imposed on them from above. In particular, they objected to the depersonalization and sped-up pace of new robotic technology. Resistance went far beyond complaining. Some employees engaged in sabotage, open rebellion, and a wildcat (unauthorized) strike. Six years after its appearance, GM discontinued the model that had once held such high hopes for meeting Japanese competition.[21]

Theory into Practice

A participative process can help build support for change efforts.

Compare that resistance to a different initiative just a few years later at GM's Cadillac plant in Livonia. Cadillac and Vega were worlds apart in terms of intended market niche. Nevertheless, GM executives hoped Livonia would help address some of the same pressures for strategic renewal: the need to produce a world-class car that would help the company regain slumping market share. As they had done at Lordstown, executives sought improved quality and increased efficiency at Livonia. Now, however, the company approached change quite differently. Management worked closely with labor through the United Auto Workers union. Instead of imposing new technology and work processes on the plant, management and the union involved hourly workers in a planning committee that would redesign the way the plant operated.

Theory into Practice

In a unionized environment, creating employee participation involves inviting the union itself into the decision-making process.

The joint worker-management planning committee created employee teams organized around a product line or function and given responsibility beyond production, including responsibility for quality control and material handling. Other design changes proposed by the planning committee—the removal of multilevel job classifications in order to improve flexibility and efficiency in the deployment of workers, extensive front-end training for all employees to gain teamwork and problem-solving skills—turned the plant into what some in the company called "a Lordstown that worked."[22] Twenty-five years later, Livonia continued to operate as a high-quality producer of Cadillac's highly regarded Northstar engine.

Imposed change encourages resistance. Individuals can feel manipulated, coerced, or even ignored. When people participate in designing change, on the other hand, they are more likely to feel they are making an informed choice about altering their behaviors. Individuals can develop commitment to the choice as well as feeling responsibility for implementing that choice. When people participate in the design of change (in the diagnosis, action planning, and implementation stages), they will be more motivated to alter their behaviors.

And, to emphasize a point made earlier, employee motivation matters. New behaviors will not be sustainable if they have been prompted by manipulation or coercion. Effective change does not seek to fool employees into setting aside their better judgment. Rather, it seeks to encourage employees to find continually new and improved ways of applying their better judgment. How can internal processes be improved? What are customers telling employees about our products and services? How might we eliminate waste and improve quality? To support behaviors that can sustain outstanding performance, effective change efforts avoid manipulation and coercion, aiming instead to enhance employee willingness and ability to contribute their own judgment.

Theory into Practice

Behavioral change seeks to motivate employees to change their behaviors; not to force, coerce, or trick them into changing.

Because motivation is internal to each employee, the change leader's challenge is complex. The task involves shaping the organizational context in such a way as to encourage and support an internal desire on a large number of employees to alter their behaviors in ways consistent with the shifting demands of the new strategy.

How that is done will be the subject of the remainder of this book. When change leaders are successful, the organizational context unleashes "people's innate curiosity and desire to experiment," says Peter Senge, which creates a powerful "engine for improvement."[23] Motivation works to build initiative and a desire on the part of the employees themselves to innovate and alter behaviors in order to achieve outstanding performance.

THE THREE FACES OF CHANGE

Not all change efforts take aim directly at behaviors. Let's return to GM. In February 2006, with the U.S. automobile industry in a state of drastic decline, America's leading auto manufacturer made some tough decisions: cutting dividends, reducing white-collar benefits, and slashing executive pay. On top of 30,000 job cuts announced the previous year, company losses totalling $10.6 billion, and share prices hitting their lowest point since the middle of the Great Depression of the 1930s, GM's CEO (chief executive officer) Rick Wagoner declined to predict when the company would return to profitability, saying only it would be "as soon as possible."[24]

In 2008, after announcing a huge loss, the company dove even deeper into turnaround, offering a "special attrition program"—an offer to buy-out contracts in order to encourage retirement—for all 74,000 of its domestic hourly workers.[25]

Theory into Practice

Not all change is behavioral.

Building a Vocabulary of Change
Turnaround an attempt to improve the immediate financial position of an organization by focusing on the income statement and the balance sheet.

GM's approach to change can be characterized as **turnaround**. Rather than focusing on new behaviors, turnaround looks at a company's assets and seeks to manage them in a new way in order to stabilize cash flow, shore up the balance sheet, and maximize shareholder wealth. GM's turnaround may have been unusual in its scope. The activities of the turnaround effort—reducing capacity, shutting down facilities, reducing levels of pay, health insurance, and pension benefits—are typical.

Is turnaround by itself enough? "Cutting costs is not a business plan," observed Gary Chaison. Turnaround does not by itself create sustained outstanding performance.

The impact of layoff announcements on the psychological state of employees—on their sense of security and belief in the future—accounts for part of the difficulty of translating downsizing into sustained outstanding performance. Employees who become insecure because of workforce reductions are less productive and less committed to the organization.[26]

Given the short-term severance and outplacement costs of workforce reductions, the savings in compensation to the organization and subsequent impact on the bottom line are often overstated. Firms that engage in downsizing cannot count on those efforts finding their way to the bottom line.[27] Downsizing provided no "quick fix" for sagging performance.

Theory into Practice

Turnaround may be necessary, but it is not sufficient to ensure long-term effective change.

That is not to say that organizations can or should ignore the goals of turnaround. As Morgan Smith and the employees of the Concord Bookshop learned, all companies, large and small, need to keep a sharp focus on matters such as profits, earnings, and return on investment. Failure to do so can quickly lead to the loss of investor confidence and increased difficulty raising needed capital. Poor financial performance can quickly erode employees' sense of efficacy and worth, thereby undermining motivation.

"Businesses have always tried to reduce costs," Carlos Ghosn, CEO of Renault and Nissan who began his own transformational efforts with serious cost cutting measures, explained. "I don't see how one can manage a business without keeping one eye glued to expenses. It's a fantasy to think otherwise . . . There have been very few

Building a Vocabulary of Change
Techniques and tools organizational processes, mechanics, and other interactions intended to produce a product or service.

Building a Vocabulary of Change
Outsourcing a deliberate decision to farm out certain value chain activities to external specialists and/or strategic allies.

successful extravagant captains of industry."[28] Turnaround efforts that initiate strategic renewal ensure that financial discipline will accompany behavioral change.

Another nonbehavioral face of change focuses on **techniques and tools**.[29] Some technique and tool changes occur in a virtual behavioral vacuum, requiring no significant alteration in patterns of behavior. In 2007, for instance, Netflix adopted a "new" technique for improving customer service. The company substituted a two-hundred-person customer service call center for its e-mail based response system.[30] True, two-hundred telephone service represents were added to the payroll. True, also, the change was viewed as a strategic response intended to differentiate Netflix from rival Blockbuster. Nonetheless, behavioral patterns among its existing employees were not altered.

One of the most common tools used to help achieve strategic renewal in recent years is **outsourcing**. Outsourcing involves the farming out of certain value chain activities—anything ranging from help desk support to logistics and manufacturing—to external vendors.[31]

IBM CEO Samuel J. Palmisano has incorporated outsourcing into the company's strategic reinvention. By moving low-value and routine technology jobs to overseas companies, IBM can focus its core activities on "the higher-value portions of our industry."[32]

Labor costs account for upwards of 80 percent of the total costs of technology service contracts, and salaries for computer programmers in India run about one-third of those in the United States. By carefully distinguishing between those routine, rules-based tasks that can be outsourced to overseas providers (India-based companies Infosys, Wipro, and Tata Consultancy are among the fastest growing independent providers), IBM can reduce labor costs by laying off U.S.-based workers. With lower-cost workers dispersed around the globe and linked by high-speed communications, IBM project managers can "search worldwide for the right people with the right skills for a job."[33]

Theory into Practice

Outsourcing is a change technique with important turnaround and transformational behavior change implications.

Companies find the technique of outsourcing to be of strategic importance for three main reasons:

1. Outsourcing saves money by transfering jobs to lower-paid workers.
2. Outsourcing enables companies to concentrate on core competencies.
3. Outsourcing offers a hedge against shifting technologies and customer preferences by lowering fixed costs and building flexibility.

Outsourcing is a technique with important turnaround (i.e., cost-savings) implications.

Although outsourcing can be used as a change tool to enhance organizational performance, its effectiveness can, and often is, undermined, by the manner in which that tool is applied. Not all activities should be outsourced, observes

Jérôme Barthélemy, and poor application can lead to increased rather than reduced costs.

In particular, effective deployment of outsourcing requires attention to the behavioral impact, particularly on employees who remain with the company. "Outsourcing has a negative impact on employees' sense of job security and loyalty," Barthélemy writes. A firm may attempt to retain key employees as a way of preserving their firm-specific knowledge. If the commitment of those employees wanes due to the outsourcing, performance will suffer. Additionally, the retained employees will now be expected to shift their task focus from service delivery to interface and coordination between vendors and users. The firm is likely to need an investment in training and ongoing support to help coordinate that required interface.[34]

Outsourcing is one of many change techniques and tools that require attention to simultaneous behavioral change in order to reap the hoped-for organizational benefits. Dorothy Rice, the vice-president for finance at Ultra Electronics Maritime Systems, found that many of her interventions—the introduction of an enterprise resource system for the firm's Canadian arm, a new "lean office" initiative that created processes for simplifying operations, and the introduction of a Balanced Scorecard—all required behavioral realignment on the part of employees.[35] The act of aligning the behaviors of employees with company strategy and customer expectation—this is the change that allowed the various techniques and tools to make a difference.

Theory into Practice

Outsourcing can be a helpful change tool, but be careful! If not applied carefully, it can undermine motivation and distrupt important linkages and relationships.

Attending to techniques and tools without paying at least equal attention to the behavior of employees—as demonstrated by GM's Lordstown experience—can be a path not just to disappointment but also to dysfunction. When employees participate in the design and implementation of new technology, as occurred at Livonia, they are more likely to alter their behaviors in ways that will help ensure effectiveness.

Theory into Practice

Effective strategic renewal efforts combine aspects of turnaround, tools and techniques, and transformational behavioral change.

We have identified three faces of change: turnaround aimed at financial improvement, tools and techniques aimed at improving internal organizational processes, and transformation of employee behaviors (summarized in Exhibit 1-4). All three offer options available to leaders in search of strategic renewal. Although leaders may opt to approach each of these "faces" as separate and independent options, effective change efforts combine the three.

Type	Target	Rationale
Turnaround	Internal resources	Improve short-term bottom-line performance
Tools and techniques	Processes	Increase internal efficiencies
Transformation	Behaviors	Enhance human capabilities

EXHIBIT 1-4   Three Faces of Change.

TRIGGER EVENTS AND CHANGE

Organizational change is typically initiated in response to a **trigger event**—a shift in the environment that precipitates a need for altered strategies and new patterns of employee behavior. For the Concord Bookshop, the increasing penetration of online booksellers into the store's market space triggered the requirement for strategic renewal. For Facebook, the more freewheeling approach to open networking employed by successful rival MySpace demanded a strategic response.

Trigger events, says Lynn Isabella, "are so named because their magnitude and potential for organizational as well as personal impact set into motion a series of mental shifts as individuals strive to understand and redefine a situation. By their very nature, they unbalance established routines and evoke conscious thought on the part of organizational members. They stir up feelings and emotions that come to affect people's reactions to the change. In short, trigger events bring people's mindsets into the arena of change."[36]

Theory into Practice

Trigger events, either external or internal to an organization, precipitate the need to alter behavioral patterns of employees.

Trigger events can be external, such as the one faced by the Concord Bookshop. Trigger events may also come from inside the organization, most typically with the infusion of new leadership at the top of the organization. When Jack Welch was promoted to CEO of General Electric (GE) in 1981, the company was enjoying decades of prosperity and success. Yet he set about, virtually from the outset, in a quest for transformational change.

To propel that change, Welch eliminated strategic business units and instead refocused resources on a small number of strategic circles (manufacturing, technology-intensive businesses, and services). He demanded that internal businesses become number one or two in their respective industries or disengage. He altered the company's budgeting process from an internal to an external focus.

Those changes, significant as they were, represented only the initial stages in a two-decade-plus transformation effort. The external environment—a deep national recession—that greeted Welch on his accession to CEO undoubtedly added force to his message that GE needed to change. Nonetheless, the transformation at GE grew largely from Welch's own views of the need for strategic renewal.

Conclusion

Strategic responsiveness to a dynamic environment requires organizational change. Change, however, is not a singular concept. The three faces of change suggest that change leaders face options. Turnaround addresses the need to improve the balance sheet and technology focuses on improved processes. By itself, however, neither will achieve the full, intended impact of strategic renewal. Effective change will also require attention to employee behaviors—patterns of action and interaction—no less than financial and technological effectiveness.

Not all employees will greet change efforts with equal enthusiasm. Employee resistance arises from a number of sources, some internal to individual employees and others externally located in the implementation processes of change leaders. By allowing employees to participate in the formulation of change plans, however, leaders will increase employee ownership over and support for those efforts.

Trigger events—either discontinuities in a firm's competitive environment, new leadership, or a combination of the two—precipitate the requirement for strategic renewal and organizational change. Recognizing the requirement for change and being able to manage change effectively are, of course, two different matters. Chapter 2 will examine the theoretical underpinnings of effective change implementation.

Discussion Questions

1. Review Exhibit 1-1. Select one of the companies. Based on the brief statement of its renewed strategy (or research the company for further details), think about how patterns of employee behavior will have to change.
2. Explore the challenges that faced Morgan Smith at the Concord Bookshop. What explanations can you offer for the high level of employee resistance that emerged from the changes?
3. What are the three approaches to organizational change? In what ways are they different and in what ways do they overlap?

4. Identify the main external forces triggering the requirement for organizational change. Pick three and discuss how they might necessitate behavioral change on the part of organizational employees.
5. Why is motivation important to behavioral change? How might leaders approach change differently if they are trying to motivate employees to change rather than forcing employees to change?

Case Discussion

Read "Two Stories of Outsourcing" and prepare answers to the following questions:

1. What is the nature of the changes sought by Auratek and K-PUB? Are they turnaround, tools and techniques, transformation, or some combination?

2. How do you account for the apparent differences in effectiveness in the use of outsourcing by these two companies?

Two Stories of Outsourcing

Two engineers, John Hearst from Auratek and Caroline Matthews of K-PUB, met at a professional conference and exchanged stories about their companies experiences with outsourcing.

John Hearst's Story

The Auratek Corporation of Burlington, Massachusetts manufactured an industry-leading data storage device, DataSafe. At the heart of the system were field-programmable gate arrays (FPGAs), the microchips that ran the DataSafe's director boards. From Auratek's perspective, the main drawback to the product was the cost to fabricate the many FPGA revisions necessary for a reliable, finished product.

To help control costs, Auratek's vice president of hardware engineering announced the creation of the Verification Group (VG). VG amounted to a step inserted between design and fabrication (manufacturing) of the FPGA. The 33 engineers hired for VG worked closely with the engineers responsible for designing the FPGAs. Their main responsibility was to identify flaws in the chip design *prior* to fabrication. The cost of the 33 engineers was approximately $3.3 million per year, and the benefits to Auratek were greatly improved quality and a decrease in the development and fabrication process (plus decreases in after-sales support).

The two groups of engineers—from both the design and verification groups—created a close and interactive relationship. They developed shared pride, mutual trust, and a willingness to pull together for long days and nights when delivery schedules required. Even as DataSafe shifted from FPGA to application-specific integrated circuits (ASICs), the transition went smoothly and efficiently.

Under further pressure to cut costs, Auratek's CEO made a public commitment to shareholders. The company would double the amount of engineering work to be outsourced. The vice president of hardware engineering, looking at the $3.3 million annual budget allotted to VG, decided that the company had the opportunity to cut costs with little risk to the overall process. VG in Burlington would be reduced from 33 to 6 engineers, and the main verification work would now be subcontracted to the Veritas Group, a large (the second largest in the world), independent R&D (research and development) services provider located in Bangalore, India.

The cost savings to be achieved by the move would be significant: approximately $2 million annually due to the reduced cost of engineering personnel in India. The vice president believed that the verification work itself was relatively routine and well within the capacity of the Bangalore-based engineers employed by Veritas. The verification engineers in Burlington would act as liaisons between the design engineers and the engineers performing verification work in India.

The project experienced problems from the outset. Misunderstandings resulted from e-mail communication between Bangalore and Burlington, and the 12-hour delay due to the time zone difference led to confusion. The Veritas engineers hesitated in raising concerns about design in order to avoid offending their American managers. Root-cause analysis of design defects all but disappeared.

Morale among the six remaining VG engineers deteriorated. Few had skills as coordinators and liaisons or an interest in changing their job responsibilities so dramatically. A number of them treated to resign. Auratek offered stock options and retention bonuses to motivate them to stay. Even so, four resigned. The remaining two verification engineers found themselves under increasing pressure to pick up the work load, not just that of the Burlington-based group, but also of the Veritas engineers in whom Auratek no longer had trust.

The results proved disastrous. Delayed product releases and lengthened time to fix defects led to a deterioration of the company's previously dominant market position in storage devices.

"Maybe we saved $2 million in salaries," concluded Hearst. "I wonder what we've lost in present and future sales."

Caroline Matthews' Story

K-PUB is an electronic publishing company located in suburban Portland, Oregon. In pursuit of the company mission, "Spread Knowledge," K-PUB targets Information Technology professionals with both printed and online material. The company barely survived the burst in the high technology market, and has since grown rapidly. Much of that growth has come from partnering with traditional publishers to put their material on the Internet.

Part of the value chain involved in placing traditional material on the Internet included the "translation" of the material from desktop publishing formats (DTP) into an XML (extensible markup language) format that could easily carry technical content. At first, that translation work was done internally, using company-developed software tools and staff. The process of translating from DTP to XML is similar to translating from one language to another. Even with the technical nature of the material (perhaps because of the technical nature), translation was often subjective, prone to misunderstanding and error. Therefore, the process required a fair amount of quality assurance checking on the final output to ensure acceptable translation.

K-PUB worked continually to improve the translation process. In particular, the company sought to enhance software conversion tools and automate more and more of the process. More recently, an initiative was launched to leverage newer software tools and rewrite the conversion tools from the ground up. Even with those efforts, the cost to K-PUB of translating a book to XML ran between $800 and $1,000, with quality assurance and rework taking up to eight hours.

After a year, K-PUB identified a private offshore provider—in Pune, India—that could perform the translation for between $300 and $400 a book. Although the process would take longer—40 hours on average compared with eight hours—company executives agreed to outsource the translation process. The longer time period, they believed, would not be critical since most titles remained "in print" and available on the Internet for between two and three years. "The revenue impact of the off-shore outsourcing has been minimal," said Caroline Matthews, "and we hope that within a year or two, this step will be completely automated so there will be no need for outsourcing."

Conclusion

"You were lucky outsourcing worked out so well for you," John Hearst concluded. "I suppose you're right," Caroline Matthews responded, although she doubted very much that luck had much to do with their companies' different experiences.

Endnotes

1. Barbara Blumenthal and Philippe Haspeslaugh's definition of strategic renewal is from Michael A. Mische, *Strategic Renewal: Becoming a High-Performance Organization* (New Jersey: Prentice Hall, 2001), p. 23.

2. Mische, *Strategic Renewal*, p. 24.

3. Peter Burrows, "The Mac in the Gray Flannel Suit," *Business Week*, May 8, 2008, p. 36.

4. José Santos, Bert Spector, and Ludo Van-Der-Heyden, "Toward a Theory of Corporate Business Model Innovation," Northeastern University College of Business Administration Working Paper, 2008.

5. *Ibid.*

6. Charles Stein, "The Trapeze Act: Reinventing a Firm," *Boston Globe*, May 8, 2005, pp. C1, C5.

7. Bert Spector, "HRM at Enron—The Unindicted Co-conspirator," *Organizational Dynamics* 32 (May 2003), pp. 207–221.

8. George Pohle and Marc Chapman, "IBM's Global CEO Report 2006: Business Model Innovation Matters," *Strategy and Leadership* 34 (2006), pp. 34–40; Joanna Barsch, Marla M. Capozzi, and Jonathan Davidson, "Leadership and Innovation," *McKinsey Quarterly* (April 2008), pp. 37–47.

9. Henry W. Lane, Bert Spector, and Dennis Shaughnessy, "A Dynamics Capacity Perspective on the Transfer of Innovations," Northeastern University College of Business Administration Working Paper, 2008.

10. D. Ulrich and D. Lake, *Organizational Capacity: Competing from the Inside Out* (New York: Wiley, 1990); J. Arthur, "The Link Between Business Strategy and Industrial Relations Systems in American Steel Minimills," *Industrial and Labor Relations Review* 45 (1992), pp. 448–506; A. A. Lado and M. C. Wilson, "Human Resource Systems and Sustained Competitive Advantage: A Competency-Based Perspective," *Academy of Management Review* 19 (1994), pp. 699–727; M. A. Huselid, "The Impact of Human Resource Management Practices on Turnover, Productivity, and Corporate Financial Performance," *Academy of Management Journal* 38 (1995), pp. 635–677; J. J. Lawler, R. W. Anderson, and R. J. Buckles, "Human Resource Management and Organizational Effectiveness," in G. R. Ferris, S. D. Rosen, and D. T. Barnum, eds., *Handbook of Human Resource Management* (Cambridge: Blackwell, 1995), pp. 630–649; J. T. Delaney and M. A. Huselid, "The Impact of Human Resource Management Practices on Perceptions of Organizational Performance," *Academy of Management Journal* 39 (1996), pp. 949–969; S. A. Snell, M. A. Youndt, and P. M. Wright, "Establishing a Framework for Research in Strategic Human Resource Management: Merging Resource Theory and Organizational Learning," in G. R. Ferris, ed., *Research in Personnel and Human Resource Management*, Vol. 14 (Greenwich, CT: JAI Press, 1996), pp. 61–90; J. E. Delery and D. H. Doty, "Modes of Theorizing in Strategic Human Resource Management: Tests of Universalistic, Contingency, and Configurational Performance," *Academy of Management Journal* 39 (1996), pp. 802–835; M. A. Huselid, S. E. Jackson, and R. S. Schuler, "Technical and Strategic Human Resource Management Effectiveness As Determinants of Firm Performance," *Academy of Management Journal* 40 (1997), pp. 171–188; David Ulrich, "Intellectual Capital = Competence × Commitment," *Sloan Management Review* 39 (1998), pp. 15–26.

11. Daniel R. Denison, *Corporate Culture and Organizational Effectiveness* (New York: Wiley, 1990).

12. John P. Kotter and James L. Heskett, *Corporate Culture and Performance* (New York: Free Press, 1992); Jim Collins and Jerry I. Porras, *Built to Last: Successful Habits of Visionary Companies* (New York: HarperCollins, 2004).

13. This story is reported in Adam Lashinsky, "Chaos by Decision," *Fortune*, October 2, 2006, p. 88.

14. This definition of resistance is from Kurt Lewin, "Group Decision and Social Change," in G. E. Swanson, T. M. Newcombe, and E. L. Hartley, eds., *Readings in Social Psychology*, 2nd ed. (New York: Holt, 1952), pp. 459–473.

15. Leon Coetsee, "From Resistance to Commitment," *Public Affairs Quarterly* (Summer 1999), pp. 204–222.

16. Kenneth E. Hullman, "Scaling the Wall of Resistance," *Training and Development* (October 1995), pp. 15–18.

17. Several authors have argued for a reconsideration of the meaning of "change resistance," suggesting even that the term "resistance" should be dropped because of its pejorative implications. See, for example, Tony J. Watson, "Group Ideologies and Organizational Change," *Journal of Management Studies* 19 (1982), pp. 259–275; and Sandy Kristin Piderit, "Rethinking Resistance and Recognizing Ambivalence: A Multidimensional View of Attitudes toward an

Organizational Change," *Academy of Management Review* 25 (2000), pp. 783–794.

18. That research was highlighted at a session, "Changing Individuals," at the 2007 Academy of Management meetings. See, in particular, Jane D. Parent and D. Anthony Butterfield, "A Model and Test of Individual and Organization Factors Influencing Individual Adaptation to Change."

19. See, for example, L. Coch and J. R. French, "Overcoming Resistance to Change," *Human Relations* 1 (1948), pp. 512–533; Lewin, *Field Theory in Social Science*; R. Likert, *The Human Organization* (New York: McGraw-Hill, 1967); Edwin A. Fleishman, "Attitude versus Skill Factors in Work Productivity," *Personnel Psychology* 18 (1965), pp. 253–266; Chris Argyris, *Intervention Theory and Method* (Reading, MA: Addison-Wesley, 1970); Warner W. Burke, *Organization Development: Principles and Practices* (Boston: Little, Brown, 1982); Frank Heller, Eugen Pusic, George Strauss, and Bernhard Wilpert, *Organizational Participation: Myth and Reality* (New York: Oxford University Press, 1998).

20. The connection between employee participation and commitment to change has been demonstrated in Rune Lines, "Influence of Participation in Strategic Change: Resistance, Organizational Commitment and Change Goal Achievement," *Journal of Change Management* 4 (September 2004), pp. 193–215.

21. James O'Toole, "Lordstown: Three Years Later," *Business and Society Review* (Spring 1975), pp. 64–71.

22. Paul Lawrence and Bert Spector, "General Motors and the United Auto Workers," in Michael Beer, Bert Spector, Paul R. Lawrence, D. Quinn Mills, and Richard E. Walton, *Human Resource Management: A General Management Perspective* (New York: Free Press, 1985), pp. 698–700.

23. Peter Senge, "It's the Learning: The Real Lessons of the Quality Movement," *Journal for Quality and Participation* (November/December 1999), p. 35.

24. Wagoner is quoted in Jeremy W. Peters, "G. M. Vice Chairman Rebuffs Critics of Turnaround," *New York Times*, April 13, 2006, p. C6.

25. Bill Vlasic, "GM Offers New Buyout to 74,000," *New York Times*, February 13, 2008, p. C1.

26. Leonard Greenlaugh, "Maintaining Organizational Effectiveness During Organizational Retrenchment," *Journal of Applied Behavioral Science* 18 (1982), pp. 155–170.

27. John W. Slocum, Jr., James R. Morris, Wayne F. Cascio, and Clifford E. Young, "Downsizing after All These Years: Questions and Answers about Who Did It, How Many Did It, and Who Benefited From It," *Organizational Dynamics* 27 (Winter 1999), pp. 78–88; Paul C. Nutt, "Organizational De-Development," *Journal of Management Studies* 41 (November 2004), pp. 1083–1103.

28. Carlos Ghosn and Philippe Ries, *Shift: Inside Nissan's Historical Revival* (New York: Currency, 2005), pp. 39–40.

29. Mark Hughes, "The Tools and Techniques of Change Management," *Journal of Change Management* 7 (March 2007), pp. 37–49.

30. Katie Hafner, "Humans Regain Jobs from Mice," *New York Times*, August 16, 2007, pp. C1, C11.

31. That definition is based on Arthur A. Thompson, Jr., A. J. Strickland III, and John E. Gamble, *Crafting and Executing Strategy: The Quest for Competitive Advantage*, 15th Edition (Boston: McGraw-Hill Irwin, 2007), pp. 175–177.

32. Steve Lohr, "At IBM, A Smarter Way to Outsource," *New York Times*, July 5, 2007, p. C1.

33. *Ibid.*

34. Jérôme Barthélemy, "The Seven Deadly Sins of Outsourcing," *Academy of Management Executive* 17 (May 2003), pp. 87–98.

35. Robert Coleman, "Navigating Strategic Change," *CMA Management* (October 2006), pp. 40–42.

36. Lynn A. Isabella, "Managing the Challenges of Trigger Events: The Mindsets Governing Adaptation to Change," *Business Horizons* 35 (September–October 1992), pp. 59–60.

CHAPTER 2

Theories of Effective Change Implementation

A dynamic competitive environment prompts organizational leaders to alter or transform their strategies. That process of strategic renewal places new expectations on employees at all levels. Roles, responsibilities, and relationships will be altered, some subtly, others fundamentally. Translating renewed strategies into altered patterns of behavior—behavior that supports the new strategy and contributes to sustained outstanding performance by the organization—that is, the change implementation challenge.

This chapter will explore theories of implementing change that can be called upon to help guide interventions. In particular, the chapter will:

- Present the three phases of the planned change theory of Kurt Lewin
- Delineate the key insights to effective implementation offered by the field of Organizational Development
- Differentiate between content-driven and process-driven change
- Explain an approach to change management that emphasizes task requirements and performance results
- Offer a framework for change implementation that encompasses multiple theories

First, we will look at an attempt by the director of a university-based hospital to respond to a deep financial crisis.

TURNAROUND AND TRANSFORMATION AT DUKE UNIVERSITY CHILDREN'S HOSPITAL

In 1996, the 135-bed Duke University Children's Hospital faced a deep financial crisis.[1] Key administrators at the hospital provided the following dire assessment:

> A decrease in Medicaid allowances and an increase in patients with capitated reimbursement* were driving revenues down. Expenses were down as cost per case for children's services ballooned from $10,500 in fiscal year (FY) 93 to $14,889 in FY96. This caused a dramatic reduction in the net margin—from (−)$2 million in FY93 to (−)$11 million in FY96. Programs were slated to be eliminated and services were targeted for reduction. Sales productivity had fallen from the 80th to the 70th percentile range. In addition, patient and staff satisfaction was at an all time low.

Jon Meliones, the hospital's chief medical director, realized that he and fellow hospital executives faced a particular challenge. "No matter how effective the chief executive officer (CEO) and chief operating officer (COO) are," he observed, "they can control only a portion of the components that drive the organization's financial performance." Physicians determined length of stay, drug prescriptions, and tests, while accepting referrals that helped determine revenues. Nurses drove quality. Any effective change would require a united effort among administrators and clinicians.

Meliones led his staff through a diagnosis of the root causes of the hospital's financial crisis. They found a particularly troubling pattern of behavior. "The problem was that our hospital was a collection of fiefdoms," said Meliones. "Each group, from accountants to administrators to clinicians, was focusing on its own individual goal rather than on the organization as a whole." Creating a shared sense of responsibility for the hospital's performance and realigning patterns of behavior would be required.

A team consisting of Meliones, the chief nurse executive, and nurse managers agreed upon an approach that emphasized the interdependence between financial performance and excellence of health care. "We want patients to be happy . . . and for them to have the best care," the team concluded. They also adopted a motto for their planned strategic renewal: "No margin, no mission." Excellent patient care *and* excellent financial performance would be the twin hallmarks of the hospital's strategic renewal.

Implementation next moved to a single unit: pediatric intensive care. Meliones and his team worked to operationalize new behaviors through a redesign of roles, responsibilities, and relationships. With the participation of doctors, nurses, the medical staff, and even accountants, the team redesigned how all members of the unit would undertake their responsibilities. The unit called on a popular measurement tool, the balanced scorecard, that looks not just at financial outcomes but also customer perceptions, internal business processes, and the ability of an organization to learn and grow, to help reinforce desired new behaviors.[2] Meliones and his leadership team returned the hospital to profitability in three years.

---

*Under capitated reimbursement, insurance companies reimburse providers at a fixed amount, typically based on some calculation of the average cost of a procedure.

THEORIES OF CHANGE IMPLEMENTATION

Organizational leaders such as Jon Meliones at Duke Children's Hospital, have multiple tools and levers at their disposal that they can apply in pursuit of effective change implementation. The question that needs to be addressed to understand effective change implementation is not just *what* levers can be applied—diagnosis, cross-functional teams, and measurement systems, in Meliones' case—but also in what order or *sequence* should those levers be called upon.

Look carefully at the sequence of Meliones' interventions:

- Involving his staff in a shared diagnosis of the root causes of the hospital's financial woes, then:
- Putting together a cross-functional team—doctors, nurses, medical staff, and accountants—with the goal of figuring out how to provide both excellent patient care and excellent financial performance, then:
- Piloting change within the pediatric intensive care unit, then:
- Redesigning the roles, responsibilities, and relationships of all unit members, then:
- Reinforcing the new behaviors with a new measurement system, the balanced scorecard.

That sequence, repeated in unit after unit, effectively transformed the hospital over a three-year period.

Would Meliones have been equally—or even more—effective if he had altered the sequence; say, by introducing a balanced scorecard earlier in the effort? To seek answers to the all-important sequencing question, we can turn to the body of theories that has been developed concerning organizational and behavioral change.

Theory into Practice

Effective change involves both content—*what* is being changed—and process—*how* the changes are being implemented.

Kurt Lewin's Field Theory in Social Science

The scientific study of change implementation can be traced back to the work of psychologist Kurt Lewin. In the aftermath of World War II, Lewin published two path-breaking essays, "Behavior and Development as a Function of the Total Situation" (1946) and "Frontiers in Group Dynamics" (1947).[3]

It may be hard to think that a social scientist working over 60 years ago—and in a past millennium, no less!—could have anything relevant and important to say about today's organizations. But Lewin offered two insights that, to this day, shape our understanding of how to alter patterns of behavior.

First, he highlighted the important, even decisive role that context plays in shaping individual behaviors. And second, he argued that the only way to motivate an individual to change his pattern of behavior is to create a sense of disequilibrium or dissatisfaction with the status quo within that individual. To fully appreciate Lewin's contribution, it is worth spending some time looking at each of these ideas.

CHANGING BEHAVIORS BY CHANGING CONTEXT   We made the point in Chapter 1 that companies often call on organizational context to help shape employee behavior. The leaders of Google, as we saw, attempted to create a context that tolerated risk-taking, even failure, in order to encourage creativity.

Lewin made the same point about context. The behavior of an individual within a group setting—social groups were the context that Lewin was concerned with—is shaped both by that individual's psychology and the group setting or context in which she finds herself.

Lewin captured that duality in a simple formula: $B = f(P, E)$. Behavior (B) is a function of the person herself (P) and the environmental context (E) in which that person operates. Person and context are interdependent variables shaping behavior.

The question Lewin addressed was: How can that context be changed? To start, Lewin insisted that what does *not* work is telling people. Giving a speech about the need for change will not motivate new behaviors.

You might be able to imagine what such a speech about the need for change would sound like. An executive explains to employees that they need to be more responsive to customers, coordinate better with international operations, bring new products to market more quickly, work more effectively across functions, and so forth. That executive might be an extraordinarily effective communicator. Nonetheless, the likelihood that telling people about the need for behavioral change will lead to real and sustained change is quite small.

When leaders rely on "lectures" to drive change—in today's organizational context, that may mean speeches, small group meetings, PowerPoint presentations, video conferences, and so forth—they fail to take into account the power of context in reinforcing the status quo. In Lewin's view, getting group members to change their behaviors, and having those new behaviors become lasting rather than fleeting, involves breaking a "social habit."

To make matters more challenging, group members tend to assign *positive value* to those existing social habits. The group **norms** that support those behavioral habits—that is, the shared expectations of how group members ought to behave—come to be viewed by group members as good things: standards to be cherished and upheld.

Whatever an individual may glean from a speech, no matter how well delivered that speech may be, he is not likely to alter his behaviors. The positive value associated with the existing social arrangements continues to exert a powerful force on the individual, "keeping the individual in line with the standards of the group."[4] The old habits have not been broken; the positive value associated with past behaviors still exerts powerful pressure; so individual behavior returns to the norm.

Building a Vocabulary of Change
Norms shared expectations of how group members ought to behave.

Theory into Practice

Telling employees why they need to change will not build motivation to change; it is necessary, but not sufficient.

The next important question, therefore, is how to exert a force that will alter not just the individual but also the social context of that individual.

CREATING DISSATISFACTION   Leaders seeking to implement organizational change are often surprised by the degree of complacency they face. Why are employees clinging to the status quo—doing things the way they always have—even in the face of declining organizational performance? Isn't it *obvious* that we need to change?

In 1999, when Carlos Ghosn took over leadership at Nissan Motors, following the auto company's alliance with Renault, he was puzzled by the apparent lack of urgency among company employees. At that moment, Nissan was $19.9 billion in debt with annual losses exceeding $250 million. Despite the obviously unacceptable level of performance, Ghosn encountered resigned acceptance among Nissan executives.

"For a company that has been losing money for seven years out of eight," he observed, "there is not enough of a sense of urgency. People should be banging their heads on the walls everywhere."[5] Instead, Ghosn observed a disturbing lack of dissatisfaction with the status quo.

Theory into Practice

Don't assume that poor organizational performance will create an urgent need to change within a company.

Potential change leaders are often stumped by same situation that greeted Ghosn when he first arrived at Nissan: why, in the face of such apparently obvious distress, do employees remain attached to the status quo? Lewin had an explanation for that.

Group membership often confers a positive sense to members; they *like* being part of the group, accept the group's norms, and are pleased with what the group has been able to accomplish in the past. And the more they assign positive value to group membership and group norms, the greater the resistance will be on the part of individual group members to alter those norms.

Group membership, then, creates a kind of inertia, or at least reluctance, to change what it is about that group that seems so positive. The task of motivating individuals to alter their established behaviors, then, is a demanding one. That is the challenge for leaders seeking change.

The act of announcing the need for change, of proclaiming new goals, of presenting a rational argument for how the changes will improve performance simply will not motivate behavioral change. What is needed, Lewin argued, is a kind of deliberate "emotional stir-up," a powerful intervention designed to "open the shell of complacency" and "unfreeze" the existent equilibrium.

Theory into Practice

To break the "social habits" that support existing patterns of behaviors, start with creating dissatisfaction, disequilibrium, and discomfort.

To be effective, then, a change leader's initial task is to create what Lewin called **unfreezing**. "All forms of learning and change start with some form of dissatisfaction or frustration," explains Edgar Schein, "generated by data that disconfirm our expectations or hopes." The emotional stir-up that Lewin pointed to will not occur simply by hearing "disconfirming information," however: "We can ignore the information, dismiss it as irrelevant, blame the undesired outcome on others or fate, or, as is most common, simply deny its validity." Ignoring or denying the reasons for change will do nothing but increase resistance.

Remember the employees of the Concord Bookshop (Chapter 1)? They resisted change, in part, because they simply did not accept the diagnosis of leadership that the store's finances were in "dire" shape. Now, contrast that approach to the one taken by Jon Meliones at the Children's Hospital. Instead of lecturing employees on why they needed to change, he involved them in a diagnostic process, allowing them to learn—just as he had—the financial situation of the hospital and to shape the appropriate response.

Imagine if Meliones had, instead, given a talk about the dire need for change, supplemented with elaborate PowerPoints. Then he would have told employees how they needed to alter their behaviors, and work together in different ways: doctors, nurses, medical technicians, even accountants pulling together to ensure outstanding performance. He would have then explained why he felt the balanced scorecard was an excellent tool for measuring their progresses and reinforcing their new behaviors. Had he approached change implementation that way, he may well have faced the same kind of resistance that greeted the efforts at the Concord Bookshop.

To truly unfreeze behavior, Schein explains, "We must accept the [disconfirming] information and connect it to something we care about."[6] If employees do not accept the validity of the stated requirement for change, they are likely to resist.

The second stage of Lewin's model involves **moving**, wherein members of the group move from one set of behaviors to another. Those new behaviors, in Lewin's view, must become permanent, for at least a desired period of time. That is the **refreezing** stage where a newly created equilibrium "is made relatively secure against change."[7] Refreezing is the stage where structures and systems align with and reinforce new behaviors. That is the stage at which measurement tools like the balanced scorecard—there are many others that we will discuss in Chapter 6—can be called upon to reinforce new behaviors.

LEWIN'S CONTRIBUTION TO CHANGE IMPLEMENTATION   Lewin is best known for his three stages of change implementation: unfreezing, moving, and refreezing (summarized in Exhibit 2-1). Equally important is Lewin's recognition that the most effective way to manage behavioral change among individual members of a group is to work *first* on changing the group's norms, then focus on individual behaviors. If "one succeeds in changing group standards, this same force field will tend to facilitate changing the individual and will tend to stabilize the individual conduct on the new group level."[8] Context exerts a powerful shaping force on individual behaviors.

Lewin urged a kind of implementation sequence. To create sustainable behavioral change, organizational leaders need to work both on the individual and the

Building a Vocabulary of Change
Unfreezing the first stage in Lewin's change model in which group members become dissatisfied with the status quo.

Building a Vocabulary of Change
Moving the second stage in Lewin's change model in which group members alter their patterns of behavior.

Building a Vocabulary of Change
Refreezing the final stage in Lewin's change model in which group members institutionalize the new patterns of behavior into a new status quo.

Stage 1: Unfreezing	Stage 2: Moving	Stage 3: Refreezing
Create dissatisfaction with the status quo	Redesign organizational roles, responsibilities, & relationships	Align pay/reward systems
Benchmark operations against other companies	Train for newly required skills	Re-engineer measurement/ control systems
Diagnose internal barriers to improved performance	Promote supporters/ remove resisters	Create new organization structures

EXHIBIT 2-1   Implementation Implications of Lewin's Change Model.

contextual level. There is a far greater leverage to be gained, however from *first* working at the contextual level.

The positive social values created by the new equilibrium will motivate individuals to adapt to the new norms. If, instead, leaders first focus on the individual level, they risk undermining their best intentions. No matter how much impact they have on changing the expectations and behaviors of individuals, those new expectations and behaviors will not endure as long as the old equilibrium continues to exert a powerful and attractive force.

Theory into Practice

In order to implement change, target group norms first and then focus on individual behaviors.

Lewin's focus was on behavior within groups rather than on organizations in their totality. His approach does not transfer in its entirety to the current work of business organizations. For example, his linear approach—first unfreeze, then move, and finally refreeze—underestimates the potential for complex group dynamics to shift significantly during the intervention process. Additionally, his notion of refreezing assumes that a group will return to a stable state once the change intervention has passed. In fact, highly dynamic environments exert constant demand for adaptation and change.[9] Nonetheless, Lewin's attention to both the impact of context on behaviors and the requirement to create disequilibrium in order to motivate behavioral change continue to inform current theories of effect change implementation.

ORGANIZATION DEVELOPMENT AND CHANGE IMPLEMENTATION

Building a Vocabulary of Change

Organizational development (OD) an approach to organizational effectiveness that calls on the fields of behavioral and social sciences to provide guidance to planned change efforts.

Lewin's work represents an early foray by behavioral scientists in the world of organizational behavior and change management. The field of **organizational development (OD)** soon coalesced around emergent learnings from the behavioral and social sciences (mainly, psychology, sociology, and systems dynamics) to inform approaches to planned organizational change. OD offers a complex and systemic perspective on how and why people behave and organizations operate. For that reason, OD provides particular insight into the process of changing people's behavior and organizations' operations.

Although different theorists and practitioners have offered their own insights into these matters, ten key perspectives and assumptions—summarized in Exhibit 2-2—underlie the field.[10] Three insights in particular help advance an understanding of effective change implementation.

ORGANIZATIONS ARE OPEN SYSTEMS   OD sees the organization as an **open system**: a kind of organism that exists in constant interaction with its external environment and between its own internal elements. Effectiveness in an open system arises

Perspective	Underlying Assumptions
1. Systems perspective	Outstanding performance depends on interactions between and among the multiple elements of organization; between the people, processes, structure, and values of the organization; and between the organization and its external environment
2. Alignment perceptive	The effectiveness of organizations will be determined by a state of congruence between people, process, structure, values, and environment
3. Participation perspective	People will become more committed to implementing solutions if they have been involved in the problem-solving process
4. Social capital perspective	To achieve outstanding performance, organizational leaders seek to create a network of interdependent relationships that provides the basis for trust, cooperation, and collective action
5. Teamwork perspective	Accepting shared purpose and responsibility for interdependent tasks enhances coordination, commitment, and creativity and supports outstanding performance
6. Multiple stakeholder perspective	Outstanding performance requires that organizational leaders balance the expectations of multiple stakeholders: shareholders, employees, customers, suppliers, host community, labor unions, trade associations, governments, etc.
7. Problem-solving perspective	Conflicts over task issues can increase the quality of decisions if they occur in an environment of collaboration and trust
8. Open communications perspective	Open and candid communication, especially upward in the hierarchy, creates the opportunity for learning and development while building trust and collaboration
9. Evolution/ revolution perspective	Organizations must develop competencies to engage in both incremental (evolutionary) and fundamental (revolutionary) change
10. Process facilitation perspective	Individuals who reside outside of the organizational hierarchy can become both facilitators and teachers of effective implementation processes in partnership with organizational members

EXHIBIT 2-2   Ten Defining Perspectives of Organizational Development.

not just out of the actions of employees but also out of *inter*actions that occur at multiple levels:

- Between the personalities and activities of various employees
- Between employees and the requirements of their tasks
- Between the tasks and the culture of the organization
- Between the culture and the intended culture of the organization
- Between the strategy of the organization and its external environment

Organizational effectiveness is best achieved when a state of fit or congruence exists between various elements of the open system (see Exhibit 2-3).

Theory into Action

Performance problems often reside in the hand-offs between employees, between tasks, between functions, and between units; these are the problems that be targeted first for change.

Building a Vocabulary of Change
Alignment the degree of congruence or compatibility between and among various elements of a system.

A view of organizations as open systems emphasizes **alignment** between the internal dynamics of an organization (how employees act and interact) with the

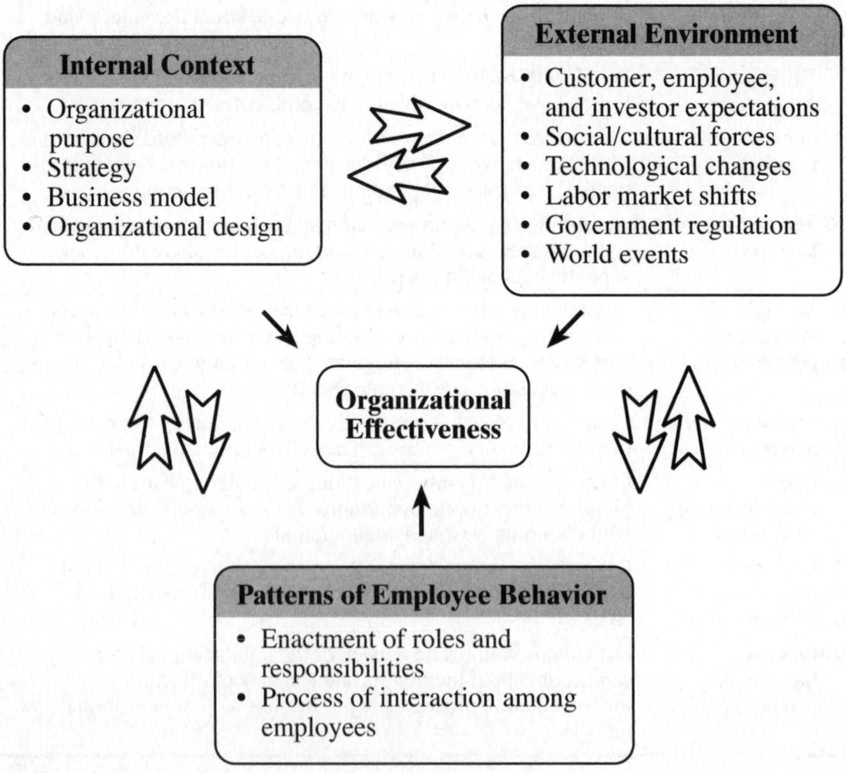

EXHIBIT 2-3   A Congruence Model of Effectiveness.

external marketplace in which the organization lives and competes. Alignment is a state of congruence between organizational sub-elements and their environment. Because the external environment changes, elements of the system must respond.

ORGANIZATIONS SERVE MULTIPLE STAKEHOLDERS   OD assumes a multiple stakeholder perspective. **Stakeholders** are individuals or groups who lay legitimate claim to the performance of the organization; they have a *stake* in how the organization is doing. Those who have a financial investment in a company possess a legitimate interest in its performance, to be sure. So do employees, not to mention customers and suppliers. The host community, whose economy is impacted by the company's performance and who share an ecosystem with that company, also has a legitimate interest in how the company is performing.

The multiple-stakeholder perspective represents, in part, an ethical view of the role of business organizations in a community's life. Businesses, in that view, do not sit above or apart from other stakeholders; they must instead play a citizenship role.

The multiple-stakeholder view also represents a perspective on effectiveness. A key source of outstanding performance lies in the willingness of organizational leaders to commit time, energy, and resources to tending to the interests of multiple stakeholders; most especially to shareholders, to customers, and to employees. That commitment translates into a responsive, adaptive organization capable of sustaining outstanding performance in a dynamic environment.

Theory into Practice

If leaders are successful at aligning the interests of multiple stakeholders—shareholders, employees, customers, suppliers, the host community, and so forth.—they can contribute to outstanding performance.

DEALING WITH CONFLICT WITH PROBLEM SOLVING, OPENNESS, AND TRUST   *Don't argue. Go along. Don't stir the pot. Get on board. Be a team player.* All of these expressions, and others you have surely heard, represent a particular view about conflict and its role in organizational life. Conflict is disruptive and dysfunction. Avoid it or soothe over it.

OD takes a fundamentally different view; it is that conflict, when managed properly, can improve effectiveness, increase innovation, and enhance adaptiveness. Not all conflict is desirable; interpersonal conflict based on personalities can be harmful. But conflict about how best to perform tasks can have a positive value on an organization.

Conflict can, for example, improve innovativeness by highlighting a diversity of viewpoints. Additionally, conflict can encourage individuals to articulate their personal points of view and assumptions while considering the viewpoints and assumptions of others. The potential benefits, therefore, involve both an enhanced grounding in reality and an increased opportunity for creativity.[11]

Theory into Practice

Don't shy away from conflict. As individuals articulate and analyze differences, they can improve organizational effectiveness.

Not all approaches to conflict produce equally desirable outcomes. Avoiding, accommodating, or even compromising when faced with conflicts around how best to perform the tasks of the organization will suboptimize the ability of organizational members to work together while achieving realistic and creative solutions. Collaboration, in which conflicting parties combine advocacy for a particular position while inquiring into the legitimate and conflicting views of others, leads to both superior solutions as well as commitment on the part of participants to implement that solution.[12]

ORGANIZATIONAL DEVELOPMENT'S CONTRIBUTION TO CHANGE IMPLEMENTATION   The insights offered by organizational development can help leaders implement behavioral change in a manner that is both effective and sustainable. The major perspectives and assumptions of the field suggest that interventions that target just one aspect of an organization—say, its structures or its pay systems or its work processes—will likely fail to deliver the hoped-for performance improvements.

Because organizations are highly interactive systems, the keys to outstanding performance reside not in any one independent component of the organization but rather at the interface between many interdependent factors. Piecemeal approaches to change will likely fail, especially over the long run, because they target discrete units or issues rather than focusing on the "joints" of the organization, the places where organizational processes and activities come together.[13]

Additionally, OD points to the importance of an implementation process that builds a sense of ownership: trust, open communication, collaborative problem solving, and participation in the change process. Questions of both what needs to be changed and how the change should be implemented can be exclusive or inclusive.

In an *ex*clusive mode, top executives exclude all stakeholders except a small group of fellow senior executives who decide what behaviors need to be targeted and how the change process should proceed. In an *in*clusive process, representatives of multiple stakeholders are all included in the diagnostic, action planning, and implementation efforts. Employee motivation to adopt and sustain required new behaviors will be enhanced, making implementation more likely to be successful in the short run and sustainable in the long run.

Theory into Practice

Be sure to create an inclusive change process—one that builds ownership of and commitment to the desired improvements.

Process-Driven Change Interventions

Given the complexity and dynamism of the competitive environment, it is not surprising that change efforts have proliferated over the past several decades: employee involvement, customer relationship management, balanced scorecard, and lean enterprise, to name just a few. These efforts represent **content-driven change** that emphasizes programmatic responses to organizational requirements.

As an alternative methodology of implementation, **process-driven change** suggests that the hows of implementation—the manner in which change is conceived, introduced, and institutionalized—will be more determinate of effectiveness than the specific content of any given change program.[14] While content-driven changes may serve as useful tools in reinforcing behavioral change, they can be ineffective as drivers and shapers of the transformation effort.

To help understand and identify content-driven change, we can look at the efforts Blue Cloud Development (disguised name), a small, software development company. After attending a conference on a new methodology for software development known as Agile, Blue Cloud CEO Shel Skinner hired consultants to introduce the methodology.

At its core, Agile emphasized multiple iterations and short time frames. Blue Cloud's traditional developmental cycle emphasized a deliberate sequence of development, with verification (testing and debugging) often occurring after a year's worth of work. "Why waste a year to find out whether our product is working," Skinner wondered. No more alpha and beta testing of new software, hoped Skinner. "Our new motto around here is, 'Release early, release often!' "

What appealed to Skinner was Agile's emphasis on teamwork, collaboration, and monthly releases. Cross-functional development teams held a daily "scrum" to ensure that all members were fully onboard with the progress and that all questions and concerns were raised in a timely manner. By bringing together business people, developers, customers' representatives, and other concerned parties in a disciplined, face-to-face encounter, Agile methodology was intended to simultaneously increase efficiency and improve quality.

After a year of applying Agile, Skinner asked his engineers to evaluate the effort. "Wonderful," said some, "what's new?" asked others, and "this is a definite step in the wrong direction" complained a few. Skinner remained unsure about whether to continue with the Agile methodology or look for a new approach to software development.

> **Building a Vocabulary of Change**
> *Content-driven change* programmatic change in which specific programs—customer relationship management, balanced scorecard, and lean enterprise, for example—are used as the driver and centerpiece of implementation.

> **Building a Vocabulary of Change**
> *Process-driven change* an approach to change implementation that emphasizes the methods of conceiving, introducing, and institutionalizing new behaviors and uses content as a reinforcer rather than a driver of new behaviors.

Theory into Practice

There are no one-size-fits-all solutions to performance problems in your organization.

Agile is just one example of a content-driven change. To help understand and identify content-driven change, we can identify a set of characteristics that are common across different particular change efforts. Content-driven change:

- *Serves as the initial centerpiece for launching and driving transformation throughout the company or unit.* At Blue Cloud, Agile became the centerpiece for promoting a whole range of changes, including bringing the voice of the customer into the development process sooner than in the past, working collaboratively across functions, and confronting and solving problems daily.
- *Is imposed by the top management.* Skinner virtually single-handedly provided the impetus and sustained commitment to the Agile effort. Even in the face of

serious questions raised at the end of year one, it was Skinner who would decide whether to continue the methodology.

- *Does not proceed from shared diagnosis*. By virtue of his position atop the Blue Cloud hierarchy, Skinner could simply impose the Agile methodology. Neither the management team nor the involved engineers participated in a process to diagnose the current approach to development and suggest improvements. Was there even dissatisfaction with the status quo? Skinner's implementation failed to ask even that question.
- *Relies on standardized, off-the-shelf solutions*. Agile was a methodology developed outside of Blue Cloud. Was it appropriate for Blue Cloud, its strategy, and product mix? That question was not asked.
- *Is imposed uniformly across the organization*. Perhaps Agile was appropriate for some software development, but did it fit all circumstances? Could new software be treated the same way as updates and improvements on existing products? Neither Skinner nor his team engaged in such a diagnoses; instead, he applied Agile across the entire company.

The characteristics of content-driven change are summarized in Exhibit 2-4.

THE LIMITATIONS OF CONTENT-DRIVEN CHANGE   The uniform nature of content-driven change creates its own set of problems. To decree that all managers in all divisions and units "should" undergo a training program or that all processes "should" use a particular methodology such as Agile ignores the diversity extant in any complex organization, including differences in customer expectations, in competitive realities, in key task demands, and/or in workforce characteristics. Applied universally across organizational boundaries, change programs can drive out creativity and usually lack the specific relevancy needed to help managers in a given unit solve their real and immediate business problems.

The fact that programs are imposed from above may reflect the commitment on the part of top management to the need for change. But the transformation effort often bogs down because that commitment is not widely distributed throughout and across the organization.[15] Only those individuals dissatisfied with the status quo—with the performance of their unit and the patterns of behavior supporting that performance—will be motivated to alter their patterns of behavior. Top-down change programs may *assume* the pre-existence of such dissatisfaction, but they do little to actually *build* dissatisfaction and direct that dissatisfaction toward new patterns of behavior.

- Serve as the initial centerpiece for launching and driving transformation throughout the company or unit.
- Are imposed by top management.
- Do not proceed from shared diagnosis.
- Rely on standardized, off-the-shelf solutions.
- Are imposed uniformly across the organization.

EXHIBIT 2-4   Characteristics of Content-Driven Change Programs.

Theory into Practice

Just because top leaders believe in the need for change doesn't mean that all employees share that conclusion.

The cost of continued reliance on content-driven change as a way of transforming the organization is significant. In addition to the inefficient use of organizational resources, each unsuccessful and discarded program makes it that much harder to effect successful transformation in the future. As one failed program leads to another, managers begin to discount and ignore all programs. Because line managers have little commitment to these efforts, what they offer—at best—is compliance. They may tolerate the program, carry out procedures to the best of their ability, but fail to provide any lasting support for program continuation. They may complete the minimal requirements expected of them by filling out the proper forms or attending the expected conferences, but *disdain* and criticize all aspects of the effort. And to the extent that they can get away with it, they may avoid the effort entirely.

Theory into Practice

Content-driven change often fails because of inadequate attention to the process of change.

THE POPULARITY OF CONTENT-DRIVEN CHANGE   Given the complexity and dynamism of the competitive environment, it is not surprising that content-driven change efforts have proliferated over the past several decades. Exhibit 2-5 offers an overview of some of the most popular change efforts.

The popularity of content-driven change can be understood in terms of the dynamics in place in many organizations. Content-driven change efforts represent actions that can be put into place *quickly*. Faced with competitive crisis, top managers want to make change quickly. Pressures for quarterly earnings coupled with impatience and high task orientation lead managers to seek a lever that will demonstrate forward movement. Although simplistic and often ineffective, change programs are highly visible and provide tangible evidence of concerted effort.

Theory into Practice

Repeated failure to implement change effectively can build cynicism in an organization, "inoculating" it against future change efforts.

Furthermore, managers like to emulate well-known success stories, and they do so by importing programs. Best-selling management books present documented studies of the transformative impact of reengineering. Why shouldn't we do that, too? As one manager said of his support for a particularly trendy change program: "We were

Change Efforts	Key Points	Company Examples
Employee involvement	Allow employees, especially lower-level employees, to participate in making decisions, scheduling and designing work, and ensuring quality.	General Motors Hampton Inn Hotels SAS Airlines
Lean processes	Redesign cross-functional workflow and processes to drive out waste and inefficiencies.	Lockheed Martin Toyota Tyco Electronics
Concurrent engineering	Integrate product design, manufacturing, and support activities into a synchronized process.	British Aerospace Carolla Development Comdial Corporation
Value-chain integration	Capture value by linking and coordinating the primary activities—inbound logistics, production, outbound logistics, marketing, and sales—of the organization.	Burcas IBM Electronics Microsoft
Balanced scorecard	Strategic planning and measurement tool that connects internal processes with financial performance.	Blue Man Productions Centex Construction Citizens Bank
Agile	Software development process emphasizing frequent releases, intense customer involvement, and cross-functional teams.	Cambridge Biotech Lotus Development Quality Tree Software
Business model reinvention	Redefine the ways in which the organization acquires and retains customers while generating profits.	Metro eBay Southwest Airlines

EXHIBIT 2-5   Popular Approaches to Change.

one of the *Fortune 500* companies and we were all into this buzzword kind of stuff, and so let's get with the program here. We don't want to be left behind."[16]

The tangibility of change programs offers another apparent advantage: they are easily measurable. Thus, they make it convenient for top managers to hold subordinates accountable. Executives can point to the number of teams or the number of managers who have attended a training program as a proxy—and not an especially useful or valid proxy at that—for accomplishment.

Theory into Practice

Content-driven change is both tangible and measurable—but that doesn't make it effective.

**PROCESS-DRIVEN CHANGE AND ITS CONTRIBUTION TO CHANGE IMPLEMENTA-
TION**   A process-driven approach to change works from the opposite direction of content-driven change. Process-driven change seeks to create a context and environment in which employees at all levels of the organization engage in a collaborative way to achieve the strategic goals of the organization. Collaborative, participative, and problem-solving approaches work to align behaviors with strategic requirements. Change programs ranging from Six Sigma to business process reengineering, the balanced scorecard, lean enterprise, and Agile may then be used to reinforce rather than drive new behaviors. The leadership task becomes one of establishing purpose and strategic direction for the organization, then creating the fertile soil out of which new patterns of behavior may emerge.

Theory into Practice

Process-driven change seeks to create an organizational climate in which employees will be motivated to adopt new behaviors consistent with the strategic direction of the organization.

Task Alignment as a Driver of Behavioral Change

Task alignment offers an approach to change intended to sharpen the connections between Lewin's requirement to alter the context and create a disequilibrium, OD-based interventions, process-driven change, and strategic renewal. Effective change implementation efforts display a common thread: management focused on the business' central competitive challenges as the means for motivating change and developing new behaviors and skills.[17]

    Task alignment takes as a starting point for change the work that needs to be undertaken in order for a unit to achieve its strategic goals and sustained outstanding performance. That was precisely the point at which Jon Meliones started his shared diagnosis at Children's Hospital.

    In a dynamic environment, strategic renewal typically requires new behaviors in order to perform those tasks. Task alignment embeds the insights of organizational development in a drive to produce outstanding performance. Employees redefine their roles, responsibilities, and relationships in order to perform those tasks.

Theory into Practice

Task alignment combines the insights of organizational development with a bottom-line focus on performance.

TASK-ALIGNED CHANGE   To understand task alignment as a performance-focused approach to change, let's visit General Product's Technical Center (a disguised name). White-collar, professional-level employees found themselves simultaneously engaged in two very different change efforts.[18] The first effort, led by upper management at the

**Building a Vocabulary
of Change**

Task alignment an approach to behavioral change that starts with the identification of the key strategic tasks of an organization or unit and then asks employees to redefine their roles, responsibilities, and relationships in order to perform those tasks.

center and encouraged by corporate executives, focused on an "employee involvement" initiative.

Intrigued by reports of improved performance due to increased employee involvement in manufacturing operations, management formed committees to address issues of urgent concern to employees. Because employees often mentioned their interest in career development, one committee discussed how to get employees more involved in their own career planning.

Top management at the center began holding regular meetings to discuss the meaning of employee involvement: Just how far should employee involvement go and over what issues should employees be involved? The head of the center, feeling that he could not be overly directive about an initiative heralding employee involvement, watched in frustration as two years of effort yielded few tangible results.

Theory into Practice

A task-aligned approach to change implementation can help create motivation to adopt new behaviors by focusing on real, immediate business problems and producing tangible results.

Farther down the organizational hierarchy, a different sort of change effort unfolded. Struggling with the requirement to speed up the new product development process, an implementation task force uncovered poor cross-functional coordination reinforced by strict functional lines and a lack of teamwork throughout the organization as the culprit. Several cross-functional product development teams were created as a result.

As teams began to produce results, relationships among functions improved, engineers and production specialists began to feel empowered, and demands for team skills were met with a training program.[19] Although the efforts of the employee involvement team spurred by upper management's desire to meet "urgent" employee concerns withered, employees' involvement increased on cross-functional teams designed to develop new products.

TASK ALIGNMENT'S CONTRIBUTION TO CHANGE IMPLEMENTATION   The dramatic differences in the impact of these two interventions highlight a flaw of many change interventions. Look at the first approach. Hearing "good things" about employee involvement and desirous of gaining the benefits that had apparently accrued to other companies, corporate management urged employee involvement initiatives. One employee involvement task force recommended placing artwork in the center's atrium as a way of enhancing the ambience of the facility. But what did employee involvement mean to managers and workers? And more importantly, how did it impact on the ability of the center to achieve and sustain outstanding performance?

The second approach started with a different premise: not *we need to bring the idea of employee involvement into the organization* but *we need to improve new product development performance and involving employees will help us do that.* By following a task alignment approach to change implementation, employees at all levels of the organization are motivated to engage in behavioral change to the extent that they appreciate how that change is related to the performance of the core tasks of the organization.

Line managers have far greater ability to diagnose business and performance problems than to engage in psychological or therapeutic analysis of individuals. By focusing on solving real business problems, task alignment takes advantage of the knowledge and expertise in the organization. Tangible performance results that accrue from task-aligned change interventions reinforce the efficacy of such efforts, which, in turn, create momentum for renewed change intervention. Results build conviction.[20] Task alignment builds commitment by focusing on real and immediate performance drivers and producing tangible results.

PUTTING IT ALL TOGETHER: BUILDING A THEORY OF CHANGE IMPLEMENTATION

Each body of theory examined in this chapter offers critical insight into the effective implementation of change. Those theories and their implementation implications are summarized in Exhibit 2-6. The challenge for change implementation becomes: how can multiple theories of change be integrated into a common approach to effective change implementation?

The change implementation model presented in Exhibit 2-7 provides just such an integrated roadmap.[21] By melding theory and practice, the model suggests both what tools can be applied and the most effective sequence for that application. It suggests that once strategic renewal triggers a new requirement for transformation, effective implementation will start with **shared diagnosis**.

Building a Vocabulary of Change
Shared diagnosis a process that creates widespread agreement about the requirements for change.

Starting Implementation with Shared Diagnosis

Trigger events often lead to strategic renewal. Driving change from strategic renewal assures that implementation aligns with requirements of outstanding performance. However, in and of itself, the decision to alter or renew an organization's strategy does not create the disequilibrium that Lewin said is required to motivate changed behaviors. Remember the Concord Bookshop from Chapter 1? Morgan Smith and the board decided to restructure the store's management to take control over financial performance. Now think of the Duke University Children's Hospital at the opening of this chapter. This time, another trigger event—changes in insurance reimbursement that created a financial crisis—created the need for change.

Think about the dramatic difference in the way in which employees responded to the call for change: fierce resistance that bordered on rebellion at the bookshop and widespread support for change at the hospital. How can we account for these radically varied responses? In order to do so, we need to look at the opening stages of the change process.

Smith and the Concord Bookshop board assumed that employees would simply accept their declaration that financial realities dictated the response. At Children's

Theoretical Approach	Main Theoretical Contribution	Help Explain How to Implement Change
Lewin's *Field Theory in Social Science*	Begin behavioral change by focusing on context and unfreezing existing social habits	• Build a pervasive sense of dissatisfaction with the status quo on the part of employees • Offer operational models for what new behavioral patterns will be • Reinforce new behavior with alterations to systems and structures
Organizational development	Organizations are dynamic, open systems	• Target entire organizational system for change • Create a climate of open discussion and upward feedback concerning the efficacy of change implementation • Call on process consultants to facilitate interventions
Process-driven change	Focus on organically developed and implemented efforts to improve organizational performance	• Do not use externally developed program as driver of change • Focus on the unique requirements of each organization and unit • Build support for change while implementing it
Task alignment	Link desired new behaviors to requirements of performing key tasks of the organization	• Analyze and identify key performance indicators and behavioral implications required for outstanding performance • Attach requirements for new behavioral to new strategic objectives of organization • Build line-management support for change effort

EXHIBIT 2-6   Key Theoretical Approaches to Change Implementation.

Hospital, Jon Meliones did not impose a solution. Instead, he involved a cross section of administrators of health care providers in a diagnostic process that surfaced the interconnection between financial outcomes and patterns of behavior.

Theory into Practice

Kicking off change implementation with shared diagnosis builds both dissatisfaction with the status quo and a commitment to enact new behaviors.

Change requires the commitment of a variety of employees. Meliones had to impact the behaviors of accountants and administrators no less than physicians and nurses. A participative and involving diagnostic process can be used to build that commitment. Broad-based participation helps overcome defensiveness and resistance to change. Dissatisfaction with the status quo is no longer a lecture from above; rather, it is an agreement among many employees concerning what needs to be changed and why.

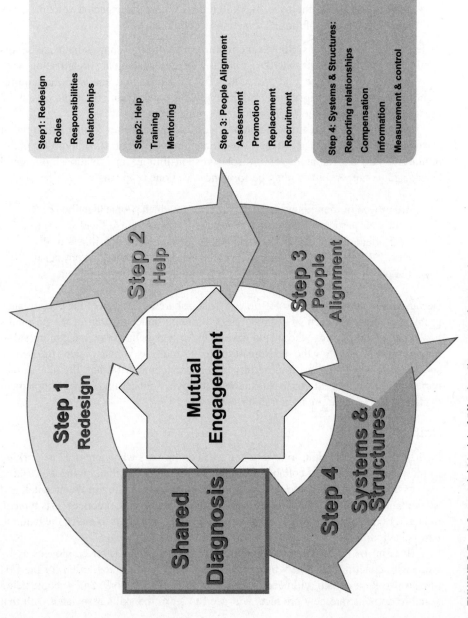

Step1: Redesign
Roles
Responsibilities
Relationships

Step2: Help
Training
Mentoring

Step 3: People Alignment
Assessment
Promotion
Replacement
Recruitment

Step 4: Systems & Structures:
Reporting relationships
Compensation
Information
Measurement & control

Step 2
Help

Step 3
People
Alignment

Step 1
Redesign

Mutual
Engagement

Step 4
Systems &
Structures

Shared
Diagnosis

EXHIBIT 2-7 A Sequential Model of Effective Change Implementation.

Moving to Redesign

Building a Vocabulary of Change
Redesign an alteration in employee roles, responsibilities, and relationships.

Once diagnosis generates dissatisfaction with the status quo, employees can participate in redesigning behavioral patterns to support strategic renewal and outstanding performance. As part of that **redesign** effort, employees seek answers to these questions:

- What can employees do to contribute to the achievement of the company's strategy (roles)?
- What are the performance outcomes for which employees will be held accountable (responsibilities)?
- With whom must employees work in order to meet the expected outcomes, and what is the nature of those interactions (relationships)?

Redesigning roles, responsibilities, and relationships through shared diagnosis serves to align behavioral patterns with the competitive realities facing the organization; with the values, goals, purpose, and principles of the organization; and with the requirements of outstanding performance. Additionally, the participation of employees in the redesign process builds their commitment to implementation.

Meliones and his team at Children's Hospital did not alter formal structures or systems, at least at the early stage of implementation. Rather, the diagnostic phase produced a new understanding of how roles, responsibilities, and relationships should be enacted to support outstanding performance. Meliones explains:

> We moved from mission-bound departments in which people identified only with their particular jobs ("I am a manager," "I am a nurse," and so on) to goal-oriented multidisciplinary teams focused on a particular illness or disease ("We, the ICU team, consisting of the manager, the nurse, the physician, the pharmacist, and the radiologist, help children with heart problems").[22]

Because these newly defined roles flowed from a shared diagnosis of the performance problems facing Children's Hospital, and a common understanding of the hospital's new strategy, employees who would have to enact new behaviors were committed to making them work. Now the redesign of the unit—multidisciplinary teams focused on specific diseases—was not imposed by upper management. Rather, the new design represented an emergent consensus among employees concerning how to implement the hospital's "no margin, no mission" strategy.

Help

At the Children's Hospital, Jon Meliones asked employees who were used to working as individuals to join in a collaborative team effort. Not only that, but he was asking doctors and nurses to become familiar with the financial situation of the hospital, and accountants to develop an appreciation of excellent health care practices. It is typical, in fact, for change efforts to ask employees to develop new skills to match the required new behaviors.

It is in the help stage of change that organizations can offer employees assistance with enacting those new behaviors. Employees being asked, often for the first time, to work on a team will need to learn the skills of teamwork. Sales people being asked to demonstrate new products will need to learn the skills associated with that new functionality. Shop floor supervisors being asked to work as facilitators with work teams will have to learn a new set of skills.

In Chapter 5, we will look at specific tools for providing that help. The point to make for now is that training can be used most effectively in a change process when it follows a participative process of redesigning roles, responsibilities, and relationships. The commitment to enact new behavior drives a desire to learn the skills required of that behavior. The skills and competencies developed in the help step of implementation are less likely to "fade out" because the organization's strategy is calling for their regular and ongoing use.

Theory into Practice

Asking employees to enact new behaviors—roles, responsibilities, and relationships—can be supported by organizational help in learning new skills.

People Alignment

After a shared diagnostic process produces a shared understanding of the renewed strategy and a commitment to change, and *after* employees engage in a process of redesigning roles, responsibilities, and relationships, implementation calls upon **people alignment**: the process of matching the attributes of employees—their skills, motivation, attitudes, and behaviors—with the strategic requirements of the organization.

Building a Vocabulary of Change
People alignment the process of matching the attributes of employees with the strategic requirements of the organization.

The process is designed, to borrow a phrase from Jim Collins' book, *Good to Great*, to get the right people with the right competencies *on* the bus and the wrong people *off* the bus.[23]

The specific interventions that can be called upon in this stage of implementation include:

- *Assessment of employees*—which can now reflect the new set of required competencies
- *Recruitment*—which seeks to attract and select new employees based on the demand for new competencies and fit with the redesigned organization
- *Promotion*—which identifies current employees whose skill makes them effective enablers of the change
- *Removal and replacement*—which deals with individuals who cannot or will not alter their patterns of behavior in ways consistent with the newly defined roles, responsibilities, and relationships

Aligning human resource capabilities with the new strategic requirements of the organization—that is, the goal of the people alignment step.

Theory into Practice

Effective change implementation requires new skills and competencies on the part of the organization's employees.

Reinforcing New Behaviors

Now comes the point in the change implementation process when leaders reinforce altered patterns of behavior through new structures, systems, and technologies. Roles, responsibilities, and relationships have been redesigned, individuals have been offered the opportunity to learn and enact new behavioral patterns and competencies, and the right people are in place.

Making formal systems alterations early in the change process risks creating resistance. Meliones and his team at Children's Hospital decided *together* to call upon a performance measurement system—the balanced scorecard—to help institutionalize the new behaviors designed at early stages of the change. The measurement system became "an essential component of our culture and supports ongoing change."[24] "Hardwiring" changes, such as structures and systems that grow organically out of employees' experiences and are not imposed from above early in the change implementation process, have a far better chance of receiving the support of affected employees.

Theory into Practice

Altering formal organizational systems and structures can come at the back end of a change implementation in order to refreeze new patterns of behavior.

Building a Vocabulary of Change
Mutual engagement the process of building a participatory dialogue among employees at all organizational levels to the requirements of and process for achieving change.

Mutual Engagement at the Core

At the center of the model and accompanying every stage is a process of **mutual engagement**.[25] Participation in decision making, as we noted in Chapter 1, helps build commitment to the outcomes of that decision-making process. The cycle of change implementation, then, needs to create opportunities for dialogue, discussion, communication, and participation as a way of building commitment to the changes. Those opportunities are what can be called mutual engagement. Mutual engagement rests on the assumption that multiple stakeholders—particularly the employees at all organizational levels whose behaviors have to change—will need to be committed to the change.

Beyond building commitment, mutual engagement provides another asset indispensable to effective change implementation. In all organizations, vital knowledge about the current state of the company's operations, about the shifting expectations of customers, about the required interface with suppliers, and about emerging technological trends and developments in the industry are embedded deeply in and widely across the firm. Employees have a unique perspective on how well the organization is meeting its strategic goals and living up to its espoused values. Employees directly experience whether management development and training efforts are producing desired and strategically-aligned patterns of behavior.

Theory into Practice

Mutual engagement at every stage of the implementation process helps assure learning and builds commitment.

How does an organization gain access to such vital knowledge? By allowing employees to influence important change decisions at each step in the implementation process, organizations invite employees to share their knowledge and ensure that decision-making proceeds in full awareness of that knowledge, as well as the consequences of the decisions on the employees who will be impacted.

We will address specific steps that can be taken to ensure mutual engagement in Chapter 3. For now, let us understand that mutual engagement requires that participating parties enter mutual engagement with two beliefs.[26] First, they must accept *mutuality*, which is the belief on the part of individual participants that the *other* participants have both the capacity and the desire to learn and to change. If a manager believes that employees are simply unwilling or unable to change, that manager will have little incentive to engage.

Second, the participating parties must accept *reciprocity*, which is the belief on the part of individual participants that *they* have something to learn from the other participants. Individuals who believe that they know what the problems are and have a recipe for attacking those problems will have little incentive to enter into an open and freewheeling exchange of ideas.

Mutuality and reciprocity grow out of values and assumptions regarding learning. Only individuals who believe that learning, adaptation, and change are core to their role and responsibilities within the organization will enter into a real, shared dialogue. At the same time, individuals must accept and welcome the participation and contribution of others as vital to that learning.

Those beliefs are not enough to ensure mutual engagement, however. Participants must also be willing and able to engage in advocacy and inquiry.[27] *Advocacy* involves the willingness and ability of individual participants to reveal positions and the assumptions underlying those positions. *Inquiry* involves the willingness and ability of individual participants to open their own positions and underlying assumptions to questions and challenges by others.

Advocacy invites individuals to reveal their ideas about *how things ought to be done* and to place on the table the data and assumptions that have led to that position. But advocacy can deteriorate into posturing, even browbeating, if it is not accompanied by inquiry that seeks alternative views, welcomes challenge, and probes one's own thinking. When these four elements—mutuality, reciprocity, advocacy, and inquiry (summarized in Exhibit 2-8)—are in place, mutual engagement is possible.

Mutuality	Belief on the part of participants that the *other* participants have both the capacity and the desire to learn and to change
Reciprocity	Belief on the part of participants that *they* have something to learn from the other participants
Advocacy	Willingness and ability of participants to *reveal positions* and the *assumptions* underlying those positions
Inquiry	Willingness and ability of participants to open their own positions and underlying assumptions to *questions and challenges* by others

EXHIBIT 2-8   The Four Elements of Mutual Engagement.

Avoiding Implementation Traps

Organizational leaders can maximize the likelihood that their implementation efforts will succeed if they orchestrate an intervention that moves sequentially through these required stages in a manner that integrates theoretical insights into specific interventions (Exhibit 2-7).

The road map offered in the sequential implementation model provides both an analytic and planning tool. It also provides insights into **implementation traps**: the application of appropriate change tools at inappropriate points in the implementation process.

Organizational leaders, for example, may call on Step 4 to initiate change. The difficulty with that, however, is that they are substituting "refreezing" for "unfreezing." When used to drive change, new structures have the effect of imposing new behavioral expectations on employees who are still attached to the "social habits." By leaping over the process of shared diagnosis and redesign, leaders who initiate change through Step 4 interventions have often failed to build commitment to new behaviors or to exploit the knowledge and insights embedded deeply and widely in their employees. Exhibit 2-9 presents different ways that change leaders can fall into the implementation trap by calling on interventions out of sequence.

Building a Vocabulary of Change

Implementation trap applying the right tools at the wrong time in the implementation process.

Trap	For Example	Why It Is a Trap
Starting at Step 4	Imposing new system or structure (e.g., global matrix, balanced scorecard measurement system)	Will be experienced as "change from above"; likely to be poorly understood and resisted.
Starting at Step 2	Driving change with training program	Because employees work in an unchanged organizational context, their learning is likely to be short-lived and will fade out.
Starting at Step 3	Recruiting new employees, removing and replacing, and replacing individuals seen to be resisters to change	Easy to make mistakes due to lack of understanding concerning what is required and who can adapt to new demands; can be viewed by employees as arbitrary, thus diminishing trust and commitment.
Starting implementation without shared diagnosis	Redesigning work (e.g., creating cross-functional teams)	New designs will be seen as unconnected to strategic reality and performance demands of organization; can lead to compliance or resistance on the part of line managers.
Ignoring mutual engagement	Driving change through top management	Leadership may be out of touch with realities of organization while employees may not understand strategic imperatives.

EXHIBIT 2-9 Change Implementation Traps.

Conclusion

The sequential model of effective change implementation represents an integration of the key insights offered by previous theorists of organizational change. The diagnosis stage, as the model suggests, becomes the opening intervention in effective implementation. For an understanding of how that diagnostic stage can be the most helpful in propelling change implementation, we can turn to an analysis of organizational diagnosis.

Discussion Questions

1. How might Blue Cloud general manger Shel Skinner have handled his attempt to introduce more efficient software development differently?
2. According to Kurt Lewin, why is it so difficult to motivate employees to alter their patterns of behavior?
3. Discuss the various ways in which change theorists have attempted to introduce performance and results into the implementation process.
4. What were the sources of resistance to change at the Concord Bookshop? What might Smith and the board have learned from that resistance?

Case Discussion

Read "The Asda Way of Working" (A) and prepare answers to the following questions:

1. Based on your understanding of the theories of effective change implementation, how would you evaluate the change leadership of Archie Norman and his top executives during their first six months at Asda?
2. Based on your understanding of the theories of effective change implementation, what specific steps would you recommend be undertaken over the next 18 months?

The Asda Way of Working (A)

Asda, the grocery store chain that Archie Norman had just been hired to lead, teetered on the edge on bankruptcy.[28] While Asda had enjoyed a long run of success in the United Kingdom, upscale competitors and down-market deep discounters had sharply eroded its customer base. Norman, an outsider to Asda who had never run any retailing operation, believed that Asda could not afford the luxury of piecemeal or incremental improvement. Everything about the organization—from the way they purchased and displayed products to the way store managers interacted with shop-floor employees—would have to change. *Everything*.

Company Background

With 65,000 employees in 205 Asda stores and another 2,000 at corporate headquarters, Asda was the fourth largest grocery store chain in United Kingdom. Asda enjoyed annual sales of $6 billion[†] and claimed 8 percent of the supermarket business, ranking fourth in market share.

[†]All figures are given in equivalent U.S. dollars.

Starting in the late 1960s, Asda pioneered the concept of large supermarkets located outside of downtown areas with expansive parking lots and low prices. Flourishing particularly in working-class areas, Asda became known as a blue-collar store, specializing in low prices in a warehouse like atmosphere ("Pile it high and sell it cheap" was a phrase commonly associated with this type of operation). The demographic of their customer base was decidedly "down-market." In that niche, Asda was quite successful, operating without any real competition. The larger grocery store chains vied for more upscale (i.e., wealthy) customers and simply could not compete with Asda on price.

Asda's problems began when top management embarked on two equally disastrous paths. First, they diverted much of the profit from the grocery operations into nonfood acquisitions: retail operations such as furniture and carpeting. And second, management moved to change their customer base from blue-collar to more upscale shoppers. As part of that upscale strategy, Asda moved out of their traditional blue-collar strongholds into wealthier suburban locations. That move had two negative effects:

1. In the wealthy suburbs, it placed them in competition with chains not burdened with the reputation of being blue-collar warehouse stores.
2. In their traditional working-class areas, they allowed competitors to steal market share from the very blue-collar base that Asda seemed to be abandoning.

Top management exacerbated the problem by spending lavishly on themselves: corporate jets, high-style corporate offices, and the like. Soon Asda products were pricier than its competitors' were. Asda began to spiral downward. While the company borrowed money to expand into new markets and open new stores, same-store sales declined and overall growth slowed. In response, Asda's board of directors fired its chief executive and brought in Archie Norman to turn Asda around.

Enter Archie Norman

Thirty-seven-year-old Archie Norman had joined the McKinsey & Company consulting organization to work in the company's retail division after receiving an MBA in the United States. From McKinsey he moved to a large retail operation where he served as chief financial officer. Norman arrived at Asda with no specific experience in the grocery business and no general management experience aside from his graduate school training.

What Norman found when he arrived at Asda was complete demoralization of the workforce; a highly politicized central headquarters; people caught up in their "chimneys"—operations people did not talk to the trading people, and nobody listened to marketing. It was a place, noted one observer, completely bereft of any notion of where it was headed or how it might weather the crisis. And that crisis was deeper and more profound than Norman had expected:

> We had so much debt we thought we would be in breach of our loan covenants shortly. Our sales were running at 2 percent below the industry like for like, and the trend was heading south. We had, if anything, worse value than our competitors. And while everyone was very loyal about it, morale was actually quite poor.

Norman inaugurated his intervention by reaching an understanding with his board of directors. The turnaround would not happen overnight, they agreed. If the board would tolerate Norman's investments in renewing the chain, he would deliver significant return by the end of the third year:

> I told the stockholders and the market analysts, that I had a three year plan that Asda should be returned to profitability and growth within that time frame. The stockholders agreed to let me make short-term sacrifices for long-term profitability.

Building a Top Team

Norman immediately set out to attract other outsiders to the top management team. Over a six-month period, he replaced two of his three direct reports,[‡] creating a team that consisted of:

- Allen Leighton, vice president, marketing,
- Phil Cox, chief financial officer, and
- Tony Campbell, vice president, trading.

Of his three direct reports, only Campbell was a holdover from the previous Asda regime. His past position had been vice president of operations. None of the new hires had any previous retail experience.

Among his direct reports, Allen Leighton emerged as the first among equals. He was friendly, outgoing, dynamic, expansive, bright, and creative—a complement to the generally more cerebral and contained Norman. Top managers suggested that nothing of significance occurred in the organization without the direct involvement and approval of Norman and/or Leighton.

The First Six Months

Norman's first task was to pull the organization back from disaster. "Archie had to convince people that there was a problem," said Phil Cox, "that our poor performance wasn't just a momentary hiccup." In speech after speech, to employees as well as investors, Norman laid out the details of what he referred to as Asda's "dark moment." He ignored frequent advice that he soften his blunt message of "gloom and doom." A regional manager shook his head after one such speech, admitting:

> None of us understood how serious our financial difficulties were. When Archie brought all this out into the open, it finally dawned on people just how close to the edge we'd been. It became clear that we couldn't just wave a magic wand and make all things right.

In the first six months of Norman's tenure, all of the top management team took up residence in a local hotel. They were often joined by Chrispin Tweddle, a consultant hired by Norman with considerable retail experience. During the day, Cox focused on Asda's financial crisis[§] while Norman toured the stores, talking to employees at all levels and taking copious notes. Then the team would sit up together until past midnight talking about a vision for a new Asda.

[‡]Before walking in the door on his first day, Norman had decided to firm the current CFO and had already reached an agreement with Phill Cox to join the company.

[§]A number of steps were taken to raise money. Nonfood operations were either sold off or, failing that, shut down; head count at corportate headquarters was reduced by 30 percent; in-store middle-manager positions were cut by 10 percent; and an 18-month pay freeze was initiated for all employees.

Every discussion was based on the shared assumption that the total organization was dysfunctional. Said Norman:

> We wouldn't survive if we simply created a little change. We had to revitalize the entire organization. We had to take the organization paradigm, which was over here, and move it over there. We assumed that however the organization worked when we got here was wrong.

In particular, the team believed they needed to address Asda's stovepiped functional culture, which made companywide collaboration a virtual impossibility. Observed Norman:

> The whole place was dysfunctional. The top management never met together except once a month at a board meeting. They never talked from week to week. And the whole organization ran down these functional pipelines.

Renewal

The process of change, which the top team came to refer to as "renewal," would occur within the 205 stores. But the team provided guidance to the renewal process in three forms: a statement of corporate strategy, an articulation of company values, and a blueprint for what came to be known as the Asda Way of Working.

STRATEGIC RENEWAL. Norman called on consultants from McKinsey to help him and his team formulate a new strategic position. Their deliberations started with gaining a thorough understanding of the grocery industry and Asda's position in it. They then formulated a strategy statement: "We will supply the weekly shopping needs of ordinary working families."

CULTURE CHANGE. The team realized early on that they would have to do more than change the old Asda culture; they would have to shatter it and then rebuild it from the ground up. To set the parameters for that new culture, they drew up a statement of company values (see Exhibit 2-10), plus a set of operational concepts that became known as the Asda Way of Working. Store-based renewal would flow from a few key concepts: greater autonomy to store management in making operational decisions and, within the stores, self-managed autonomous teams focusing on particular product lines such as produce, bakery goods, and so forth.

In a speech laying out the Asda Way of Working to store managers, Norman said, "I see a day when our stores consist of clusters of businesses, each with their own profit-and-loss responsibilities." A store manager, who had been with Asda in the pre-Norman era, reflected on the message he heard concerning the Asda Way of Working: "What they told me was to involve everybody in everything. As long as you're doing that, you're going to get the best out of people."

This sense of empowerment and responsiveness "will be a unique source of advantage," insisted Norman, "against the militarized and straight-jacketed competition."

1. *Equality*. Our staff are our colleagues and our colleagues are our staff. We need to start treating our people differently. Toughness and hierarchy must not get in the way of our need to develop people and involve them in our business: quite simply to make Asda a better place to work. The time has come to recognize that the world is changing. We cannot deliver better sales and better service without our staff. They demand respect. They want involvement. The are our competitive advantage. But they will only be our competitive advantage if they think of Asda as the best place to work because of what we can offer them, and I don't mean money. Paying people money is the easiest thing in the world, but it is not management. We must offer them a better place to work they can feel part of, a place they can believe in.

And to reinforce the change, I want to ensure today that we burn the symbols of the past. Let's start with our language: we talk about staff as if they are a different breed from management. We are all in this together, and these hierarchical distinctions must go. From now on there is one word and one word only for people employed at Asda. It is colleagues.

2. *Sales*. Selling will be a universal Asda responsibility. Every one of our 65,000 employees is here to help the selling effort. Asda is a natural selling company. It is what we used to be about and it is what we will be about again. It fits with the idea of how we will run our stores and it fits with the spirit of the company. We have to get away from the idea that grocery is a commodity. There is no such thing as a commodity in our business. Selling and service can make anything special.

It is vital to remember that selling is the only real motivation in retail. There is no fun in pushing paper. There is no fun in just enforcing disciplines unless they are going to drive the sales. That is why I want every one of our 65,000 colleagues to know that selling is the most important thing we do. And I want every colleague in every area of the business to know how the sales are going in his or her store or trading area and for the company as a whole.

3. *Service*. Through selling we will serve our customers better. We need not just good but legendary customer service, service that constantly amazes out customers. How do we achieve this? The only way to do it is to recruit the right staff and motivate them to sell.

4. *Value*. What we sell is better value. We can believe in it because by selling it we are doing our customers a favor.

5. *Cost*. We hate waste of any kind. Waste is not an allowable option. We must reduce waste—to be lower cost, to provide better value.

6. *Improvement*. Our job is to improve the business. Everyone is here to help improve the business every day and in every way. That's the one job description that really matters. This is your obligation and your duty. I want to see every aspect of our business moving forward. We have lost the habit of innovation in this company. Why? Because innovation is risky. If you innovate, you make mistakes. We got into the habit when mistakes were made of looking for a head in the basket. Let me be clear: if you are not making mistakes, you are not innovating. And that's the time you should worry.

EXHIBIT 2-10   Statement of Values.*

*This statement of Asda Values comes from a speech delivered by Norman to regional managers.

Moving Renewal into the Stores

With his top management team in place to provide a general sense of direction, Norman turned his attention to the 205 stores. Renewal must become a reality within those stores, and Norman thought about how to proceed. As he considered his options for action, Norman analyzed several key issues.

1. Because Asda's previous management had underinvested in the stores, the physical plant had deteriorated precipitously. Asda's new management estimated that each store required an average investment of $3.25 million to become a state-of-the-art facility, but they wondered about the connection between the required plant retooling and the cultural upheaval implied by the value statement and the Asda Way of Working. Should the two processes be coupled or separated? If handled together, would physical revamping and cultural renewal simply be too much change for any one store to handle?

2. Norman wondered whether somebody—either an individual or a group—should be assigned responsibility for oversight and coordination of the renewal efforts within the stores. Or was Asda likely to achieve greater innovation by allowing each store to find its own way to define and apply renewal?

3. While Norman had shaken up his top management group, he knew that the functional stovepipes that had prevented collaboration in the past still existed. Could real innovation occur within a functional structure? How would he address the lingering constraints still being felt because of the company's past culture?

4. Ultimately, Norman knew, everything about how the stores operated would have to change. But how much change should occur and how fast? Could he focus on all the stores at once, or should he concentrate on a small number of pilot stores?

5. Part of the concern over the pace of renewal had to do with the depth of managerial talent—or, more precisely, the lack of depth—at Asda. At the corporate level, the 16 managers who reported directly to members of the top management team were all Asda "veterans." The same could be said of the 205 store managers. Could individuals who had survived, or even thrived, under the old culture make the transition required of the new strategy, values, and way of working? Conversely, large-scale termination at the managerial level might prove disastrous: depriving Asda of much needed grocery industry experience, undermining already shaky morale, fostering risk-averse behavior, and stifling innovation. Plus, there was hardly a large queue of talented managers seeking employment at Asda.

Finally, Norman wondered about his own role in the renewal effort. Already his colleagues on the top management team had reached consensus on his personal management style, and "controlling" was the most frequently applied label. Among the evaluations offered:

- He must have learned the lesson as a young boy that if you want to do anything right, you have to do it yourself.
- In truth, and I'm sure Archie would admit this, his preferred style is a controlling style. The issue of devolving power does not sit comfortably with him.
- The only thing you will never hear Archie say is, "I think you're wrong, but do it anyway."

Norman offered the following self-assessment:

I do believe I give people the right to argue and challenge. But I still make decisions, and I don't want to delude people into thinking I don't. I simply won't tolerate any deviation around basic values and strategy.

While expressing his desire to avoid the "cult of personality" at Asda, Norman realized that he would play a large role in determining the shape and direction of the renewal effort. The challenge going forward was to ensure that role be positive and productive.

Endnotes

1. Information in this case is based on Jon N. Meliones, Richard Ballard, Richard Liekweg, and William Burton, "No Mission No Margin: It's That Simple," *Journal of Health Care Finance* 27 (Spring 2001); Jon Meliones, "Saving Money, Saving Lives," *Harvard Business Review* (November–December 2000); and *ITWeek.com*, January 1, 2001.

2. Robert S. Kaplan and David P. Norton, "Trans-forming the Balanced Scorecard from Performance Measurement to Strategic Management: Part I," *Accounting Horizons* 15 (March 2001), p. 87; Robert S. Kaplan and David P. Norton, "Using the Balanced Scorecard as a Strategic Management System," *Harvard Business Review* (January–February 1996), p. 3; Robert S. Kaplan and David P. Norton, "Integrating Shareholder Value and Activity-Based Costing with the Balanced Scorecard," *In Context* (Boston: Harvard Business School Publishing, 2001), p. 4.

3. These essays and others are collected in Kurt Lewin, *Field Theory in Social Science: Selected Theoretical Papers* (New York: Harper and Row, 1951).

4. *Ibid.*, p. 226.

5. Emily Thornton, "A New Order at Nissan," *Business Week*, October 11, 1999, p. 54.

6. Edgar H. Schein, "Kurt Lewin's Change Theory in the Field and in the Classroom: Notes Toward a Model of Managed Learning," *Systems Practice* 9 (1996), p. 28.

7. Lewin, *Field Theory in Social Science*, p. 229.

8. Lewin, *Field Theory in Social Science*, p. 231.

9. Critiques of Lewin's theories can be found in Ralph Stacey, "Management and the Science of Complexity: If Organizational Life is Non-linear, Can Business Strategies Prevail?" *Research and Technology Management* 39 (1996), pp. 2–5; Wanda J. Orlikowski and Debra Hofman, "An Improvisational Model for Change Management: The Case of Groupware Technologies," *Sloan Management Review* 38 (Winter 1997), pp. 11–21; and Alexander Styhre, "Non-linear Change in Organizations: Organization Change Management Informed by Complexity Theory," *Leadership and Organization Development Journal* 23 (2002), pp. 343–351.

10. Based, in part, on Michael Beer and Bert Spector, "Human Resource Management: The Integration of Industrial Relations and Organization Development," in Kendrith M. Rowland and Gerald R. Ferris, eds., *Research in Personnel and Human Resources Management: A Research Annual*, Vol. 2 (Greenwich, CT: JAI Press, 1984), pp. 261–297.

11. That perspective on conflict is fully explored in Richard E. Walton, *Interpersonal Peacemaking: Confrontations and Third-Party Consultation* (Reading, MA: Addison-Wesley, 1969).

12. Kenneth W. Thomas, "Conflict and Conflict Management," in Marvin D. Dunnette, ed., *Handbook of Industrial and Organizational Psychology* (Chicago: Rand McNally, 1976), pp. 889–935.

13. Michael Beer and Bert Spector, "Organizational Diagnosis: Its Role in Organizational Learning," *Journal of Counselling and Development* 71 (1993), pp. 642–650.

14. On the importance of process-driven change, see Beer, Eisenstat, and Spector, *The Critical Path to Corporate Renewal*; Richard P. Rumselt, "How Much Does Industry Matter?" *Strategic Management Journal* 12 (1991), pp. 167–185; Robert Macintosh and Donald MacLean, "Conditioned Emergence: A Dissipative Structures Approach to Transformation," *Strategic Management Journal* 20 (1999), pp. 297–316; Richard H. Axelrod, *Changing the Way We Change Organizations* (San Francisco: Berrett-Koehler, 2000); L.C. Harris and E. Ogbonna, "The Unintended Consequences of Culture Interventions: A Study of Unexpected Outcomes," *British Journal of Management* 12 (2002), pp. 31-49.

15. Bert Spector, "From Bogged Down to Fired Up: Inspiring Organizational Change," *Sloan Management Review* 30 (Summer 1989), pp. 29–34.

16. Beer, Eisenstat, and Spector, *The Critical Path to Corporate Renewal*, p. 40.

17. *Ibid.*, pp. 45–46.

18. This case is detailed in Beer, Eisenstat, and Spector, *The Critical Path to Corporate Renewal*.

19. *Ibid.*, p. 52.

20. Robert H. Schaffer and Harvey A. Thomson, "Successful Change Programs Begin with Results," *Harvard Business Review* (January-February 1992), p. 83.

21. The framework presented here builds on one presented earlier, in Beer, Eisenstat, and Spector, *The Critical Path to Corporate Renewal*.

22. Meliones, "Saving Money, Saving Lives," pp. 59–60.

23. James C. Collins, *Good to Great: Why Some Companies Make the Leap and Others Don't* (New York: Harper Business, 2001).

24. Meliones is quoted in *ITWeek.com*, January 1, 2001, p. 1.

25. The concept of mutual engagement is developed in José Santos, Bert Spector, and Ludo van-der-Hayden, "Toward a Theory of Corporate Business Model Innovation," Northeastern University College of Business Administration Working Paper, 2008.

26. Based on Mary Ann Hazen, "Dialogue as a Path of Change and Development in a Pluralistic World." A paper presented at the Academy of Management Meetings, Chicago, IL, 1999.

27. The notion of advocacy and inquiry as a requirement for learning is discussed in Chris Argyris, *Flawed Advice and the Management Trap: How Managers Can Know When They're Getting Good Advice and When They're Not* (New York: Oxford University Press, 2000).

28. The case is based on research conducted for Bert Spector, *Taking Charge and Letting Go: A Breakthrough Strategy for Creating and Managing the Horizontal Company* (New York: Free Press, 1995).

CHAPTER 3

Mutual Engagement and Shared Diagnosis

Effective organizational change requires an alteration in patterns of employee behavior. At the outset of change implementation, leaders can engage employees in a process of shared diagnosis. The goal of mutual engagement in a process of shared diagnosis is to unfreeze "social habits" and create a sense of dissatisfaction with the status quo. That process of shared diagnosis built on mutual engagement constructs the appropriate platform for the upcoming change.

This chapter will describe and analyze mutual engagement and shared diagnosis. In particular, the chapter will:

- Describe the role of diagnosis in assessing behaviors and values and in creating dissatisfaction with the status quo
- Discuss the use of a systemic framework for guiding diagnosis
- Explore ways to overcome the "climate of silence" that blocks mutual engagement
- Provide the key ingredients of a diagnostic intervention
- Define the role played by after-action reviews in created quick learning and improvement

First, we will look at the six-year effort by a CEO intent on energizing transformational change.

BRINGING GE's "MAGIC" TO HOME DEPOT

An air of ambiguity surrounded Robert L. (Bob) Nardelli's six-year tenure as CEO of Home Depot, America's second largest retail chain.[1] Between December 2000 when he arrived from GE's Power Systems division and January 2007 when he abruptly resigned, Nardelli presided over expansive growth (from $42 billion in revenues in

2000 to $81 billion in 2005) and a disheartening decline in stock price (from $37 a share to $23). Home Depot's archrival, Lowe's, meantime, gained market share and enjoyed a 210 percent increase in stock price.

From the moment he arrived at Home Depot, Nardelli announced his goal of transformational change, saying, "What effectively got Home Depot from zero to $50 billion in sales wasn't going to get it the next $50 billion." What worked so well in the past, he insisted, would not work as well in the future.

Founded in 1979 by Bernie Marcus and Arthur Blank, Home Depot's "big box" approach to hardware and appliance retailing allowed the company to become the youngest business ever to reach $40 billion in sales (in 1999). The founders carefully balanced the advantages of size—economies of scope and scale—with a culture that promoted local customer responsiveness. That delicate balance rested on the shoulders of highly autonomous store managers. "Whether it was an aisle, department, or store," said a manager, "you were truly in charge of it." Decentralized merchandising and store-based human resource policies (hiring, training, and promoting) created inefficiencies, but also built a bond between the stores and their customers.

After Nardelli was passed over at GE to be Jack Welch's successor, Marcus and Blank hired him to lead Home Depot to a new generation of growth. Nardelli acknowledged his lack of retailing experience by observing, "Is retail different? Sure it is. But there are certain fundamentals in running a business that are pretty portable."

Nardelli imported GE's legendary focus on operating efficiencies and discipline. Merchandising and human resources were centralized, leading many of the entrepreneurial managers who had been attracted to Home Depot in its early days to leave. Some of Nardelli's tactics—using a closed circuit store-based television system to observe store operations from his corporate office, accepting GE-style compensation packages (Nardelli received $28.5 million in 2005), and drastically increasing the stores' reliance on part-time workers (up from 26 to 50 percent)—hurt employee morale. Customer satisfaction declined precipitously. When a University of Michigan survey placed customer satisfaction at Home Depot dead last (Home Depot's decline in customer satisfaction was the largest decline registered by any company in any industry in the survey's history), Nardelli called the results "a sham."

Rival big-box merchandiser Lowe's achieved a much higher level of customer satisfaction. In stark contrast to Nardelli's reliance on part-time workers, Lowe's built an in-store workforce made up of 80 percent full-time employees. Same-store sales at Lowe's rose faster than did Home Depot's.

The full reasons for Nardelli's January 2007 resignation, labeled by *Business Week* as "stunning," were not disclosed. Nardelli had another stunning announcement to make. Nine months after his departure from Home Depot, he was named to head the newly restructured auto company, Chrysler, that had just been purchased by Cerberus Capital Management.

DIAGNOSING THE ORGANIZATION

The desire on the part of executives such as Bob Nardelli to hit the ground running with solutions, particularly when their organizations are mired in poor performance, may be perfectly understandable. The tendency to believe that what has worked for them in the past can provide a kind of recipe for the future is also strong. GE has been a great success; why not import some of that "magic" to Home Depot?

Taking that approach fails to create mutual engagement and shared diagnosis that is so critical in shaping and guiding change. It can lead to solutions that are inappropriate to the target organization and are not supported—perhaps even actively resisted—by employees.

Theory into Practice

Effective change starts with action but not with solutions.

The desire for quick solutions can lead executives to overlook the critical elements of learning and commitment that can be built through mutual engagement and shared diagnosis. The dynamics of every organization are unique. Additionally, an organization's external competitive forces are likely to be in a state of flux. Therefore, applying a recipe—what worked somewhere else in the past will work here now—can be overly simple, misleading, and even dysfunctional.

GE's best practices may not have been applicable to Home Depot. As we saw, the act of imposing those practices evoked resistance and turnover. Lack of mutual engagement—of holding an honest conversation among employees about what needed to change, why, and how—led to low levels of employee commitment to the new culture sought by Nardelli.

Diagnosis is meant to create learning about the real, current, and unique dynamics impacting the organization's performance. When combined with mutual engagement, it is designed to create deep and wide commitment to the desired outcome.

Theory into Practice

Don't expect formulas—solutions that have worked in the past and are imposed on the current situation—to work for your organization. That approach to change can be overly simple, misleading, and dysfunctional.

At its most fundamental level, diagnosis is about learning: learning *what* needs to be changed and *why*. The notion of *shared* diagnosis goes one step further. For change implementation to occur effectively many employees at multiple hierarchical levels and in varied units need to change in the same direction. A diagnostic process engaged in by an individual, no matter how insightful, highly placed, or influential that individual may be, will not lead to coordinated change. It is only when the same diagnosis is shared by multiple individuals that change implementation can move forward effectively.

Theory into Practice

The most effective change implementation starts with a diagnosis that is shared by many employees at multiple organizational levels.

Altered and renewed strategies, new business models, and shifting external realities typically call for new skills, competencies, and patterns of behavior. The sequential implementation model depicted in Exhibit 2-7 starts with diagnosis in order to identify both the current state of skills, competencies, and behaviors as well as the requirements for future outstanding performance. Mutual engagement by employees generates awareness of the gap between the status quo and the desired future state. That awareness, in turn, provides the source of dissatisfaction and the drive for change.

Recall from Chapter 2 Lewin's warning that "lectures" about the status quo—speeches on the need for change or PowerPoint presentations on the new strategy, for instance—will not be sufficient to create within employees the disequilibrium necessary to motivate change. Instead, effective change starts with a diagnostic process that engages employees in a learning process. Executives learn why the status quo is unsatisfactory; so, too, do employees at all levels and in all units.

In addition to generating learning, mutual engagement in shared diagnosis can create a consensus among the stakeholders not just about *what* needs to be changed but also *how* to bring about that change. Engaging employees in the process of collecting and learning from data and then using that learning to shape an intervention can help build real commitment to implementing change.

Building a Vocabulary of Change

Diagnosis the process of learning about the dynamics of the organization in order to take action intended to improve performance.

As an alternative to initiating change by announcing a solution, leaders can instead begin with diagnosis. **Diagnosis** is the process of learning about the dynamics of an organization's functioning. It is meant to engage employees in the process of identifying both the current state and the desired future state of the organization.[2] Employees collect data and engage in a dialogue concerning the meaning of the data. The diagnostic process provides a roadmap for change; mutual engagement in diagnosis helps build motivation on the part of employees to alter their behaviors.

Theory into Practice

Use diagnosis as the preliminary stage in implementing change.

Requirement for a Systemic Framework

Diagnosis can be guided by a broad, systemic view of the firm.

Building a Vocabulary of Change

Diagnostic framework a roadmap to analyzing alignment that makes explicit both the key elements of an organization that need to be aligned and the interconnections and interdependencies among those elements.

Organizations are composed of multiple units and functions, line and support staff functions, and processes that link various activities. There are also design elements, both formal and informal, that organizations call upon to—they hope—align employee behavior with strategy. Additionally, organizations live in a dynamic world: new competitors, technologies, business models, customer expectations, changing government rules and regulations, shifting environmental imperatives.

A **diagnostic framework**—a roadmap for guiding mutual engagement in shared diagnosis—should help to identify all the key variables that impact the performance of an organization. But it must do more. None of these elements, after all, exist in a vacuum. Just think: employee behaviors are shaped by organizational design, which should serve the company's business model and reflect its strategy and purpose. And all of the elements, in turn, must find success within an ever shifting external environment.

Understanding that organizations exist in constant interaction with a dynamic external environment leads to an important insight: An organization whose internal processes are perfectly well suited for one kind of competitive environment may find those same processes becoming a burden in a new, shifting landscape.

Theory into Practice

In order to set the stage for effective implementation, diagnosis can do more than target specific elements of the organization; it can focus on the entire organization.

Take the Federal Bureau of Investigation (FBI). The FBI built its reputation battling crime and arresting criminals. The mission of the FBI—"G-men battling notorious criminals"—created a culture and a set of structures and policies that gave absolute primacy to criminal investigations and special agents in the field. A highly decentralized structure allowed agents to focus their attentions locally. Additionally, the FBI preferred internally generated data, often distrusting and rejecting information supplied by external agencies and sources.

The attacks of 9/11 on New York and Washington created a sea change in the mission and goals of the FBI. Gathering information and *preventing* attacks—that was the new critical task. Recognizing that the new mission would require altered patterns of thinking and behaving, FBI Director Robert Mueller took steps to transform the bureau.

When organizations such as the FBI attempt to undergo strategic renewal, leaders can call on a diagnostic framework to focus attention on the multiple elements that contribute to success. But an effective framework can do more; it can delineate and help make explicit the interactions and interconnects among the elements. If employee behaviors do not reflect strategy—let's say, salespeople spend most of their time selling products that are no longer core to the company's strategy, or functional employees continue to work mainly within their functions rather than across functions when the company's strategy calls for rapid new product development—a framework can drive employees into analyzing the linkages that have created those misalignments.

Theory into Practice

Use a common organizational framework to shape mutual engagement and shared diagnosis.

No framework can, of course, explicate all the interconnects, causes and effects, and actions and reactions that occur within an organization and impact performance. That is why relying on a framework is only a preliminary step in the diagnosis. Mutual engagement and open, honest dialogue will build on the framework and enrich participants' understanding of organizational dynamics.

There are numerous frameworks available for judging alignment.[3] The goal of any framework is to provide a common guide to participants as they seek to understand the interconnected linkages that affect organizational performance. David Nadler has suggested that for a framework to be effective and useful, it should adhere to certain criteria:[4]

1. The framework should be *explicit* so that all the elements and interconnections are stated and described. Otherwise, those using the framework will not be able to evaluate either its meaning or its usefulness.
2. The framework should be *operationally defined* so that "constructs, variables, relationships, and effectiveness criteria are defined in terms of the operations needed to measure them."[5]
3. The framework should be *empirically validated*. The consultant must be sure that the constructs and relationships explicated in the framework represent the latest and best state of knowledge.
4. The framework should also have *face validity*; that is, it "must make sense in the light of the day-to-day experiences of organizational members."[6] Without face validity, employees are more likely to respond with skepticism, even denial, and resist acting on any conclusions.
5. Finally, a framework should be *generalizable*, that is, applicable to differing organizations in differing competitive and technological environments. Generalizability might be especially useful in a complex, multiple product organization where the framework can be applied to all the varied units.

What makes a framework effective is that it leads people toward systemic thinking that can focus diagnosis on disjunctions that are impeding implementation of the renewed strategy and achievement of outstanding performance. A framework helps employees understand that outstanding performance can be achieved or sustained only with alignment between and among all the elements. It builds a common understanding and language that can form the basis of a shared diagnosis.

STARTING WITH MUTUAL ENGAGEMENT

The mutual engagement that forms the core of an effective change implementation effort starts at the diagnostic step. Employees can have the opportunity to engage in a dialogue that focuses on performance and the impediments and barriers to achieving an organization's strategic goals.

Building a Vocabulary of Change
Dialogue a structured, collective discussion among two or more parties with no predetermined conclusion.

Dialogue is a structured, collective discussion among two or more parties. Dialogue builds mutuality because the purpose of dialogue is to move beyond the understanding of any one individual and create an enriched and shared understanding and the multiple participants.

Dialogue is meant to be more than one-way communication, more even than a simple conversation. Because the goal of dialogue is learning, it is a process that leads to unexpected conclusions. The process of participating in dialogue enriches both the understanding and the commitment of all parties to the implications and conclusions of that dialogue.

Theory into Practice

Creating a dialogue offers the opportunity for an open and honest conversation among employees.

Achieving an open, honest dialogue, especially in a hierarchical organization, can be difficult. Success in creating a dialogue depends on a number of factors. Because dialogue occurs in an organizational context, that context must be one that enables rather than impedes openness.

Organizational Enablers of Dialogue

Dialogue does not occur within a vacuum. It is up to organizational leaders to help create and maintain a context that allows, encourages, and enables an open and candid dialogue. Speaking openly and honestly can be a risky undertaking. Employees often feel inhibited when asked to speak up concerning organizational problems and barriers to outstanding performance.

That seemed to be the case when newly named CEO Carleton (Carly) Fiorina presented her reorganization plan to Hewlett-Packard (HP).[7] Plagued by poor performance in its computer and printer business, HP's board hired Fiorina from Lucent. Appreciating the urgency of the situation, Fiorina hit the ground running. Her first public appearances were well staged and electric. What she had in mind was clear: Overcome HP's decades-old drive toward decentralized divisions and autonomous decision making, embrace the Internet, revitalize the sales force, trim costs, and energize employees.

Fiorina also had a clear idea of how she would achieve her goals, which she revealed at her first strategic meeting just a month after her arrival. To reverse the company's "sacred" emphasis on decentralization, she proposed a simpler, more centralized structure: two "back-end" divisions (designing, manufacturing, and distribution—one for printers, the other for computers) and two "front-end" marketing and sales operations—one for consumers and one for corporations. The company would also begin to focus on far fewer products. ("This is a company that can do anything; it is not a company that can do everything.") Finally, the culture would change dramatically and immediately from entitlement based to performance based. "Let me make something very clear," Fiorina told executives. "You will make your numbers. There will be no excuses. And if you can't make your numbers, I will find someone who will."

Fiorina asked for the support of HP's top executives on her centralization and reorganization plan, and she got it. That is not to say, however, that they all *agreed* with her. "I don't know anyone who was in favor of it [her back-end/front-end reorganization plan] other than Carly," said one. "She came in with a recipe," said another, "and come hell or high water, she was going to use it." Carolyn Ticknor, head of laser printing, recalled, "I was a deer caught in the headlights when she [Fiorina] described the front and back end."

The phenomenon that inhibits or even eliminates opportunities for the free and open exchange of ideas and views is known as organizational silence.[8] **Organizational silence** refers to the pervasive set of assumptions on the part of employees that candid

Building a Vocabulary of Change
Organizational silence the lack of truthful dialogue in organizations caused by the widespread assumption on the part of employees that candid feedback and the open exchange of ideas will have either no positive impact or negative consequences to the individual, or both.

feedback and open, shared dialogue is to be avoided. As we saw at HP, it is not just employees at lower hierarchical levels who can feel inhibited. Managers and executives can also hesitate to speak openly and honestly, even when they do not understand, agree, or both with the policies being promulgated from the top.[9]

Theory into Practice

Don't confuse passive acceptance with agreement.

Organizational silence hinders mutual engagement. Silence, note Elizabeth Wolfe Morrison and Frances Milliken, undermines an organization's ability to engage in learning. Learning requires engagement, participation, and openness. Pervasive silence—the unwillingness to engage, to participate, and to be open—inhibits learning and makes effective change implementation more difficult.

Theory into Practice

Leaders can ask themselves—has their organization bred a "climate of silence" that discourages subordinates from speaking up and discourages bosses from seeking feedback?

Organizational silence—even in hierarchical organizations—is not an inevitability. Leaders can help their organizations overcome silence by paying attention to particular dynamics that may block openness. Hierarchy, as we know, creates power distance: distinct differences in power based on hierarchical position. The problem is, large power distance—say, between a boss and a subordinate or a CEO and a division vice president—can encourage silence.

When one participant in the dialogue possesses significantly more organizational power than the other, both parties tend to filter their communication. The boss may be less than totally candid with her subordinates. Do they really need to know this information, she may ask herself? And what will they do with the information? The subordinate may think twice about what he says to the boss. What will my boss do with this information? Will it somehow be used against me? Both parties tend to withhold, or even distort, intending to protect and/or advance their self-interest.

As a result of power distance, participants with greater power tend to rely on advocacy at the expense of inquiry, while participants with lower power are more prone to inquire rather than to advocate. The unwillingness/inability to advocate one's own views reduces the likelihood that individuals will modify their views. Large power distance, then, may lead to compliance; it is not, however, conducive to the creation of a shared understanding.

Theory into Practice

A large power distance between parties in a dialogue inhibits openness and risk taking while distorting communications.

In a hierarchical organization, some power distance is inevitable. Filtering cannot be avoided entirely. Nevertheless, organizations have undertaken a number of approaches meant to lessen the distance and increase the effectiveness of the dialogue. One approach to reducing power distance involves *delayering*; that is, eliminating multiple levels of hierarchy.

Many of today's business units have significantly reduced the number of supervisory and managerial levels existing in a plant. In a traditionally organized automobile parts plant, for instance, shop floor workers in a unit reported to a supervisor who reported to a general supervisor who reported to the unit superintendent who reported to the production manager who reported to the manufacturing manager who reported to the plant manager. If the worker found herself on second or third shift, a shift superintendent was inserted between the shift workers and the production manager. With far fewer levels—at GM's Livonia plant, for instance, shop floor workers report to team leaders who report directly to business unit managers—the distortion that arises from filtering is reduced significantly.

Decentralizing pushes decision making down to lower levels and can occur separately or be combined with delayering. By granting lower-level managers the autonomy to make decisions, those managers have the opportunity to involve their direct staff in diagnosis, thus eliminating hierarchical levels that more typically exist between workers and managers.

Many organizations have taken the symbolic step of creating an *egalitarian culture*, eliminating many of the perquisites often associated with hierarchical status:

- Doing away with executive parking and cafeterias is a now-common characteristic in new work facilities.
- Putting the entire workforce on salary erases the distinction between hourly and salaried employees.
- Informal attire and forms of address (calling everyone by his first name, for example), and an end to opulent executive offices removes obvious external signs of status.

These symbolic actions will have little if any positive impact if they are experienced by employees as empty gestures or even as contradictions to an otherwise hierarchical, highly differentiated power structure. If, on the other hand, they are experienced as manifestations of a deeply embedded egalitarian culture, they can help reduce perceived power differentials and enable open dialogue.

Third-party facilitation can also be a powerful antidote to power differentials. In a structured dialogue where multiple hierarchical levels are involved, facilitators can suggest—and even enforce—communication rules meant to establish openness and trust. Third-party facilitators can create what Richard Walton calls "situational" power equity.

Most power equalization steps focus on power differences based on hierarchical position. Power distance can also exist *horizontally*. Horizontal power distance involves units that, in essence, compete for power within the organization.

The most obvious example would be unions and management. Most often one side retains more organizational power than the other. When management—typically but not always the advantaged side—wishes to enter into a collaborative partnership with the union, it will have to pay careful attention to the need to make union representatives relatively equal partners. That is why, for instance, leaders at GM's Livonia plant ensured that the union was significantly represented at every phase of the decision-making process.

Less obvious but equally important are the power distances that can develop over time between functional units within an organization. "Engineering is king." "Marketing is everything." "We're completely numbers driven." All of these slogans are expressions of precisely this type of inequity among functions.

Horizontal power distance can be harmful to open dialogue. Communication can be filtered and ideas dismissed. A powerful research and development function can make it difficult for sales and marketing people to inject the customer perspective into the dialogue about product design decisions. An overly dominant finance function might block the voice of employers and customers. An isolated but influential research and development department might offer new products that business units feel are unattractive to their local markets.

A well-balanced top management team with shared purpose and mutual responsibility will help maintain mutual engagement, ensuring that all voices are respected and influential. In that circumstance, the voices of multiple functions and units are more likely to come through unfiltered in a diagnosis concerning barriers to outstanding performance.

Building a Vocabulary of Change

Psychological safety a belief on the part of employees that the organizational climate is conducive to taking personal risks, especially around dialogue.

Steps to equalize power (summarized in Exhibit 3-1) help set the organizational context for dialogue. Organizations seeking to encourage mutual engagement will also need to create what is known as **psychological safety**—a belief on the part of employees that the organizational climate is conducive for taking personal risks, especially around dialogue. Leaders can look at all the elements that create or undermine trust between and among stakeholders. Creating a psychological safety zone in which all employees feel safe from threat and reprisal for both advocating and inquiring will help nurture a context in which mutual engagement can and will continue.

Ultimately, in a change implementation process, leaders can help banish the barrier of silence to committing themselves to the desirability, even the necessity of entering into a dialogue with employees. To return to the HP situation, six years after

Steps	Lead to
Delayering	Removing hierarchical barriers that create distance and distort communications
Decentralizing	Pushing down decision making to close gap between decision makers and "doers"
Egalitarianism	Removing "artifacts" of status differentials
Third-party facilitation	Structuring effective "rules-of-engagement" around feedback and dialogue
Representation	Inserting voice from multiple levels, both vertical (managers, shop floor employees, etc.) and horizontal (union and management, various functions, etc.) into dialogue
Teamwork	Building shared purpose and mutual responsibility to ensure equal participation and influence by all members in dialogue

EXHIBIT 3-1 Power Equalization Steps.

announcing the reorganization plan, the company's board demanded Fiorina's resignation. The board again looked outside of HP for a replacement; this time selecting Mark Hurd of NCR. When reporters asked Hurd about his plans to revitalize the company, he responded that it was too soon to tell. "We'll look at the entire enterprise," he said. "I can't give you any guarantees on anything," he added.[10]

Instead of committing to solutions, leaders can commit to a process of mutual engagement and learning, thus inviting employees at all levels to cross barriers of silence and participate in a dialogue.

THE CONSULTANT ROLE

Mutual engagement in diagnosis requires more than just motivation, willingness, and safety. It also requires skills. Those skills are different from the functional competencies—marketing, sales, technology, operations, and so forth—that are required in the typical workday of an employee.

Participating in an open dialogue where views—both positive and negative—are freely expressed and performance-focused might prove both unusual and uncomfortable. Participating in such a dialogue, not to mention facilitating the participation of others might be alien to an employee's experience.

Theory into Practice

Leaders can call on a consultant to introduce and teach skills required of mutual engagement and diagnosis.

Employees *can* learn these skills. In fact, one of the goals of change can be to develop such skills and competencies among employees. But because diagnosis calls for new roles and skills that have yet to be developed, it often proceeds with the help of a consultant. A **consultant** is an individual possessing a broad range of diagnostic and developmental skills who facilitates a change intervention.

Consultants may arrive from outside the organization: professional consultants or academics with a specialization in organizational change and development. They may also come from within the firm: specially trained employees, often within the company's human resource or organization development staff. Whether internal or external, the task of the consultant is the same: to facilitate diagnosis and dialogue and to do so in a way that allows employees to develop those skills themselves.[11]

Building a Vocabulary of Change
Consultant an individual possessing a broad range of diagnostic and developmental skills who contracts with the organization's leaders to facilitate an intervention.

GETTING STARTED WITH ORGANIZATIONAL DIAGNOSIS

To increase the effectiveness of diagnosis as an opening stage of organizational change, the process can follow the principles outlined in Exhibit 3-2. It is now time to explore the specific steps that can be pursued based on these principles. These steps involve:

- *Collecting data* on the organization and its environment
- Entering into a *dialogue of discovery* that makes sense of and provides insight into the data that has been amassed

Systemic focus	Targets the entire organization and guided by a framework that focuses on interactions
Consultant facilitated	Specially trained individual(s) bring external perspective and required skills
Client-oriented	Employees participate in all stages as full partners in order to build commitment and competency
Data-based	Participants agree on the validity and strategic importance of data collected about performance
Honest conversation	Employees engage the requirements of shared dialogue: mutuality, reciprocity, advocacy, and inquiry
Psychological safety	Active steps taken to overcome climate of organizational silence

EXHIBIT 3-2   Principles for Organizational Diagnosis.

- Receiving and providing *feedback* on what has been learned
- *Institutionalizing dialogue and diagnosis* so that they become an organic and ongoing part of the organization's activities.

Each step enhances mutual engagement and helps build commitment to change.

Data Collection

Effective diagnosis is data driven; that is, infused with and informed by valid information concerning the factors that impact the performance of the organization and its ability to implement its renewed strategy. A diagnostic framework, such as the one provided in Exhibit 2-3, will point to the target areas for data collection.

Theory into Practice

Make sure that diagnosis flows from valid data about the organization.

Data are more than a collection of cold, hard facts. Data amassed through the diagnostic process can have a powerful impact on the ensuing change by motivating employees to alter their behavior in ways that will support strategic renewal. The motivational impact of data occurs as feelings are aroused and forces unleashed that bring about behavioral change. The act of collecting data potentially becomes a key way of mobilizing the considerable energy needed to abandon the status quo.

So the challenge of data collection becomes twofold:

1. To collect data on the key elements impacting an organization's capacity to support the new strategy and to achieve and maintain outstanding performance; and,
2. To do so in a way most likely to build motivation and commitment on the part of employees.

There are three basic forms of data collection: questionnaires, interviews, and observation. Each holds strengths and weaknesses, especially in light of that dual requirement.

Theory into Practice

The process of collecting data can help build motivation and commitment to altering patterns of behavior.

QUESTIONNAIRES   The most popular form of collecting data involves written questionnaires. **Questionnaires** are self-administered paper-and-pencil or computer-based data-collection forms. Questionnaires often stress areas of behavioral interaction such as communications, goals, and coordination. Employees may be asked, for instance, to rate the clarity of the organization's strategy, the quality of information that is shared, or the nature of supervision. Although questionnaires can be developed internally, they are more typically packaged by an external consulting firm or an academic center. Exhibit 3-3 presents a sample from one such questionnaire.

Questionnaires can be administered to a large number of employees and results compiled in a short time period. Because they are administered and returned anonymously, questionnaires can help overcome the climate of silence by allowing employees a greater sense of freedom and protection. They can provide a valuable benchmark for the organization to measure itself against. When administered to multiple units, they can offer comparisons and highlight units in the organization where results are especially positive or negative. When administered to the same unit over time, they can track progress or regression.

There is a downside to the use of questionnaires in a change process. The preconceived categories represented in the questionnaires may measure theoretical constructs that are relevant to the developer of the questions, but they may not necessarily speak to the true needs of the organization. Questionnaires, write Jack Fordyce and Raymond Weil, "do not create the kind of personal involvement and dialogue that is so valuable in changing hearts and minds. The information generated by questionnaires tends to be canned, anonymous, ambiguous, and detached—i.e., cool data rather than hot."[12] Because of that lack of personal involvement and deep sentiment, managers may be more likely to respond with token reaction rather than significant response.

Theory into Practice

Be careful about the overuse of employee questionnaires in collecting data about organizational effectiveness. They do not create mutual engagement.

That is not to say that questionnaires have no important role to play. By providing a benchmark measurement against either other organizations or against best-practice units within the organization, questionnaires can help build dissatisfaction with the status quo and awareness of the need for change.

From time to time organizations consider it important to analyze themselves. It is necessary to find out from people who work in the organization what they think. This questionnaire will help the organization that you work for analyze itself.

Directions: DO NOT put your name anywhere on this questionnaire. Please answer all questions. For each of the statements, circle only one number to indicate your thinking.

> Agree Strongly – 1, Agree – 2, Agree Slightly – 3, Neutral – 4,
> Disagree Slightly – 5, Disagree – 6, Disagree Strongly – 7

[A sampling of 10 questions is reproduced]

1. The goals of this organization are clearly stated.
    1   2   3   4   5   6   7

2. My immediate supervisor is supportive of my efforts.
    1   2   3   4   5   6   7

3. This organization is not resistant to change.
    1   2   3   4   5   6   7

4. The leadership norms of this organization help its progress.
    1   2   3   4   5   6   7

5. I have the information that I need to do a good job.
    1   2   3   4   5   6   7

6. The manner in which work tasks are divided is a logical one.
    1   2   3   4   5   6   7

7. The opportunity for promotion exists in this organization.
    1   2   3   4   5   6   7

8. The structure of my work unit is well designed.
    1   2   3   4   5   6   7

9. I have established the relationships that I need to do my job properly.
    1   2   3   4   5   6   7

10. All tasks to be accomplished are associated with incentives.
    1   2   3   4   5   6   7

EXHIBIT 3-3   Organizational Diagnostic Questionnaire.

Excerpted from "Organizational Diagnosis Questionnaire," available at www.rollins.edu/communication/wschmidt/odquestionaire.htm, © 1999 Rollins College. Used by permission.

Building a Vocabulary of Change

Diagnostic interviews a form of data collection in which a trained diagnostician meets with an employee, or small groups of employees, to solicit information pertaining to the performance of the organization.

INTERVIEWS   Other methods of data collection can provide far richer and more detailed insight into the dynamics of an organization. **Diagnostic interviews** involve a trained diagnostician sitting down with an employee, or occasionally small groups of employees, and soliciting information. Interviews can provide far richer data than questionnaires.

Diagnostic interviews can be either structured or unstructured. In structured interviews, the interviewer prepares a set of questions to be asked of all respondents. In an unstructured interview, a small number of general questions—"What are the organizational barriers to achieving your strategic objectives?" or "What are the goals of your unit and what are the organizational barriers you perceive for achieving those goals?" for example—are intended to precipitate what Andrew Manzini calls "the respondent's own definition of relevant problems and issues."[13] What follows those broad questions is an open dialogue between the interviewer and the interviewee that helps determine the direction of the remainder of the interview.

Theory into Practice

Use diagnostic interviews and behavioral observation to collect rich and valid data about how employees behave and how the organization functions.

In addition to generating data, open-ended interviews offer the opportunity to clarify the data as they are being generated. The interviewer can ask questions of the respondent and probe more deeply: *What did you mean by that response?* Or, *can you tell me more about why you think that is true?* Because unstructured interviews can become a forum for personal issues that have little to do with improving organizational performance, interviewers will need to keep focus on pertinent, performance-related issues.

Professional consultants can conduct these interviews. There is also an advantage to training employees as interviewers. The involvement of employees in the data collection process enhances their commitment to the changes suggested by the process. Also, organizational members inevitably know more about the hidden but critical aspects of organizational life than would any outsider. They bring, in other words, their own expertise to the process. Finally, by participating in the data collection process, employees are gaining the skills necessary to engage in ongoing data collection and diagnosis in the future.[14]

OBSERVATIONS   Apart from questionnaires and interviews, another source of data is **behavioral observation**.[15] The diagnostician can watch actual behaviors of employees: the meetings of top management teams, efforts of work groups to solve problems, interactions between boss and subordinate, and so forth. Behavioral observation has the advantage of eliminating self-reports by focusing directly on behaviors. The observer remains apart from the behaviors themselves, acting as a sort of a nonobtrusive fly-on-the-wall. Or, the observer may involve himself in the behaviors being observed. The participant-observer becomes immersed in the actual behaviors of employees as a way of reaching a deep understanding of their behaviors.

A broad literature in the social sciences exists on the strengths and weaknesses, validity and pitfalls, even the ethics of the participant-observer role.[16] For a well-trained observer, the interactions that result from participation in meetings, problem-solving groups, and the like can provide an indispensable source of data concerning the cognitive and emotional state of key organizational stakeholders.

SUMMARIZING DATA COLLECTION METHODS   The three types of data collection (summarized in Exhibit 3-4) do not have to be thought of as mutually exclusive. Used together—interviews and observations to collect rich data and questionnaires to validate data on a wider scale—the various methods of data collection provide invaluable

Building a Vocabulary of Change
Behavioral observation a form of data collection in which a trained diagnostician can watch actual behaviors of employees.

Methods	Advantages at Initial Stage of Change	Disadvantages at Initial Stage of Change
Questionnaires	• Can be administered to large number of employees • Can be processed quickly • Data is collected anonymously • Can be used to create benchmarks and make comparisons across organizations and over time	• Based on preconceived ideas about what issues and areas should be examined • Can over simplify vague and complex issues like culture • Do not expose root causes of problems • Do not create commitment to outcomes or motivation to change
Diagnostic interviews	• Collect rich data • Begin process of creating dialogue • Teach communication and active listening skills to employees	• Require up-front investment in training interviewers • Data may be hard to summarize and quantify • Lack anonymity
Behavioral observation	• Provides current work-based behavior as data • Offers deep and rich data on interactions among people • Can surface underlying emotions that impact behavior	• Act of observation will impact behaviors of those being observed • Time-consuming data collection process • Requires highly skilled observers

EXHIBIT 3-4   Data Collection Methods for Organizational Diagnosis.

input into the next stage of the diagnostic process: creating a dialogue about the organization's functioning.

Building a Vocabulary of Change
Discovery the process of analyzing and making sense of data that has been collected as part of an organizational diagnosis.

Creating a Dialogue of Discovery

Data collection is only the preliminary step in diagnosis. In the **discovery** stage, employees engage in an analysis of the data, make sense of what they have learned, and consider the steps to take to act upon that learning. When diagnosis is the first step of a change process, the responsible leaders of the organizational unit being targeted—if it is the entire organization, then the responsible leaders are the top management team—can be engaged in that discovery.[17] The involvement of the individuals, groups, and teams required to take action enriches the understanding of the data while simultaneously building their commitment to the resulting change. Because their own behaviors will likely be part of the collected data, their mutual engagement in the discovery process and commitment to respond to their learnings become particularly valuable.

Determining *who* to engage is the first requirement of the discovery process. A blend of individuals representing a multitude of perspectives on the organization (say, representatives from various functions and units and from multiple hierarchical levels) will help ensure a broad, systemic view. The next vital question in designing the discovery process is *how*.

Theory into Practice

Mutual engagement in the discovery stage will help both to assure the validity of the conclusions and build commitment to corrective actions.

Mutual engagement in the discovery process can take place in face-to-face meetings: employees gathered in the same room when possible and connected via electronic means when necessary. Face-to-face interaction provides the richness required to help understand the complexity of the opportunities and problems to be addressed.

When employees themselves have been involved in the data collection process, they can deliver their data directly to the responsible individuals. The consultant can facilitate that exchange by setting ground rules for productive and open dialogue. The leadership group hearing the feedback, for example, can be allowed to ask clarifying questions but be stopped by the consultant if their responses represent defensiveness or denial.[18]

Mutual engagement in discovery is critical to determining the effectiveness of the change process. To ensure the systemic nature of the discovery process—that is, a focus on how the multiple elements of the organization do or do not align—the consultant can use a framework such as the one presented in Exhibit 2-3. A discovery process guided by a systemic diagnostic framework will channel energy, in Michael Harrison and Arie Shirom's words, "toward decisions and actions likely to provide the broadest organizational benefits."[19] By creating disequilibrium with the status quo, discovery provides a vital staging for the upcoming change process.

Closing the Loop

Employees who have engaged in the data collection and discovery phases will expect to learn how their efforts have been translated into action. There is an expectation, in other words, that feedback will be part of the diagnostic process. **Feedback** refers to the process of receiving information concerning the effectiveness of one's actions and performance.

Building a Vocabulary of Change
Feedback the process of receiving information focused on the effectiveness of one's actions and performance.

Theory into Practice

Mutual engagement can be enhanced when top management feeds back to employees what it has learned from the diagnostic process and uses that feedback as an opportunity to generate more learning.

The entire diagnostic process involves feedback, of course. By receiving data from the organization about performance and about the manner in which various organizational elements align, or do not align, in order to implement strategy, management benefits from rich and valuable feedback. In the discovery phase, management receives feedback not just about the particulars uncovered through data collection but also about the perceived meaning, importance, and performance implications of that data.

Feedback can also occur following discovery. Managers can report to employees on the conclusions reached as part of that process and on the plan of action intended to address what has been learned. When groups of employees participate directly in collecting data, the feedback loop can be closed directly if upper management communicates directly with those participants.

As top management reports its conclusions, mutual engagement can continue as employees react to the plan of action. The feedback loop can thus become continuous and ongoing. Two mechanisms advance the feedback process:[20]

1. The feedback from the top management group empowered to lead the change can occur in face-to-face sessions in order to increase the richness of the process as well as to create responsibility and accountability for taking actions.[21]
2. The learning from the discovery process as well as the change plans that result can be presented as tentative rather than final, thus inviting additional dialogue and discovery.

Closing the feedback loop will work to keep mutual engagement continuous during the change process.

After Action Reviews

A form of mutual engagement and diagnosis that has become popular in recent years involves a process of looking back. In an **after-action review (AAR)**, organizations take an "action" that has just occurred—some event of strategic import—and diagnose the dynamics of that action. The goal is to engage participants in a "just-in-time diagnosis" that leads to quick performance improvement.

An example of such an AAR occurred when Wall and Somerset (disguised name) fumbled a potential contract with a large corporate client. The cause of the difficulty was as simple to understand as it was difficult to accept. Sales and technical support had been unable to agree on either the scope of the product or its development and maintenance costs. As a result, the price quoted to the client fluctuated wildly. Worse still, the lead salesperson had been unable to explain to the client just what the cost drivers were and why the price had been so difficult to fix.

Wall and Somerset CEO Carol Peters expressed frustration, of course, but also determination. The client was scheduled to ask for a new bid in six months. To make sure that Wall and Somerset would be better positioned to succeed this time around, she called on all the participants in the past effort to engage in an AAR.

First developed by the U.S. Army at the Center for Army Lessons Learned, AARs are a structured effort to collect data, identify deficiencies, sustain positives, and improve performance.[22] The army's own definition is instructive, labeling the AAR "a professional discussion of an event, focused on performance standards, that enables soldiers to discover for themselves what happened, why it happened, and how to sustain strengths and improve on weaknesses."[23] In particular, the AAR offers an approach to shared diagnosis and mutual engagement that attempts to compress the elapsed time between action, learning, correction, and action. For Wall and Somerset, the need to learn was pressing. For soldiers involved in military operations, that need is even more urgent.

The AAR is based on the premise that an action is not "learned" unless and until it leads to new behaviors. The review follows the principles of shared diagnosis and mutual engagement by involving those who participated directly in the "action"—in the case of Wall and Somerset, those individuals involved in putting together the proposal to the client—in gathering and interpreting data and then building an action plan for future success. Because those involved in the initial action are also engaged in the analysis and planning, their commitment to future improvements are enhanced.

The specifics of the army's AARs involved eight key components:

1. The review takes place either during or immediately after the event under study.
2. The review starts with a shared understanding of the objectives and aims of the event.
3. The review focuses on the overall performance of the targeted group.
4. The review is conducted by the participants in the event.
5. The review is governed by open-ended questions such as, What occurred? Why? What can we do about it?
6. The review identifies strengths and weaknesses.
7. The review leads to new actions.
8. The lessons of the review become part of future training.[24]

For any organizational setting—whether it be the army or a business firm—the AAR approach to shared diagnosis and mutual dialogue offers an opportunity to learn, interpret, and act quickly. Wall and Somerset was able to overcome internal barriers to collaboration by forming a small cross-functional engagement task force and offer a successful rebid. Although AARs are, by definition, sharply focused on specific actions and activities, the resulting learning can be amassed by organizations as a way of sharing learning.

Theory into Practice

After-action reviews provided an opportunity for a sharply focused and timely mutual engagement that can lead to quick corrections.

Conclusion

If the need for change is urgent, executives may be tempted to rush toward a "solution." That instinct, while understandable, is likely to harm the effectiveness of the change implementation process. Mutual engagement in dialogue and diagnosis helps generate vital data. The process can also create commitment to learning and motivation to change on the part of participants, while building diagnostic competencies into the organization.

In order to target the performance of the entire organization and its ability to implement a renewed strategy, diagnosis can be shaped and guided by a systemic framework. With the facilitation of a consultant, employees can engage in data collection and a dialogue of discovery concerning those elements and their fit with each other, with the strategy, and with the external environment.

Creating a dialogue within the organization is hampered by many organizational factors. Power distance encourages participants to filter information rather than to be completely open. Organizational silence discourages honesty and must be overcome by organizational leaders. Only by creating a sense of psychological safety will employees willingly engage in a candid exchange of information and insight concerning the performance of the organization.

Once dialogue and diagnosis have been engaged, implementation can proceed. Dialogue and diagnosis likely will target patterns of behavior, asking if employees at all levels of the organization are enacting their roles and responsibilities in a way that is aligned with the demands of the strategy and the requirements of outstanding performance. The ability of an organization to create and sustain a climate of openness and honest conversation depends a great deal on the culture of the organization and the values of that organization's managers. Chapter 4 will focus explicitly on an understanding of values and culture.

Discussion Questions

1. How might Bob Nardelli have structured his early efforts at Home Depot? Pay particular attention to how he might have used the principles of mutual engagement and shared diagnosis.
2. What are the potential advantages of relying on a systemic framework for guiding diagnosis? Are their any potential disadvantages?
3. Why is open dialogue so difficult to achieve in many organizations?

4. In what specific ways can an executive actively promote a sense of psychological safety among employees to engage them in an honest conversation about performance?
5. How might the three forms of data collection be used together in the opening stages of a change process?
6. How can an organizational make sure that diagnosis becomes a regular and ongoing element of the way they do business?

Case Discussion

Read "Managing Transformation at National Computer Operations" and prepare answers to the following questions:

1. Prepare an implementation plan for change that would enable Gar Finnvold to create a fully competitive computer service within two years.

2. How could Finnvold conduct an organizational diagnosis that would lead off his implementation? Be specific about how he could ensure mutual engagement.

Managing Transformation at National Computer Operations

Gar Finnvold knew his organization needed to change, to transform itself over the next two years.[25] His 1,000 employees had enjoyed for their entire careers what amounted to monopoly status. They had been the exclusive provider of computer support services to the immense, global enterprises of the U.K.-based National Banking Group. All that was about to change. National Bank's newly appointed chairman had decreed that, starting in two years, all bank operations would be free to purchase their computer services from any vendor who could supply excellent value. Finnvold's operation would be competing against the best in Europe. At the same time, Finnvold would be free to market his computer operations on the outside, to build a customer base external to the bank.

Finnvold's excitement at the challenge of transforming his National Computer Operations (NCO) into a truly world-class competitor was matched by his anxiety (see Exhibit 3-5 for a partial organization chart). As the longtime manager of computer

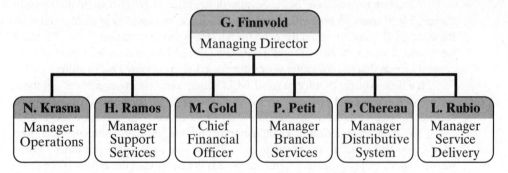

EXHIBIT 3-5   Partial Organization Chart—National Computer Operations.

operations, he understood only too well that NCO was unprepared to compete, not internally and certainly not externally. Internal bank customers had complained for years of the high-cost/low-responsiveness culture of the NCO. Buffered by their monopoly status, NCO's computer technicians didn't worry much about whether the customer perceived them as providing value. We understand better than the customer both what that customer needs and how much they should be willing to pay for it. We'll define value.

In two years, Finnvold knew that equation would be reversed. Given a free market choice to seek the best provider of computer services, would they reup with NCO? Not likely, he thought.

At least inside the bank, NCO enjoyed a substantial cost advantage over potential external interlopers. National tax laws exempted bank operations from having to pay a nearly 20 percent tax on internally provided services. That tax advantage evaporated when NCO left the safety of the bank to hunt external customers.

What's more, no one at any level in NCO possessed real general management experience. No one, Finnvold included, had ever run a freestanding commercial enterprise with all that implied: managing costs, customers, and operations within a fiercely competitive environment. Was two years even close to enough time to undergo the radical transformation required to make such a venture successful?

NCO Operations

Listen to how Peter Kapok, a longtime NCO manager, described what his organization was like in the 1980s: "We weren't client oriented. We very much told our clients what they could and couldn't have. We came to work for ourselves and did pretty much what we wanted. We simply didn't consider ourselves working for a client." The notion that customers might define the ultimate value of their services was alien to NCO.

Henri Vieuxtemps, who entered the computer operations in 1988, recalled his amazement at how little the operation resembled a true business. "What surprised me," he said, "was that money was no object. Service was not a major consideration." What might be called the arrogance of technology permeated NCO's approach to the business. "We spent money on technology that really didn't matter," continues Vieuxtemps, "not to the customer anyway. It was just something that appealed to *us*. In fact, we didn't think of internal clients as customers at all. They were just other departments in the bank."

Vieuxtemps may have believed that the culture of NCO was fundamentally flawed, but to many of his fellow managers, things were going quite nicely. National Bank, after all, had eliminated the need for NCO to respond to market forces. Think of the situation in which NCO found itself: Guaranteed customers who would always cover the costs that the computer operation passed along, assured profitability.

It's little wonder that for most of NCO's managers, effectiveness was not measured by organizational performance or client satisfaction. Their focus turned inward instead. *How can* I *build up* my *functional domain? Enhance* my *personal career?*

"We were an organization of little empire builders," Kapok observed. "The more people you had working for you, the more likely you were to get promoted. There were few performance measures, and almost no coordination of our efforts." The functional silos of the organization were so powerful, said Kapok, that NCO's own staff "didn't quite consider ourselves working for the same operation. If someone from one unit went to someone from another to ask for help, they were considered a nuisance. We certainly never considered the impact of any of this on our costs."

NCO's high spending, "customer—what customer?" attitude could only lead to resentment on the part of client operations within the bank. That resentment finally boiled over into open rebellion. The bank's new chairman hired a consulting firm to evaluate internal computer operations. The findings were as disturbing as they were predictable. "They confirmed our worst fears," recalled an NCO manager. "We were moribund."

Until the consulting report provided irrefutable evidence to the contrary, computer operations managers felt they did an excellent job of providing these services to the bank. "If you had asked us how we were doing," admitted Gar Finnvold, "we would have said, 'We meet our customer service levels most of the time. We are improving our unit costs year-on-year. And *of course* we're adding value.' " It was only later that Finnvold came to recognize that customers held a view of NCO's effectiveness that stood in diametric opposition to the opinion of NCO's managers. "Our customers were saying, 'You're too expensive. Your damn system is always breaking down. And *what* added value?' "

At the time of the consulting report, computer operations were billing approximately \$240[*] million annually (within an overall annual information technology expenditure of \$1.5 billion), almost entirely to internal bank customers. Although NCO offered myriad services, including processing, project management, and technical support and consultancy, they pointed with pride to two distinct competencies. The first was facilities management. "NCO can take the responsibility for all or part of a company's Information Technology requirement," announced their official literature, "which can include every aspect from providing the workforce and premises to the systems and services." The second vital core competency was disaster recovery. "NCO provides planning and backup facilities for unforeseen crises or disasters such as fire and flood. Planning and backup facilities can be provided either separately or together and can be offered in either a 'hot start' or 'cold start' environment."

The Challenge

The bank's new chairman quickly recognized that NCO customers and managers held completely different views of value. He knew that his first task was to force NCO

---

[*]Figures given in equivalent U.S. dollars.

managers to adopt the customer perspective. The way to do that, he reasoned, was to inject market forces into NCO's protected, monopoly-like world.

Using the consulting report as a driver, he first designated NCO as a profit center. He made clear that NCO would be expected to pare costs severely. Within a year, NCO dramatically downsized its workforce from 1,500 to 1,000. The chairman then called on Gar Finnvold to oversee more sweeping change, change that would be governed by two new ground rules:

1. NCO could actively and aggressively market its services to external customers.
2. In two years, all of the bank's internal units would be allowed to purchase computer services from outside vendors.

NCO, in other words, would have to become fully competitive in order to survive.

Finnvold said he welcomed the challenge, particularly the notion of becoming a true market competitor. "I had this gut feel that we should try to sell external from day one," he said. "If we didn't, we'd never learn the lesson of what being commercial is all about. It was the way out of our cocooned environment." He believed that there were external customers waiting to snatch up NCO's services. The facilities management business was expected to grow 50 percent annually worldwide. NCO planned on being part of that growth. "We thought we really had things to sell and that we were the best," said Finnvold.

Endnotes

1. Information on this case is from Dean Foust, "What Worked at GE Isn't Working at Home Depot," *Business Week*, January 27, 2003, p. 40; "The Best Managers," *Business Week*, January 10, 2005, pp. 56–67; Miriam Gottfried, "Repair Job," *Forbes*, December 26, 2005, p. 132; Jennifer Reingold, "Bob Nardelli is Watching," *Fast Company*, December 2005, pp. 76–83; Brian Grow, "Renovating Home Depot," *Business Week*, March 6, 2006, pp. 50–58; Ram Charan, "Home Depot's Blueprint for Culture Change," *Harvard Business Review*, April 2006, pp. 60–70; "Nardelli Out at Home Depot," *Business Week Online*, January 4, 2007.

2. Many of the concepts in this chapter are based on Michael Beer and Bert Spector, "Organizational Diagnosis: Its Role in Organizational Learning," *Journal of Counseling and Development* 71 (July–August 1993), pp. 642–650.

3. See, for example, Paul E. Lawrence and Jay Lorsch, *Developing Organizations: Diagnosis and Action* (Reading, MA: Addison-Wesley, 1969); Jay R. Galbraith, *Designing Complex Organizations* (Reading, MA: Addison-Wesley, 1973); David A. Nadler and Michael L. Tushman, "A Diagnostic Model for Organizational Behavior," in Edward E.

Lawler and Lyman W. Porter, eds., *Perspectives on Behavior in Organizations* (New York: McGraw-Hill, 1977); Michael B. McCaskey, "A Framework for Analyzing Work Groups," in Leonard A. Schlesinger, Robert G. Eccles, and John J. Gabarro, eds., *Managing Behavior in Organizations: Text, Cases, Readings* (New York: McGraw-Hill, 1983), pp. 4–24.

4. David A, Nadler, "Role of Models in Organizational Assessment," in Edward E. Lawler III, David A. Nadler, and Cortlandt Cammann, *Organizational Assessment: Perspectives on the Measurement of Organizational Behavior and the Quality of Work Life* (New York: Wiley, 1980), pp. 125–126.

5. *Ibid.*

6. *Ibid.*

7. Information on Hewlett-Packard is from Peter Burrows, *Backfire: Carly Fiorina's High-Stakes Battle for the Soul of Hewlett-Packard* (New York: Wiley, 2003) and George Anders, *Perfect Enough: Carly Fiorina and the Reinvention of Hewlett-Packard* (New York: Penguin Putnam, 2003).

8. Elizabeth Wolfe Morrison and Frances J. Milliken, "Organizational Silence: A Barrier to Change and Development in a Pluralistic World," *Academy of Management Review* 25 (October 2000), pp. 706–725.

9. Moskal, "Is Industry Ready for Adult Relations?"

10. Hurd quoted in Laurie J. Flynn, "Hewlett Chief Has No Plans but Says All Is on the Exhibit," *New York Times*, March 31, 2005, p. C11.

11. Beer and Spector, "Organizational Diagnosis."

12. Jack K. Fordyce and Raymond Weil, "Methods for Finding Out What Is Going On," in Wendell L. French, Cecil H. Bell, Jr., and Robert A. Zawacki, eds., *Organization Development: Theory, Practice, and Research* (Dallas, TX: Business Publications, Inc., 1978), p. 121.

13. Andrew O. Manzini, *Organizational Diagnosis: A Practical Approach to Company Problem Solving and Growth* (New York: AMACOM, 1988), p. 39.

14. Beer and Spector, "Organizational Diagnosis."

15. Lawler, et al., *Organizational Assessment*, pp. 337–343.

16. See, for example, Severyn Bruyn, *The Human Perspective in Sociology: The Methodology of Participant Observation* (New Jersey: Prentice-Hall, 1966); Robert Bogdan, *Participant Observation in Organizational Settings* (Syracuse, NY: Syracuse University Press, 1972); Patricia A. Adler and Peter Adler, "Observation Techniques," in Norman Denzin and Yvonna S. Lincoln, eds., *Handbook of Qualitative Research* (Newbury Park: Sage, 1994), pp. 377–392; James P. Spradley, *Participant Observation* (New York: Holt, 1997).

17. David A. Nadler, *Feedback and Organization Development: Using Data-Based Methods* (Reading, MA: Addison-Wesley, 1977).

18. Beer and Spector, "Organizational Diagnosis."

19. Michael I. Harrison and Arie Shirom, *Organizational Diagnosis and Assessment: Bridging Theory and Practice* (Thousand Oaks, CA: Sage, 1999), p. 25.

20. Beer and Spector, "Organizational Diagnosis," p. 648.

21. See also Nadler, *Feedback and Organization Development*.

22. The material on after action reviews comes from Department of Army, *A Leader's Guide to After-Action Reviews*. (Training Circular 25 20) (Washington, D.C.: Headquarters, Department of Army, September 1993); Lloyd Baird, John C. Henderson, and Stephanie Watts, "Learning from Action: An Analysis of the Center for Army Lessons Learned (CALL)," *Human Resource Management* 36 (Winter 1997), pp. 385–395; Paul Wright, "Learn as You Go Through the After Action Review," *Knowledge Management Review* (March–April 1998), pp. 4–6; Lloyd Baird, Phil Holland, and Sandra Deacon, "Imbedding More Learning into the Performance Fast Enough to Make a Difference," *Organizational Dynamics* (Spring 1999), pp. 19–32; Marilyn J. Darling and Charles S. Parry, "After-Action Reviews: Linking Reflection and Planning in a Learning Practice," *Reflections* 3 (2001), pp. 64–72; and 72.

23. *A Leader's Guide to After-Action Reviews*, p. 1.

24. Based on Wright, "Learn as You Go," p. 4.

25. All names are disguised. This case is based on research conducted for Bert Spector, *Taking Charge and Letting Go: A Breakthrough Strategy for Creating and Managing the Horizontal Company* (New York: Free Press, 1995).

CHAPTER 4

Organizational Redesign

Diagnosis exposes the current realities and culture of an organization to discussion and analysis. Combined with mutual engagement, diagnosis provides both the motivation for and target of change. In Step 1 of effective change implementation, employees engage in a process of organizational redesign to help shape required new behaviors. Redesign provides a sense of direction for the change effort.

This chapter will analyze the complexities of design choices made to support change implementation. In particular, this chapter will:

- Define organizational design and differentiate between formal and informal design elements
- Explore the main challenges posed by organizational redesign
- Analyze the requirements for building coordination and teamwork in an organization
- Discuss the dynamics of changing the design of an organization in order to impact patterns of behavior

First, we will look at the problems caused by the lack of integration at a large European airline manufacturer.

CROSS-BORDER INTEGRATION AT AIRBUS

In 2006 Airbus suffered a very public humiliation with significant delays in the production of its A380 superjumbo jet. The double-deck, wide-bodied plane was designed to be the largest passenger jet ever built, boasting 50 percent more interior floor space than its nearest competitor. The goal of Airbus was to break the dominance of Seattle-based Boeing over the jumbo jet marketplace. Given the nature of that ambition, it would also be an intensely complex engineering and building feat.

The parent consortium, the European Aeronautic Defense and Space Company (EADS), went through three CEOs in search of a solution to the delays, settling on Louis Gallois. What Gallois found when he arrived was a company divided along national boundaries. Poor coordination created havoc within the A380 project.

For the past three decades, Airbus had divided itself into centers of excellence that would allow for depth and focus on specific aspects of the aircraft manufacturing process. The avionics center was in France, cabin design and installation occurred in Germany, wings were manufactured in the U.K., and tail sections were built in Spain. That system allowed for both multinational participation and technological focus.

For the multibillion dollar A380 project, however, the focus on technological excellence and national pride interfered with the company's ability to deliver a well-designed aircraft. "Rear-fuselage sections of the A380 built in Hamburg," the *New York Times* reported, "arrived in Toulouse in 2004 without the requisite electric wiring for the planes' in-flight entertainment system."[1] That hand-off glitch proved to be just the beginning. The computer modeling software used in Germany was incompatible with what was in use by the French center of excellence. Making matters worse, Gallois took a number of steps, from banning the use of national symbols in all PowerPoint presentations to the formation of transnational teams to redesign Airbus into a truly transnational organization. Gallois' stated goal was to create a well-integrated single company. "I am always interested in new ideas," insisted the CEO.

Finally, the A380 made its maiden commercial flight in 2007. Even then, the number of planes Airbus was able to deliver to commercial carriers fell far short of promises. In the end, delays cost Airbus an estimated $65 billion in profits.

ORGANIZATIONAL REDESIGN

Building a Vocabulary of Change
Organization design the arrangements, both formal and informal, that an organization calls upon in order to shape employee behavior.

In order to deliver the A380, Louis Gallois needed to create integration across the various national centers of excellence within the multinational Airbus consortium. To achieve that goal, he called on organizational design. **Organization design** refers to the arrangements, both formal and informal, that an organization calls upon to help shape employee behavior (see Exhibit 4-1).

Formal aspects of design include rewards and performance measurements as well as the reporting relationships depicted on an organization chart. Informal aspects of design relate to how people perform the required tasks of the organization and how they collaborate and work with others, both inside the organization (within their own groups as well as across groups and functions) and outside (with suppliers and customers, for instance). Informal design addresses questions of focus and coordination, of where decision-making authority will be located,

Formal	• Compensation and measurement
	• Reporting structures
Informal	• Defining roles and responsibilities of employees
	• Defining relationships within the organization and between the organization and external stakeholders

EXHIBIT 4-1 Design Elements.

and the necessary balance between the requirement for flexibility and the need for control.

Changing Informal Design First

Effective change implementation separates the two aspects of design, targeting informal design *before* seeking to alter formal design.[2]

Theory into Practice

Effective change implementation starts first with informal redesign in order to shape new behaviors; formal design changes can follow as a way of reinforcing new patterns of behavior.

That distinction between informal and formal design can, at times, be confusing. Job design is informal, while job descriptions are formal. Broadening the scope of an individual's responsibilities can be informal, but changing that same individual's position on an organization chart is formal. Expecting individuals to work on a team is informal, while paying them team-based bonuses is formal.

To appreciate the distinction between formal and informal design elements, we can look at a specific example: the change efforts undertaken at Asda, the British supermarket chain highlighted at the end of Chapter 2. Facing bankruptcy as the result of poor strategic decisions made by its leadership team, the chain's board brought in a new CEO with the goal of revitalization. The CEO and his top team elected to place their hopes for the revival of the chain in the hands of the 205 store managers, those responsible for making sure that the stores met the expectations of their customers while generating profitable revenues.

In the earliest stages of Asda's transformation, the informal design of the store managers changed radically. They were now asked to spend more of their time and energies looking outside of the store—at their customers and competitors—rather than inside. *Stop being supervisors and start being strategic leaders*; that was the direction provided by the company. In order to succeed, they would have to push more and more responsibility down to the individual department managers.

The roles and responsibilities of store managers changed dramatically. However—and here is the point—nothing in the formal design system changed, at least not at first. Job descriptions were not rewritten; pay systems were not changed; reporting relationships were not altered; measurement systems remained the same. Over time, those formal structures would all be altered, but not early in the process.

At the beginning, nobody in the company knew exactly what the store manager job would evolve into; they only knew it would be changed. Informal redesign—new definitions of how the store manager job would be played out—created a fluid, even experimental situation. Different roles were tried out as transformation moved from one store to the next.

Informal design fits more effectively at the early stages of change precisely because it is informal. No policies or procedures are altered. Nothing is written in stone or committed to formal documents. Instead, informal design involves experimentation, trying out new roles.

What will work? What will not work? Louis Gallois did not alter the organization chart at Airbus. Reporting relationships remained unchanged. Instead, he focused on informal redesign—redefining roles, responsibilities, and relationships—in order to create greater cross-border collaboration. At a later stage, when new behaviors have been instilled, formal structures and systems can be changed, if required, to reinforce and institutionalize those behaviors.

Piloting Redesign

Design choices represent an attempt by organizational leaders to address the challenges inherent in managing in dynamic environments. Shifting customer expectations, disruptive technologies, new competitors, and renewed strategies provide the impetus for *re*design. If all those elements remained the same, then the design that worked effectively in the past would continue to prove useful in the future.

Building a Vocabulary of Change
Organizational redesign the process of changing an organization's design in response to shifting dynamics in the organization's environment.

However, a truly static environment does not, in reality, exist. New competitors enter and exit the marketplace. New technologies replace existing processes. Customer expectations shift. Companies age; they expand and contract. Strategies change. No design solution, no matter how useful it may be at any one time, is impervious to the need for change.

Changing an organization's design, a process known as **organizational redesign**, presents its own set of implementation challenges. Optimally, redesign occurs in a systemic and strategic way: aligning multiple design elements with the renewed strategy of the firm. Often, however, organizational leaders embark upon redesign in a much more haphazard, piecemeal manner.

Theory into Practice

The most effective way to change organizational design is to be systemic and strategic rather than piecemeal and haphazard.

Why is it that leaders often approach redesign in such a suboptimal way? For one thing, comprehensive redesign can be intimidating, write Michael Goold and Andrew Campbell: "It's immensely complicated, involving an endless stream of trade-offs and variables."[3] In addition, organizational redesign can be divisive, often pitting individuals against each other and devolving into power plays.[4] Organizational leaders may prefer to avoid the potential for discomfort and confrontation inherent in comprehensive redesign.

Given the potential for discomfort, it is not surprising that executives often stick with their existing designs long after shifting circumstances seem to demand change. They may tinker, making marginal design change, while leaving the core of the organization intact. *"The status quo had worked well for us in the past,"* they may conclude. *"Why stir up all the potential conflicts in order to change?"*[5]

In a dynamic environment, commitment to past design arrangements can become a prescription for disaster and downfall. Airbus' nationally oriented centers of excellence may have served the company well in the past. For the huge A380 super-jumbo jet, however, greater integration across organizational and national boundaries was required. When a diagnostic intervention reveals that existing design arrangements undermine performance, organizational leaders may wish to avoid that potential trap and decide that the negative performance consequences outweigh any perceived "advantage" of conflict avoidance.

The requirement for system and strategic changes poses what seems to be a dilemma. Organizational redesign, to be effective, targets the entire organization. Targeting an entire organization is difficult, however. In a large, complex company, it is downright impossible. The way out of this apparent dilemma is through change pilots. **Change pilots** are individual units or processes that can provide the opportunity for change. They are, in essence, change laboratories.

An example of piloting change occurred at Midwest Data Services (MDS), a service provider of backroom administrative support—electronic notifications, payments, remittances, and so on—to mutual funds operations.[6] MDS's CEO Tom Glazer readily admitted that MDS's performance in the area of customer service left much to be desired. Revenues for MDS were up, but that was mainly a factor of general industry growth. "There were a lot of mistakes made," said Glazer. "Quality wasn't where anybody wanted it to be. And this was in the industry as a whole."

> **Building a Vocabulary of Change**
> *Change pilots* small units or specific processes which can be targeted at the early stage of change implementation to experiment and learn.

Theory into Practice

When implementing change, seek early wins through pilot projects.

Malibu Equity, a small but prestigious customer, agreed to stay with MDS, but only if Glazer could guarantee a "ten-fold quality improvement" in MDS's support processes. Glazer committed to a major effort to improve the processes with the 20-person MDS unit that handled Malibu's account. The employees worked together to identify key processes and "deliverables"—specific, measurable outcomes that the customer expected from each process—that would be required to improve quality.

One of the insights gained by Glazer from his early discussions with Malibu Equity dealt with the emphasis on processes. A **business process** is an interconnected set of activities that converts inputs to outputs. The question with a business process is not just how does a department perform a particular task, but also how do the various individuals and groups within the department work together to ensure that the task is done in the most efficient manner possible with the highest quality possible. Process improvement asks a simple but powerful question: how does each activity add value from the perspective of the customer?

> **Building a Vocabulary of Change**
> *Business process* an interconnected set of activities that convert inputs to outputs.

The 20-person department in MDS worked together for four months. Employees asked what the end product or "deliverable" was for each process within the department. Next, they sought to understand what activities occurred throughout the department as part of those processes. In learning about the process, they asked:

why were activities that make up the process carried out the way they were? Finally, they worked to learn where problems occurred within these steps and why.

The mere fact that the process was being seen as a continuous flow rather than as a set of discrete activities was an eye-opener for department employees. "We really had never seen this process as a flow before," said an employee. "It was, 'I'm in this box, I do my work, then my job's done.'" Perhaps the single most surprising discovery from the perspective of employees is that "even when each of the functions performed their assigned tasks perfectly, the end result of the process could still be a botched mess."

Now the unit could redesign the work in such a way as to create a stream of activities in order to eliminate quality problems and speed up responsiveness. "As far as the client is concerned," stated an employee, "the process should be *seamless*."

Once again, we see the pattern where no formal design changes occur. The focus here was on redefining relationships within the unit; how one task related to the other. At the same time, we can note that Glazer did not attempt to change the entire design of MDS all at once. Instead, he piloted the change *within a single unit*. Given the visibility of the unit and the change efforts, Glazer was soon able to leverage its successes into other departments and units of MDS.

Theory into Practice

Change "pilots" offer an opportunity to focus attention, experiment, and learn before diffusing change throughout the larger organization.

Change pilots offer the opportunity to engage in systemic change within a small, contained unit. In selecting a target for early pilots, organizational leaders can consider the following characteristics:

- Select a self-contained unit or process with a clear customer and measurable outcomes.
- Select a unit or process of strategic importance to the company.
- If the organization's strategy is changing, select a unit or process if possible that exemplifies the desired future state.
- Most importantly, select a unit or process where success is most likely.

Early successes can build credibility and momentum, leading to more widespread transformation.

Theory into Practice

In selecting change pilots, select units where the change is most likely to be successful; early success builds credibility and momentum.

An understanding of the key issues involved in informal design will help focus the attention of leaders, so let us turn next to an analysis of those key informal design elements that will be addressed in a change process.

UNDERSTANDING DESIGN CHALLENGES

Although all organizations are unique in terms of purpose and strategic direction, they face some common design challenges:

- All organizations require some level of differentiated activities: focusing on different tasks and customers and operating in different competitive environments.
- At the same time, integrated activities will provide organizations with the benefits of efficiency and the ability to move knowledge and resources across and around their various activities and units.
- All organizations, regardless of their histories, strategies, and competitive environments, rely on some type of control mechanisms to help shape employee behaviors. They need to deploy control mechanisms, however, without losing requisite levels of creativity and innovative response from the employees whose behaviors they are attempting to influence.
- All organizations must decide how and where to allocate decision-making rights and responsibilities.

Before embarking on a change implementation effort, organizational leaders need to appreciate these three challenges: the challenge of integration and differentiation, of control and creativity, and of allocating decision-making rights.

The Challenge of Differentiation and Integration

To understand the challenge of differentiation and integration, we can turn to the shifting strategic choices made by the management at SAP America.[7] SAP America is a subsidiary of Germany-based SAP AG, producer of the integrated software architecture that dominated the enterprise systems market.

In the mid-1990s, the American division faced a number of organizational challenges. Their U.S.-based strategy had supported growth through highly autonomous regional markets. Each region developed its own processes and procedures for selling and supporting SAP software.

SAP's products, however, developed a reputation in the marketplace for being expensive, complex, slow to install, and confusing to maintain. New SAP America president Jeremy Coote felt the need to focus in a more collaborative way on supporting customers. In particular, he was convinced that SAP's professional consultants, whose job it was to help clients plan, install, and support the systems, needed to share knowledge and coordinate their efforts.

Here is where past design decisions—especially the heavy emphasis on regional autonomy—provided a barrier. Regional autonomy, which offered flexibility in response to local customers, hampered coordinated national consulting support. SAP's consultants from different regions failed to leverage learning. Consultants responded to the same customer issues in the Northeast and Southwest, for instance, without communicating with each other or sharing knowledge.

After collecting performance data from the regions and setting goals for the upcoming year, Coote worked with his newly hired national manager of professional consulting to redefine responsibilities while defining nationally agreed-upon consulting roles. SAP also involved consultants at an early stage of all new product development and implementation plans.

SAP America made a strategic choice early in its U.S. operation: to emphasize regional autonomy as a way of spurring rapid growth. The idea—an idea that, the evidence indicates, was perfectly valid—allowed regional managers to focus their resources and shape their responsiveness to match the particular needs of their regional customer base.

To pursue that strategy, SAP created a design high in **differentiation**, which refers to the degree to which different functions, departments, and units in an organization are allowed to develop their own approaches in response to their particular goals and unique competitive environments.

Building a Vocabulary of Change

Differentiation the degree to which different functions, departments, and units in an organization are allowed to develop their own approaches in response to their particular goals and unique competitive environments.

Theory into Practice

Use high differentiation to enable different functions, departments, and units in an organization to develop their own responses to their particular goals and unique competitive environments.

Paul Lawrence and Jay Lorsch's classic study, *Organization and Environment* (1967), defined the dynamics and challenges of differentiation and integration.[8] Highly

Goals	A sales function may have the goal of increasing revenues, while a manufacturing function may have the goal of reducing costs.
Time orientation	A research department will likely have a long-term orientation toward research and development, while a sales function will want new products that it can sell by the end of the quarter.
Interpersonal style	Research scientists might believe that they can maximize creativity and contribution by focusing all their individual attention on their task, while manufacturing managers might desire to create rich interpersonal relationships among key individuals to maximize quality.
Formality	An assembly operation is more likely to be governed by tight rules and strict procedures, while a research and development laboratory would find such rules stifling to creativity.

EXHIBIT 4-2   Dimensions of Differentiation.

Based on Paul R. Lawrence and Jay W. Lorsch, *Organization and Environment: Managing Differentiation and Integration* (Boston: Harvard Graduate School of Business Administration Division of Research, 1967) pp. 9–11.

differentiated designs, they found, become reinforced not just in terms of distinctive processes and procedures, but also in terms of cognitive and emotional orientation of employees. Comparing one highly differentiated unit to another, they found that individuals within those units not only *worked* differently but *thought* and *behaved* differently as well. Exhibit 4-2 presents the four distinct dimensions of differentiation.

Because of the particular and differing nature of the tasks, each unit develops its own way of working, of thinking, and of behaving. In complex organizations, differentiation relates not just to functional distinctions but also to product and/or geographic divisions within SAP America. The consultants within each region developed their own patterns of thinking and behaving.

Differentiation is necessary but not sufficient to implement strategic renewal and achieve outstanding performance. The differentiated parts must also work together if the overall organization is to perform at an exceptional level.

Low levels of integration confronted Jeremy Coote at SAP America: an inability to achieve coordination across highly differentiated consulting operations. Likewise, delays in delivery of the A380 superjumbo jet, which we read about at the beginning of the chapter, grew from the inability of national centers of excellence within Airbus to coordinate their activities.

Integration refers to the required level of coordination across differentiated functions, units, and divisions. Collaboration among differentiated units must occur, conflicts must be resolved, and unity of effort must be achieved. Within business units, differentiated functions can, and often do, fail to achieve the required level of integration. The same is true for multiple divisions in large corporations where poor coordination across business can hamper efficiencies.

Building a Vocabulary of Change
Integration the required level of coordination across differentiated functions, units, and divisions.

Theory into Practice

Use integration to enable the organization to achieve efficient operations among different functions, departments, and units.

During the dot-com boom of the 1990s, Internet-based businesses learned the importance of integration. Here's one typical example. With Internet orders pouring into an e-business unit of a large retail toy chain, the traditional functions of logistics, warehousing, and distribution strained to the breaking point, causing a near disaster in customer relations. "They act as if they weren't expecting a Christmas surge," complained the e-business managers, while "they"—the managers of the more traditional functions—retorted, "It would have been helpful if *they* would have kept us in the loop."[9] High levels of differentiation had not been matched with requisite integration.

Theory into Practice

Levels of differentiation need to be matched by appropriate levels of integration.

Building a Vocabulary of Change
Environmental complexity the number of external factors that impact how the organization operates.

An organization's external environment determines just how much differentiation and integration are required. Differentiation is determined by the degree of

	Low	High
High	Low differentiation hampers an organization's responsiveness to a complex environment	In highly complex, dynamic environments, effective firms operate here
Low		SAP America's consulting service was operating here

Integration (row axis label)

Differentiation

EXHIBIT 4-3   The Challenge of Differentiation and Integration.
Framework based on Lawrence and Lorsch, *Organization and Environment.*

Building a Vocabulary of Change
Environmental dynamism the rate of change that is occurring in a firm's external environment.

environmental complexity; that is, the number of external factors that impact how the organization operates. How many competitors are there? How many different types of customers? These and other factors help determine complexity, and the greater the complexity, the greater the amount of differentiation an organizational design must account for.

Increasing dynamism in the external environment creates an increased requirement for integration. **Environmental dynamism** refers to the rate of change: How frequently do shifts in the external environment—customer tastes, new technologies, and so on—occur? In a highly dynamic environment, knowledge must spread quickly and efficiently within the organization. That is why SAP America faced an integration challenge: the need to become more efficient at moving knowledge between its operating regions.

The design challenge is to achieve integration without sacrificing differentiation. Particularly when an organization's environment is both complex *and* dynamic, it must be designed to operate in a high-differentiation/high-integration mode (see Exhibit 4-3). That is not easy, said Lawrence and Lorsch, because the demands of differentiation and integration exert a contradictory force. "The states of differentiation and integration are inversely related," they noted. "The more differentiated an organization, the more difficult it is to achieve integration."[10] Differentiation, after all, reflects independence and autonomy, while integration demands some subordination of autonomy on behalf of interdependence.

Theory into Practice

Organizations operating in a complex and dynamic competitive environment must develop increasingly sophisticated mechanisms for integration to match the requirement for high differentiation.

Differentiation is a relatively easy achievement for organizational design: Most people respond positively to autonomy. But how is integration achieved? A number of possibilities present themselves:

- Cross-functional teams to achieve integration across differentiated functions. The challenge becomes even greater for complex, multiunit corporations
- Global teams to help with cross-national coordination
- A strong sense of common purpose and direction combined with a unified commitment to core values and business strategy
- Common, well-understood values applied across different business units

The particular design challenges presented by multidivisional organizations will be explored later in this chapter.

The Challenge of Control and Creativity

A second design challenge relates to the apparently paradoxical requirements for control and creativity. **Control** refers to design elements called upon to establish order, create predictability, and ensure efficiencies of operation. Traditional controls rely on a number of design features: fixed job descriptions with strict individual accountability; a heavy emphasis on rules, procedures, and hierarchically based differences of status and authority; and information distributed on a strict "need-to-know" basis.[11]

Traditional controls are especially congruent with a business strategy that emphasizes predictability and standardization. Explicit rules and procedures will be useful when shaping consistent behaviors among employees. Fast-food chain McDonald's has achieved great success by proscribing in careful detail virtually every movement and action of its behind-the-counter employees. Stephen Robbins notes that United Parcel Service (UPS) drivers also follow strictly delineated procedures: "It's also no accident that all UPS drivers walk to a customer's door at the brisk pace of 3 feet per second and knock first lest seconds be lost searching for the doorbell."[12] When the core tasks of an organization are largely routine and repetitive, traditional control designs may be more than adequate for the task.

Traditional controls, on the other hand, may hamper an organization's ability to achieve high degrees of flexibility and creativity. In order to enhance creativity and flexibility, organizations can call on **organic controls**: controls that rely less on specific rules and procedures and more on shared values, clarity of organizational strategy, a common understanding about risks to be avoided, attention to performance outcomes, and expectations of interactive and open dialogue.

Building a Vocabulary of Change
Control design choices called upon to shape employee behavior in alignment with the requirements of outstanding performance.

Building a Vocabulary of Change
Organic controls an approach to shaping employee behavior that emphasizes shared values, a common understanding of strategy, loosely defined roles and responsibilities, and overall organizational performance.

Theory into Practice

Traditional mechanistic control tools can create predictability and standardization but can undermine creativity, flexibility, and collaboration.

Sun Hydraulics is a Florida-based company that designs and manufactures screw-in hydraulic cartridge valves and manifolds for industrial and mobile markets. This may seem like an industry that would lend itself to traditional controls: lots of rules and procedures. Instead, since its founding in 1970, Sun has leaned heavily on organic controls. "Our workplace is as distinctive as our products," the company proclaims on its web page, "and provides just as many advantages. We have no job titles, no hierarchy, no formal job descriptions, organizational charts or departments. We have open offices, promoting open communication. Each member of our technologically skilled, cross trained workforce is trusted to take the initiative and invent new ways to serve you better."[13]

Sun's reliance, to an almost exclusive extent, on organic rather than traditional controls provides it with both "a motivated work force" and a company "always on the lookout for emerging market needs and creating innovative ways to fill them."[14]

Companies that use organic controls expect employee behaviors to be shaped by company strategy and objectives as well as widely shared performance information. A number of companies in a wide range of industries—Southwest Airlines, Nordstrom, United Services Automotive Association, and W.L. Gore among them—have decided that greater reliance on organic controls will increase the capability of employees at all organizational levels to serve customers, improve their satisfaction with their work, and reduce employee turnover—all of which will lead directly to improved customer satisfaction and enhanced competitiveness.

Theory into Practice

Organic controls, which are intended to increase employee flexibility and creativity, rely on shared values and clarity about overall strategy and performance expectations.

The Challenge of Allocating Decision-Making Rights

Building a Vocabulary of Change
Decision-making rights the determination of who should make what decisions in organizations.

At what level of the organization are decisions made about how to allocate resources, what businesses to be in, when and how to enter new markets, or what strategies to pursue? How about deciding what discount to give to a favored customer, which supplier to use, or how to allocate work schedules in order to meet a pressing order?

All of these decisions must be made *somewhere* in the organization. However, because they represent different levels of decision making, they are likely to occur at different levels of the organization.

Organizations have multiple points of decision making. The question of who makes what decision is therefore a key design challenge. **Decision-making rights** involve what Nitin Nohria describes as "the rights to initiate, approve, implement, and control various types of strategic or tactical decisions."[15] The ideal design, Nohria adds, is one that grants decision-making rights to those "who have the best information relevant to the decision."[16]

Just where does the "best information" reside? That is a judgment call for organizational leaders to make. That call can be based on a combination of company values and strategic intent. When Robert McDermott became CEO of United Services Automotive Association (an insurance company serving current and past U.S. armed forces officers and their families), he decided on a strategy that would convert customers into partners. That strategy would, he believed, take full advantage of the nature of his customer base.

In order to implement his planned strategic renewal, McDermott placed considerable discretionary decision-making rights in the hands of employees at the lower end of the traditional hierarchy. Telephone receptionists, for instance, had a great deal of liberty concerning how to deal with clients who phoned in their claims. Granting decision-making rights to individuals who dealt directly with customers, McDermott reasoned, would create a codependent bond with customers and improve performance.

Pushing down operational decision making to employees with the "best information" is intended to unleash motivation and creativity. At the same time, McDermott recognized that allocating decision making to frontline employees needed to occur within a controlled environment. The controls that McDermott designed were organic in nature, placing special emphasis on "the necessary education and training base" to support that allocation.[17] Clarity of purpose and strategy, and of values and performance expectations can support the allocation of decision-making rights to lower hierarchical levels.

Theory into Practice

Allowing frontline employees to make autonomous decisions is intended to unleash motivation and creativity among those organizational members with the "best information" to make decisions.

The Special Challenge of Multidivisional Organizations

Multidivisional organizations present special challenges regarding the allocation of decision-making rights. Divisions may be organized around products, services, customer groups, or geography (greater attention will be devoted to divisional structures in Chapter 8). Historically, General Motors operated Chevrolet, Buick, Cadillac, and its other car divisions as highly autonomous units focused on different market niches. Likewise, Cisco Systems created three highly autonomous "lines of business"—enterprise, small/medium business, and service provider—to allow divisions to focus on very different marketplaces.

The underlying rationale for divisional structures is to allow for maximum focus on the unique competitive environment faced by each unit. Business-unit managers possess a greater understanding than do corporate personnel of their own operational, customer, and regional issues. As a result, business units will be able to adapt in a speedy manner to shifts in their marketplace. Additionally, divisional autonomy promotes what Jay Lorsch called "entrepreneurial zeal" among market-focused divisional general managers.[18]

There are, at the same time, compelling reasons for the corporation to expect collaboration and integration across divisions. Collaboration allows the corporation to exploit opportunities for **synergies**—the advantages of efficiency and effectiveness conferred by the combined effect of interaction and collaboration among multiple units. For that reason, corporate executives will expect to make some decisions that apply to all divisions.

Building a Vocabulary of Change
Synergies the advantages of efficiency and effectiveness conferred by the combined effect of interaction and collaboration among multiple units.

The challenge for executives of multidivisional corporations is to seek synergies across divisions while maintaining an adequate level of divisional autonomy. Jay Lorsch and Stephen Allen have suggested a number of integrative devices that can be used to exploit synergies—planning and budgeting systems, regular interface meetings among divisional and corporate executives, task forces, and measurement and reward systems for divisional managers tied to corporate performance—that can help to achieve that dual objective.[19]

Theory into Practice

The challenge for multidivisional organizations is to allocate a high level of autonomy to separate divisions as a way of achieving marketplace responsiveness while simultaneously making corporate-level decisions that allow the exploitation of synergies across the divisions.

Building a Vocabulary of Change
Employee commitment the internalized desire of employees to expend energy and discretionary effort on behalf of the goals of the organization.

BUILDING COMMITMENT

Design choices represent attempts by organizational leaders to align employee behavior behind renewed strategies and shifting realities. Louis Gallois needed to design high levels of collaboration in order to overcome delivery delays in the A380. Jeremy Coote needed to integrate the efforts of professional consultants to help customers apply SAP's complex software applications. How much effort, energy, creativity, and persistence employees commit to the achievement of organizational goals is also determined, in large part, by design.

High **employee commitment** exists when employees sense a strong overlap between individual goals and the shared goals of the organization. Highly committed employees find a sense of purpose within their organization's mission and actively seek out opportunities to fulfill that mission.[20]

Organizations able to achieve high commitment can gain a great many performance advantages:

- Highly committed employees are more likely to communicate with each other and to act in a collaborative manner.
- Productivity, quality, and creativity are all positively associated with high commitment.
- Additionally, from the change perspective, highly committed employees will be motivated to alter their own patterns of behavior based on the requirements of outstanding performance.[21]

From the perspective of organizational performance, the advantages of achieving high employee commitment are substantial.

Theory into Practice

High employee commitment can improve organizational performance by enhancing productivity, creativity, collaboration, and the willingness to change.

Clarity of organizational goals	Employees at all levels and in all units are provided with an understanding of the goals and values of the organization as well as its strategic choices.
Influence mechanisms	A variety of formal (elected board of representatives) and informal (open doors and accessible managers) mechanisms enable wide participation in the dialogue and decision making of the organization.
Teamwork	Teams designated to perform interdependent tasks.
Shared information	Employees kept informed about how the organization is performing, including the dissemination of data such as financial performance, costs, profitability, information on competitors, and feedback from customers.
Organic controls	Control exerted through peer pressure, organizational culture, and expectations of outstanding performance reinforced through performance feedback.
Individual developmental opportunities	Employees provided an opportunity through a combination of mechanisms—job mobility, task variety, facilitative supervision, and formal training—to develop competencies consistent with their own needs and those of the organization.

EXHIBIT 4-4   Informal Design Elements for Building High Commitment.

In recent years, a number of companies in widely diverse industries—manufacturing and assembly (Lincoln Electric, for example), service (Stake n Shake, for example), retailing (Nordstrom, for example), transportation (Southwest Airlines, for example), and software (SAS, for example)—have made design choices intended to increase employee commitment. In each case, the purpose is similar: improved productivity, increased quality, and greater flexibility and adaptation.

The specifics concerning how to build high employee commitment differ from company to company and industry to industry. However, some generalized approaches characterize high-commitment designs, including:

- Clarifying organizational goals, strategy, and values
- Allowing employees greater access to managers
- Creating teams
- Wide sharing of performance information
- Reliance on organic rather than traditional controls
- Offering employees opportunities for individual development

These informal design mechanisms intended to build employee commitment are summarized in Exhibit 4-4.

Perhaps most fundamental to designing for high employee commitment is the manner in which work is performed. Organizational leaders seeking to engage in redesign as a way of building high commitment will benefit from a basic understanding of the options available for job design.

Building a Vocabulary of Change

Job design organizational expectations for how tasks will be performed in order to meet both individual task requirements the overall performance requirements of the organization.

Rethinking Job Design Choices

How will individuals perform the jobs to which they have been assigned? That question is addressed through **job design**, which refers to organizational expectations for how tasks will be performed in order to meet both individual task requirements and the overall performance requirements of the organization. At first glance, it may seem there are as many answers to that question as there are jobs in an organization. A closer examination, however, reveals a set of underlying principles that shape job design choices and impact the commitment, adaptability, and performance of jobholders.

In search of high commitment, managers began to ask a new set of questions about job design. What if managers sought to *increase* rather than eliminate initiative? How might they think about designing jobs in order to enhance their potential to evoke initiative and motivation? Richard Hackman and Greg Oldham offered a job characteristic model to suggest alternative job design options meant to enhance motivation and initiative.[22]

All jobs, they said, regardless of specific organizational levels or assigned responsibilities, can be understood as having the same core dimensions. By enhancing or enriching work on any or all of those dimensions, jobs will become more motivational. Exhibit 4-5 presents the five universal job dimensions as well as sample actions managers can take to enrich work and increase employee commitment.

Theory into Practice

By enriching jobs along any or all of five characteristics—skill variety, task identity, task significance, autonomy, and feedback—organizations can increase the motivation and commitment of employees performing those tasks.

Managers seeking to change job design as a way of affecting employee commitment now had something of a road map. Take *skill variety* as an example. Instead of having an employee perform a single job over and over again, the skills required of that worker in the performance of his job could be enlarged. A machine worker, for instance, might be asked to meet with suppliers or customers. By adding some measure of discretion to that employee's scheduling—say, providing that employee with a monthly production schedule but allowing the individual to make decisions concerning daily and weekly production schedules—managers could also enhance *autonomy*.

Providing regular information about the quality of work and the progress being made toward achieving the goal adds greater *feedback*. Communicating regularly to that employee about how her effort contributes both to the overall product or service being offered by the company and how that product or service helps advance the strategic purpose of the business enhances *task identity* and *significance*. The job characteristics model offered a systematic way of redesigning jobs in order to build employee commitment and achieve outstanding performance for the organization.

Job Dimension	Description	Enrichment Action
Skill variety	The degree to which a job requires a variety of different activities in carrying out the work, involving the use of a number of different skills and talents.	Enlarging task requirements to involve multiple and varied skills.
Task identity	The degree to which the job requires completion of a "whole" and identifiable piece of work; that is, doing a job from beginning to end with a tangible outcome.	Combining individuals into a team with shared responsibility for the final product.
Task significance	The degree to which the performance of the task has a substantial impact on outcomes that are deemed to be important to employees, to the organization, and/ or to society as a whole.	Communicating regularly and clearly how individual and group effort contributes to overall performance of the company.
Autonomy	The degree to which the job provides substantial discretion to the individual in scheduling work and determining procedures for carrying it out.	Allowing individuals or groups to schedule work and assign specific tasks consistent with achieving performance goal.
Feedback	The degree to which carrying out work activities required by the job results in the individual acquiring direct and clear information about the effectiveness of his or her performance.	Communicating frequently concerning progress toward work goals.

EXHIBIT 4-5   Using Job Enrichment to Increase Commitment.

BUILDING TEAMWORK

Given the growing complexity and interdependence of today's workplace, it is not surprising that teams have emerged as a common design element. Pacific-Bell, General Mills, Pratt and Whitney, and Texas Instruments are among the many companies that adopted teams as a way of enhancing coordination and achieving outstanding performance.[23]

Teams, which are interdependent groups with shared responsibility for an outcome, come in many forms: product development teams, project management teams, customer service teams, and process innovation teams such as the ones cre-

Building a Vocabulary of Change
Teams interdependent groups with shared responsibility for an outcome.

Work team	By sharing responsibilities, developing multiple skills, and performing varied tasks, motivation and quality are enhanced.
Product development team	Through concurrent rather than sequential development activities, speed to market and innovation are enhanced while costs associated with rework are diminished.
Problem-solving team	By bringing together individuals from multiple functions, problems associated with handoffs and cross-functional interactions can be creatively addressed.
Project management team	The multiple functions and tasks of the value chain are linked in order to enhance quality, coordination, and customer responsiveness.

EXHIBIT 4-6   Team Types.

Building a Vocabulary of Change

Cross-functional teams teams made up of representatives from multiple organization functions typically intended to achieve required coordination along a chain of interrelated activities and processes.

ated by Tom Glazer at MDS. A summary of the main team prototypes is presented in Exhibit 4-6.

Cross-Functional Teams

Traditional organizations are often made up of a collection of freestanding functional silos. Activities such as market research, design, engineering, manufacturing, quality checking, distribution, and sales all take place within discrete domains. Although those functional units provide required differentiation, organizations also need to achieve integration across functions in order to be effective.

Cross-functional teams, which are teams that span multiple organizational functions, provide a way of achieving that integration. Cross-functional teams address: the difficulty of highly differentiated functions in pulling together into seamless, well-integrated processes. By creating cross-functional teams, organizations seek to eliminate handoff problems that produce waste, high cost, quality problems, and sluggish response time. The teams are intended to create a seamless, interconnected web of activities.[24]

Theory into Practice

Use cross-functional teams to help create seamless, well-integrated processes.

Creating Teamwork

Although the creation of teams has become something of a management "fad," there is no question that effective team*work* can offer a powerful boost to performance: improved quality, on-time delivery, even lower costs.

Creating teams, of course, is not the same as designing for effective teamwork, however. Putting employees together in a group and labeling them a team will not, in

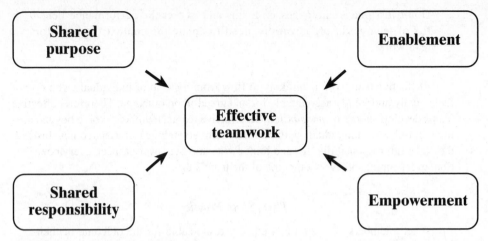

EXHIBIT 4-7   Team Effectiveness Model.

and of itself, lead to teamwork. An implementation effort that creates teams but not teamwork will fail to generate the desired performance improvement.

Effective teamwork derives from four design factors:

1. Shared purpose
2. Shared responsibility
3. Team empowerment
4. Team enablement

Absent these four elements (summarized in Exhibit 4-7), the organizational context will not support real teamwork.

The first requirement of effective teamwork is that team members transcend the individual or functional agendas each member brings to the effort and create a *shared purpose*. Team members agree both on what their goal is and why that goal is important.

Creating shared purpose can be a slow and difficult process. Individuals who have spent much of their professional lives within a function or unit adopt, often unconsciously, a particular lens through which they view all organizational problems. When they become members of a cross-functional team, their agenda—at least initially—is to optimize the interests of their own function or unit, often at the cost of others. Effective teamwork starts with the need to create a central purpose focused on companywide goals and equally accepted by all members.

Theory into Practice

Don't just place employees on teams and expect the performance benefits of teamwork; organizations need to create the context required for
teamwork.

Effective teamwork is unlikely to flow from a group of individuals who do not
feel equally and jointly accountable for an agreed-upon outcome. Therefore, effective
teams develop *shared responsibility*. On effective teams, members evolve beyond seeing themselves as individuals with narrowly defined and measured outcomes. Instead,
they take full responsibility for and joint ownership over every aspect, every contribution, every input, and every outcome of the team's task.

Theory into Practice

When members of a team feel equally responsible for the outcome of their
efforts, teamwork is enhanced.

The creation of a cross-functional team creates the possibility that its activities
will come in conflict with the traditional functional organization. Therefore, the third
design requirement is for *team empowerment*. Unless affirmative actions are taken to
equalize power, the functional organization will likely overwhelm. That is because the
functional organization is entrenched in tradition and is imbued with hierarchical
power. Unless upper management takes affirmative steps to equalize that power base,
cross-functional initiatives will be discouraged, even crushed.

Theory into Practice

At least in the early stages of change, organizations need to make sure teams
are buffered from traditional hierarchical power and are allowed to work
across functions.

Finally, *team enablement* represents the confluence of forces, other than traditional organizational power, that allows a team to operate effectively. Working on a
team provides a member with a new set of competencies. There are certainly business skills involved. In order to master all aspects of a task or process, team members will have to become conversant, if not expert, in a wide range of skills typically
assigned to functional specialists. Additionally, individuals who previously had little if anything to do with the process of strategic planning and implementation may
become part of the process that was previously left solely in the hands of upper
management.

Theory into Practice

In order to encourage teamwork, organizations can take care to ensure that
team members have the appropriate skills to perform the task effectively.

Effective teamwork also requires that team members possess a set of behavioral competencies, including critical thinking, brainstorming, problem solving, nondefensive communications, process facilitation, and conflict management. Many employees lack those skills. They have, after all, spent the better part of their lives learning how to work, think, and act as individuals. If an organization intends on enabling teams to operate effectively, then they have to provide individuals with the required competencies of teamwork.

Not surprisingly, as companies evolve toward increasing reliance on teamwork, they increasingly require training for these required skills. Much of that training focuses on providing employees with multiple skills to enable them to understand all parts of the organization so they can operate more effectively in a cross-functional environment.[25] Training in specific teamwork skills also becomes vital. One of the most striking findings of a recent international study of high-performing companies (rated by profits, productivity, and quality of output) was that 100 percent of the high performers had trained their employees in problem-solving techniques compared to less than 20 percent of the low performers.[26]

Ultimately, no matter how successful an organization might be in creating teams, the success of teamwork depends on a culture and a context within the larger organization that supports coordinated efforts: recruiting and developing individuals with teamwork competencies; holding team members jointly accountable for joint ef-

Conclusion

Organizational design refers to the ways an organization defines roles that employees enact and relationships among employees both within their own functions, units, and divisions as well as across those boundaries. No matter how well designed an organization may be at any one time, a dynamic competitive environment is likely to demand that the design be reconsidered.

Poor coordination, high levels of dysfunctional conflict, slow decision making, and low responsiveness to shifts in the external environment are all symptomatic of an organization whose design has outlived its functionality. When a diagnostic intervention reveals that these types of issues hinder the implementation of an organization's strategy or the achievement of outstanding performance, leaders will need to consider addressing the redesign challenge as the next sequential step in the change process.

That does not mean, however, that *all* design issues need to be addressed at an early stage of change implementation. Organizational design has two interrelated but separate components. Formal aspects of design relate mainly to reporting relationships as depicted on the "official" organization chart and systems such as pay and performance measurement. Informal elements of design relate to how an organization meets the challenges of differentiation and integration, of controls and creativity, and of decision-making allocation. Informal design also encompasses how an organization seeks to build employee commitment and coordination.

Both elements of design—formal and informal—need to be addressed in a change implementation process. It is useful, however, to separate the two sequentially: addressing informal design challenges first and formal design challenges later. Effective change implementation requires experimentation and learning. No leader knows precisely what solutions will be needed. Even if she did, the impositions of solutions from above would engender resistance.

When design changes are informal, employees at multiple levels and from numerous units and divisions can try things out. Ideas on how to approach the challenges posed of differentiation and integration, the tension between control and creativity, and the allocation of decision-making rights can be tested: maintained if they succeed, discarded otherwise. As experimentation and learning unfold, employees can seek to "refreeze" (Lewin's term—see Chapter 2) desired behaviors by calling on more formal design mechanisms.

The next step in the change implementation process involves addressing an organization's human resource policies and practices, both as a way of helping to develop required new behaviors and of reinforcing those behaviors among the organization's employees.

Discussion Questions

1. Why do organizations find it so difficult to address the requirements of differentiation and integration simultaneously?
2. What are the advantages and disadvantages of allowing for high levels of autonomy within divisions of multidivisional organizations? What are some effective means of coordinating efforts among divisions?
3. Why is it so difficult to achieve high levels of employee commitment within today's business organizations? List the factors that are working against commitment

and the potential benefits to be achieved through high commitment.
4. Some people have argued that there is far too much emphasis on "teamwork" in today's business world and that the danger is that individual creativity and initiative is being sacrificed. Do you agree or disagree? Explain.
5. The chapter argues that change efforts should address informal design before addressing formal design. Do you agree with that theory? Explain your thinking.

Case Discussion

Read "Performance Plus" and prepare answers to the following questions:

1. What steps should Steve Cook, as general manager, take to ensure that the Performance Plus teams delivers a high quality product on time?

2. What have been the main causes of the difficulties being experienced by Performance Plus team members?
3. Looking particularly at the Strong Bond question, how would you suggest that issue be resolved?

Performance Plus

"What happens over the next four months is vital to our division," said General Manager Steve Cook in January. "We missed our financial targets last year—not by much, but enough to get the corporate folks nervous. Now I've promised the market that we're going to have this new package of offerings for book publishers with a lot of new capabilities. There are some exciting growth opportunities for us here. And believe me, there are some big competitors out there who would be only too happy to see us fail."

Still, Cook insists, quality is his number one priority. "We may not be the biggest, he said, "but we've developed an excellent reputation. I would never do anything to sacrifice that reputation. I'd rather miss my deadline than come out with a substandard product offering, believe me."

New Product Development at the Company

Maine Papers is a century-old developer and manufacturer of specialty papers. After several years of declining performance in a general industry recession, new corporate leadership had succeeded in turning around the Maine Papers' performance.

Corporate leadership had announced, as part of its strategic renewal, a desire to increase the revenues from internally developed new products.

Maine Papers currently derives 30 percent of its revenues from products generated within the previous five years, and the CEO has announced his intention of reaching 60 percent in three years. That announcement has placed considerable pressure on each of the divisions to improve their new product development processes.

Book Publishing Division

The Book Publishing Division, of which Steve Cook is general manager, is subdivided into three units:

- *trade books*—both best-sellers aimed for a mass market and professional books designed for practicing specialists like managers, doctors, or scientists, distributed through mega-book stores like Barnes and Noble and Borders and Internet providers like Amazon.com
- *textbooks*—intended for classroom use and sold through college bookstores
- *auxiliary materials*—workbooks and teachers' guides distributed directly to teachers using compatible textbooks

The Division also includes Finance and Marketing (see Exhibit 4-8 for a partial organization chart). Manufacturing is a centralized corporate function that is shared among the Maine Papers' eight divisions.

As Cook reflected on the new product development process within the book publishing division, he realized that changes would have to occur:

The world of book publishing has changed recently. It used to be that trade books, professional books, and a textbook were different markets. We had difficult production values for each, even different marketing people.

Cook noted important changes that, he believed, had rendered the Division's past approach unsuitable for the future:

There's been so much consolidation in the publishing industry that there's no such thing as a separate trade and professional and text book market. These giant publishers do everything, so they're looking for opportunities to cross-sell. The Internet has worked to consolidate distribution channels. Everyone—from the casual reader who likes to follow the *New York Times* best seller list to the practicing physician to the college students—gets his books through Amazon.com. Finally we see a lot of books that used to be classified as trade books being used in college classrooms. Take a look at an outline for a course in a college of business. You might not even see a traditional textbook anymore. The same management book or CEO autobiography that was on the best seller list last week might be in a college course tomorrow.

With the approval of his top management team, Cook announced a goal of introducing a full-service program, Performance Plus, that would have a robust functionality

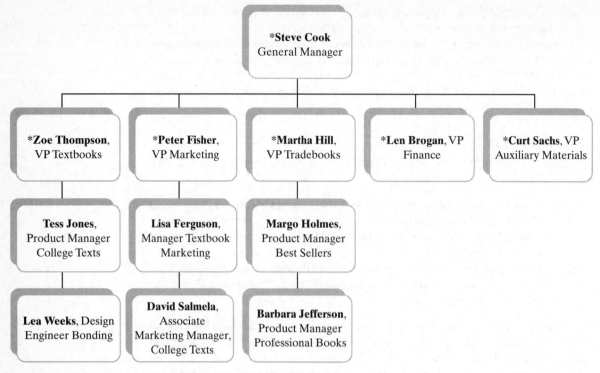

EXHIBIT 4-8 Partial Organization Chart—Book Publishing Division.
*Indicates Management Committee member.

and meet the needs of the trade, professional, and textbook market. To achieve that goal, he had organized a cross-functional Performance Plus team. Says Cook:

> The world has changed, and we have to learn how to respond. Plus, we have to get a lot quicker at getting new products up and running. Everyone in this Division has heard the CEO say we need to reach that 60% goal. So the Performance Plus team is an opportunity to learn how to do product development quicker and better and also giving our customers the opportunity to find all their solutions right here with us.

Performance Plus Team

Just over a year ago, Cook had pulled together the Performance Plus team to develop a product that would appeal to all book markets. He asked Tess Jones (product manager, college texts) to act as a project leader. Her tasks include coordinating meetings, requesting resources, and keeping the management committee informed on team progress. All team members retained their "normal" job responsibilities while meeting with the team every Tuesday afternoon after lunch. While Cook had made no change in the formal organization chart, he did understand that management styles, including his own, would have to change.

Individual team members offered quite different perspectives on the workings of the Performance Plus team. Lisa Ferguson (marketing manager, textbooks*),* for example, has assumed a great deal of personal responsibility for the project:

> Because I'm in marketing, I feel responsible for the overall; success of this new service program. To be honest with you, I wasn't entirely convinced we should be going to market with a single program aimed at these different customers. But once that decision got made, I understood that it was my job to make sure we go to market with the right product so that our customers are happy and I can show a profit. So I guess I kind of consider myself a mini-general manager overseeing the project.

Tess Jones has been designated project manager:

> This is a big deal for us. Performance Plus should replace about 30 percent of our current revenue and offer great growth opportunities. It's my job to make sure all the right pieces come together at the right time.

Lea Weeks (design engineer, bonding) is particularly keen on adding a newly developed feature—Strong Bond—to the finished product:

> One of the biggest complaints about college texts is that the binding falls apart before the end of a term. Students don't take especially good care of their books and within a couple of months they have pages falling out. This has become a greater problem as the cost of text books rise. More and more colleges are using the same texts for a year: in some programs, a text might be used over two years and then be replaced. We have got to go to market with Strong Bond—it's state-of-the-art.

Not everyone on the team shares Weeks' enthusiasm. Says David Salmela (associate marketing manager, college texts):

> I don't know that the Strong Bond is all that important to our customers. Remember, our book publishers really don't mind when a book becomes obsolete after a year. They don't want a lot of used books cluttering up the market place. So maybe Strong Bond is something to look at down the road, but I don't want to miss our May deadline.

Barbara Jefferson (product manager, professional books) is especially concerned with meeting deadlines:

> We've spent time and money on developing Performance Plus. The Company has models that show us that going 50% over budget during product development to get a product out on time reduces profits by only 4%, but staying on budget and getting to market six months late reduces profits by 33%.

Margo Holmes (product manager, best sellers) is concerned about potential delays caused by the as-of-yet unresolved debate over Strong Bond:

> Look, we're not manufacturing's only product. They have to schedule us into a tight schedule. To us, Performance Plus is a big deal; to them, it is just one product among many. We're running this company lean and mean these days. So we've got to resolve this Strong Bond question one way or the other.

Looming Deadline

It is January, and Performance Plus is behind schedule in terms of both design and production. The team continues to work to meet the May deadline. Steve Cook is aware of the difficulties:

> I know the team is having some problems right now and I fight the temptation to jump in and resolve the problems for them. But I believe I've got the right people, they're moving in the right direction, and they'll come up with the right answer. I need to show them that I have faith in them.

He knows, of course, that if production does not start soon, he risks missing the promised launch date. And he knows that the market expects not just a new product, but one that bears the traditional quality of Maine Papers.

Endnotes

1. Nicola Clark, "Turnaround Effort Is Challenging at Airbus, a Stew of European Cultures," *New York Times*, May 18, 2007, p. C1.
2. Michael Beer, Russell A. Eisenstat, and Bert Spector, *The Critical Path to Corporate Renewal* (Boston: Harvard Business School Press, 1990).
3. Michael Goold and Andrew Campbell, "Do You Have a Well-Designed Organization?" *Harvard Business Review* (March 2002), p. 5.
4. *Ibid.*
5. Danny Miller has documented the tendency of once-successful companies to avoid design change. See *The Icarus Paradox: How Exceptional Companies Bring About Their Own Downfall* (New York: Harper Business, 1990).
6. All names are disguised. This case is based on research conducted for Bert Spector, *Taking Charge and Letting Go: A Breakthrough Strategy for Creating and Managing the Horizontal Company* (New York: Free Press, 1995).
7. Information on SAP America is from "ASAP's a Wrap," *Managing Automation* (February 1998); Colleen Frye, "SAP Soothes Implementation

Worries," *Software Magazine* (1997); and David A. Garvin, *SAP America* (Boston: Harvard Business School Publishing, 1996).
8. Paul R. Lawrence and Jay W. Lorsch, *Organization and Environment: Managing Differentiation and Integration* (Boston: Harvard Graduate School of Business Administration Division of Research, 1967).
9. These quotes come from a consulting engagement by the author.
10. Lawrence and Lorsch, *Organization and Environment*, p. 157.
11. See Richard E. Walton, "From Control to Commitment in the Workplace," *Harvard Business Review* (March–April 1985), pp. 5–12.
12. Stephen P. Robbins, *Essentials of Organizational Behavior* (New Jersey: Prentice-Hall, 2005), p. A-3.
13. www. sunhydraulics.com.
14. *Ibid.*
15. Nitin Nohria, *Note on Organization Structure* (Boston: Harvard Case Services, 1991), p. 2.
16. *Ibid.*, p. 3.
17. McDermott is quoted in Thomas Teal, "Service Comes First: An Interview with USAA's Robert

F. McDermott," *Harvard Business Review* (September–October 1991), p. 119.

18. Jay W. Lorsch, *Note on Organization Design* (Boston: Harvard Business School Publishing, 1975), p. 15.

19. Jay W. Lorsch and Stephen A. Allen III, *Managing Diversity and Interdependence: An Organizational Study of Multidivisional Firms* (Boston: Harvard University Graduate School of Business Administration Division of Research, 1973), pp. 53–79.

20. Daniel Goleman, *Working with Emotional Intelligence* (New York: Bantam Books, 1998), p. 118.

21. Robert M. Marsh and Hiroshi Mannari, "Organizational Commitment and Turnover: A Prediction Study," *Administrative Science Quarterly* 22 (March 1977), pp. 57–72; Walton, "From Control to Commitment in the Workplace"; Gary J. Blau and Kimberly B. Boal, "Conceptualizing How Job Involvement and Organizational Commitment Affect Turnover and Absenteeism," *Academy of Management Review* 12 (1987), pp. 288–300; Stephen L. Fink, *High Commitment Workplaces* (New York: Quorum Books, 1992); Mark A. Huselid, "The Impact of Human Resource Management Practices on Turnover, Productivity, and Corporate Financial Performance," *Academy of Management Journal* 38 (1995), pp. 635–661; Julian Gould-Williams, "The Effects of 'High Commitment' HRM Practices on Employee Attitude: The Views of Public Sector Workers," *Public Administration* 82 (2004), pp. 63–81.

22. J. Richard Hackman and Greg R. Oldham, *Work Redesign* (Reading, MA: Addison-Wesley, 1980).

23. Susan Albers Mohrman, Susan G. Cohen, Allan M. Mohrman, Jr., *Designing Team-Based Organizations: New Forms for Knowledge Work* (San Francisco: Jossey-Bass, 1995).

24. The notion that coordination across functions, units, and divisions lies at the core of organizational effectiveness has received a great deal of attention in recent years. See, for instance, Edwad E. Lawler, III, "Substitutes for Hierarchy," *Organizational Dynamics* 17 (1988), pp. 5–15; Christopher A. Bartlett and Sumantra Gloshal, *Managing Across Borders: The Transnational Solution* (Boston: Harvard Business School Press, 1989); D. Keith Denton, *Horizontal Management: Beyond Total Customer Satisfaction* (New York: Lexington Books. 1991); John A. Byrne, "The Horizontal Corporation," *Business Week* (December 20, 1993), pp. 76–81; Jay R. Galbraith, *Competing with Flexible Lateral Organizations* (Reading, MA: Addison-Wesley, 1994).

25. David Nadler, "Ten Years After: Learning About Total Quality Management." A paper delivered at the Total Quality Management conference sponsored by the Management Centre Europe, Brussels, October 1993.

26. International Quality Study, *Best Practices Report: An Analysis of Management Practices That Impact Performance* (Cleveland: American Quality Foundation and Ernst and Young, 1992).

CHAPTER 5

Developing Human Resources

The need to enact a new strategy in response to a dynamic competitive situation places new demands on employees. Redesigned roles, responsibilities, and relationships may require that formerly individualistic employees become team players, for instance; that formerly internally focused employees become responsive to customers; that formerly functionally oriented employees become collaborative with people from other functions; that formerly technically oriented employees adopt a general management perspective; that formerly autocratic managers become facilitators and coaches; that formerly parochial employees become global. Each and every one of these changes calls for altered patterns of behavior and new skills to support those behaviors.

In Steps 2 and 3 of effective change implementation, organizations focus on the skills, competencies, appraisals, development, recruitment, selection, removal, and replacement of employees. The goal of these steps is to ensure that the organization has employees with the skills and motivation necessary to implement new strategies and sustain outstanding performance.

First, in Step 2, the organization seeks to help develop in employees the necessary skills and competencies. Then, in Step 3, the company aligns the talents, skills, attitudes, and behaviors of employees with the strategic requirements of outstanding performance.

This chapter will explore the relationship between human resource development and the dynamics of implementing change. In particular, this chapter will:

- Define human resource development and its role in implementing strategic renewal and organizational change
- Understand how to match selection and recruitment with the shifting requirements of behavioral change
- Analyze how an organization can help employees gained the new skills required of the change effort
- Present the particular choices available to organizations as they seek align employee competencies with the requirements of the organization as part of their change effort
- Analyze the role and usage of removal and replacement in implementing change

First, we will look at an attempt by a grocery chain to drive strategic renewal through the behaviors of its store-level employees.

CHANGING EMPLOYEE BEHAVIOR AT GRAND UNION

The Grand Union grocery store chain faced a formidable challenge: national discount super stores.[1] Historically, the company pursued a low-cost, discount-priced strategy in the northeastern United States. But now, new competitors invading the northeast dwarfed them in both store size (the smallest of the new super stores was twice the size of the largest Grand Union) and purchasing power.

With the discount-priced segment increasingly dominated by the likes of Wal-Mart, top management decided it was time to respond to these new competitive realities by redefining Grand Union's strategy. Instead of battling Wal-Mart head on, Grand Union would reconfigure stores to feature top quality products, national brands, and ethnic foods. What the company lacked in size and market power they would make up for with high quality products and customer responsiveness.

Bill Reffett, the company's senior vice president of human resources, realized that this new strategy required new behaviors on the part of store employees—all store employees at all levels. After surveying store personnel, Reffett produced a before-and-after profile:

Employee Group	Behaviors *before* change	Behaviors *after* change
Bag packers	• Ignore customers • Lack of packing standards	• Greet customers • Respond to customers • Ask for customers' preference
Cashiers	• Ignore customers • Lack of eye contact	• Greet customers • Respond to customers • Assist customers • Speak clearly • Call customers by name
Shelf stockers	• Ignore customers • Don't know store	• Respond to customers • Help customers with correct information • Knowledgeable about product location
Department workers	• Ignore customers • Limited knowledge	• Respond to customers • Know products • Know store
Department managers	• Ignore customers • Ignore workers	• Respond to customers • Reward employees for responding to customers
Store managers	• Ignore customers • Stay in booth	• Respond to customers • Reward employees for service • Appraise employees on customer service

The question faced by Reffett and Grand Union's top management team was simple but vital: how best to move employees from "before" to "after."

HUMAN RESOURCE DEVELOPMENT AND CHANGE

Identifying new behaviors required of a strategic renewal is one thing; developing those behaviors among current employees is another. Grand Union was fully staffed with employees recruited and trained to work in the previous culture. Even assuming that store managers and employees could be motivated to initiate the "before" to "after" switch, did they have the requisite skills to be successful?

Did a department manager, say from produce, know enough about the store's layout to be able to help a customer locate a brand of cereal? That, it seems, would be an easy enough competency to develop. But what about the cashiers who preferred, all their working lives at Grand Union, not to look into a customer's eyes? Could that behavior be easily changed? Or the store manager who preferred sitting inside the manager's booth rather than roaming around the store interacting with both customers and employees. How easy was that behavior to alter?

At the end of the day, Grand Union failed to make the required changes, failed to keep up with the competition, and failed as a company. To ask the question—what might Grand Union have done to bring about the required new behaviors in employees—we need to turn to human resource development.

Building a Vocabulary of Change

Human resource development the creation of required knowledge, skills, and attitudes within an organization to enable the effective implementation of shifting goals and objectives.

Human resource development involves the creation of required knowledge and skills within an organization to enable the effective implementation of shifting strategies.[2] Effective change requires fusion between the development of people—the selection, training, evaluation, promotion, even removal of employees—and the shifting goals of the organization.

In developing required competencies, leaders can select a "make" or "buy" approach. *Making* implies developing the needed new set of competencies and behaviors in current employees. Making assumes that employees are both capable of and motivated to acquire and utilize new skills and engage in new behaviors.

Not all employees can or will make that shift, of course. Additionally, the time required may be too long. Leaders, therefore, will also have to consider a buy approach. *Buying* involves injecting the organization with new employees who possess the desired set of competencies.

In his experience of leading change at Michelin Tires, Renault, and Nissan Motors, Carlos Ghosn developed a marked preference for the "make" appoach to changing behaviors. "It is more of a challenge to me to change people from within," he observed. "It is more long-lasting and beneficial—more powerful—to change people than to change persons."

Despite that preference, the choice between making and buying (summarized in Exhibit 5-1) is rarely either/or. Effective changes typically involve some combination of the two. Getting the make/buy mix "right" means doing them both appropriately and doing them in the appropriate sequence. That matter of sequencing will be addressed later in the chapter.

Theory into Practice

In order to develop required human resource competencies, organizational leaders need to align the selection, training, development, and removal of employees with the behavioral requirements of the desired change.

Option	Steps	Advantages	Disadvantages
Make	Training Altered incentives	Takes advantage of existing knowledge/ skill base	May be slow Not all current employees willing or able
Buy	Recruitment Selection	Can quickly add required knowledge/skills	May undercut morale/commitment of existing employees

EXHIBIT 5-1   Make/Buy Options for Changing Human Resources.

HELP EMPLOYEES DEVELOP COMPETENCIES TO SUPPORT CHANGE

When organizations seek to redefine their strategy—Grand Union moving from low end to upscale groceries, for instance—they face the requirement of developing new competencies among their employees. Thus, once the required new behaviors and their supporting competencies are defined in Step 1, effective change implementation seeks to help employees gain the new competencies and skills. That is why training and development provides the key intervention in Step 2.

Training

Quite a lot of training occurs in organizations. U.S. companies alone spend more than $60 billion a year on training, plus another $180 billion on informal day-to-day instruction. Not all of that training, of course, is designed to be a part of strategic renewal and change. Training is often called upon to teach basic literacy, update technical skills, as well as to develop management skills in individuals leaving functional areas and assuming management responsibilities. In these cases, training programs are intended to improve individual performance within current organizational arrangements rather than change the organization.

To be part of a change effort, training programs need to contain two components.

The first is a *knowledge component*: an awareness of the forces demanding strategic renewal and change and the options available to the organization in response to those forces. What are the relevant changes in the external environment? What are the design choices available to the organization? and what are the strengths and weaknesses of those choices? Understanding both the reasons for abandoning the status quo and the options available to the organization in the future helps motivate employees to change.

Theory into Practice

Training can help convey to employees how their competitive environment is changing and why their own behaviors need to be altered.

The second component of training involves *skill development*. As the organization moves toward greater collaboration and teamwork, for example, people will have to acquire a set of skills associated with teamwork: effective communications, conflict management, trust building, norm setting, diversity awareness, negotiations, and so on.[3] Traditional training approaches such as classrooms, lectures, and discussion groups are effective at achieving the knowledge component; far less so at skill development.

Theory into Practice

Training can, under the right circumstances, help employees gain new behavioral competencies.

Building a Vocabulary of Change

Experiential training training programs that focus on behaviors and typically include role playing and feedback.

As a way of impacting behavior, organizations can supplement traditional knowledge-based training with **experiential training**. Traditional training programs emphasize the delivery of knowledge from the instructor to the learner. Experiential learning, on the other hand, focuses on behaviors while allowing participants to try out the new behaviors required of the change effort.

When General Motors' Livonia plant (see Chapter 1) needed to reorient behavior to focus on teamwork and collaboration, they engaged employees in experiential training. Trained facilitators provide real-time feedback to participants and often model the very behaviors the organization is now seeking. Experiential learning occurs in a protected environment, allowing participants to experiment with new behaviors.

Building a Vocabulary of Change

Training fade-out the failure of behaviors learned as part of a training exercise to transfer to on-the-job experience or behaviors that disappear over time.

The problem with experiential learning is that new behaviors acquired in a training program often disappear quickly once the participants return to their jobs. That phenomenon is known as **training fade-out**. The extent to which the learning gained from a training opportunity is transferred back into the work environment is impacted by three factors:

1. Supervisory/managerial support—Does the employee's supervisor/manager endorse, encourage, provide feedback, and reward new behaviors, or does that supervisor/manager discourage or oppose the application of new skills and behaviors?
2. Peer support—Do the employee's peers support the application of new skills and behaviors, inquire about that learning, provide feedback, and encourage, or do they ignore, discourage, and even attempt to prevent the application of new skills and behaviors?
3. Work conditions—Does the employee have the opportunity to use new skills and behaviors when back on the job, or are new skills and behaviors overtly or covertly discouraged by time pressures, inadequate resources, and/or unchanged responsibilities?[4]

An organizational context that encourages, even demands, the use of new behaviors will lead to greater peer and supervisory support and help to prevent fade-out. Most importantly, to avoid the fade-out problem, participants need to understand and believe that the competencies transferred as part of the training process are required to enact behaviors required of the new strategy.

Theory into Practice

Watch out for fade out—whatever is learned in a training opportunity can lose its impact over time.

Development

One of the most important opportunities for developing new competencies and skills among existing employees arises from a simple but powerful mechanism: feedback. The challenge in using feedback in order to develop new competencies is two fold:

1. To make sure that the feedback is offered in a way to maximize its impact on behaviors.
2. To make sure that the feedback moves employees toward new behaviors rather than reinforcing old behaviors.

Organizations can, under the right circumstances, use the traditional tools of performance feedback and appraisal to help support change implementation.

PERFORMANCE FEEDBACK   In a change implementation process, expectations and definitions of outstanding performance are in flux. It becomes valuable, then, for employees to evaluate the performance of employees for four reasons:

1. It allows an assessment of the current state of the firm's human asset.
2. It helps identify the gap between what skills and organization currently possess and what gaps need to be filled.
3. It identifies poor performers and potential future leaders.
4. It targets required development and training efforts.

From the data generated by the performance evaluation process, organizations can construct developmental tools—training, career pathing, mentoring, etc.—as well as guide future recruitment and selection.

Individual employees also gain value from performance feedback. An assessment of their effectiveness can offer employees invaluable answers to a number of questions:

- How is my effort being perceived and received by the organization?
- What is my future with the company?
- What gaps do I need to address between my efforts and the organization's expectations?
- What set of experiences do I need to construct for myself in order to advance my own aspirations?

The desired goal of the process is alignment between the future needs of the organization and the desires and motivations of employees.

The evaluation process takes place simultaneously in two different forums. The first involves informal, ongoing, often real-time feedback, and the second involves a more formal process, typically a performance appraisal conducted in accordance with organizational guidelines. Informal feedback can occur in both obvious and obscure ways. Regular, real-time feedback discussions between superiors and subordinates or among peers can occur spontaneously and/or as part of the culture of the organization which creates expectations that evaluation and performance dialogue will occur regularly and routinely.

Organizations typically seek to supplement such informal feedback with a more formal approach to effectiveness evaluation: the **performance appraisal**. Although firms implement performance appraisals quite differently, there are some generalizations that can be made. Performance appraisals tend to:

- be regularly scheduled events, occurring annually, semi-annually, or even quarterly
- be individual, one-on-one sessions between a supervisor and a subordinate
- be guided by a form designed by the organization's human resource department
- involve some sort of grading system, covering both specific performance elements and an overall evaluation of effectiveness
- be designed for both administrative purposes—documentation of poor performance, distribution of performance-based rewards, etc.—and developmental purposes

One other salient characteristic of most performance appraisal systems: as implemented, they tend to be highly *in*effective, failing to enhance desired behavior and even leading to deteriorating performance. Extensive research has demonstrated that both appraisers and appraisees are highly dissatisfied with their performance appraisal experience.[5] Appraisers fear that, except in the case of a "superior" performance rating, they will be doing more harm than good, leaving the employee demoralized, demotivated, even alienated.

Apparently, those fears are justified. Managers often report that subordinate performance actually *deteriorates* as a result of conducting a performance appraisal, and indicate that the only reason they conduct such interviews is to comply with company mandates. Employees report greater uncertainty *after* the performance appraisal than before. Most likely, that confusion results from a mismatch between the informal feedback described earlier and the formal feedback offered as part of the performance appraisal.

When performance appraisals become exercises in compliance, as they apparently do with great regularity, they are unlikely to generate commitment on the part of employees to increased effectiveness.

Theory into Practice

Formal performance appraisals often fail to bring about the desired behavioral change.

Employee commitment is also impacted by issues of validity and accuracy. Is the performance appraisal actually assessing what it claims to be assessing, and is it doing so accurately? Employees often leave an interview doubting whether either validity or accuracy has been achieved, and empirical evidence suggests that their suspicion is well founded. Supervisory ratings are regularly and significantly distorted by subjectivity, personal bias, deliberate distortion, and unintended but common rating errors.[6]

To increase employees' perceptions that the feedback they are receiving from the appraisal process is valid—and thus increasing their commitment to enhancing their own high performance behaviors—organizations have tried a number of innovations.

One—the **360° feedback**—attempts to expand the data and bring multiple points of view into the effectiveness appraisal process. Peers, subordinates, even customers are invited to contribute data on an employee's effectiveness relating to both dimensions: task performance and behavioral patterns consistent with the organization's culture.

Approximately 90 percent of Fortune 500 companies use some form of 360° feedback for purposes of employment evaluation, development of needed competencies, or both.[7] The effectiveness of 360° feedback will be enhanced if the organization's culture emphasizes openness and learning, de-emphasizes strict power distinctions based on hierarchy, and places a high value on customer responsiveness.

Another innovation relies heavily on self-appraisal, where the appraisal discussion is based on the subordinate's view of him or herself. When employees perceive themselves to be active participants in the appraisal process, they are more likely to alter their behavior in ways desired by the organization.[8] Both self-appraisal and 360° performance appraisals represent attempts by organizations to increase employee acceptance of the feedback, thus leading to improved behavior and performance.

Building a Vocabulary of Change
360° feedback performance feedback gathered from peers, subordinates, supervisors, and customers.

Theory into Practice

Self-appraisal and data from multiple sources can help increase the validity and effectiveness of performance feedback.

TOP MANAGEMENT DEVELOPMENT   Concentrating on the development of new competencies at lower and middle levels of the organization is a necessary component of strategic renewal and change; it is not, however, sufficient. Effective change will also demand new behaviors from executives at the top of the organization.

Theory into Practice

Behavioral change requires attention to the behavioral pattern of those at the top of the organization as well as lower-level employees.

Greater coordination, higher levels of innovation, speedier response to a dynamic marketplace—all these outcomes are associated with the behaviors and interactions of top managers. Both behavioral and cognitive training interventions are useful in developing new skills among executives, but Richard Boyatzis has suggested that on-the-job experience is far more effective in developing required competencies.[9]

At the CEO level, corporate boards often pursue a "buy" rather than "make" strategy in search of change. Insiders, especially those who have stayed with the company long enough to rise to the top, are products of the culture that have been targeted for change. A change in business fortunes requires a change in top leadership, which means, in turn, injecting the top of the organization with "new blood."[10] Outsiders such as Louis Gerstner at IBM and Archie Norman at Asda have been effective at implementing significant and successful change.

Experience suggests, however, that outsiders are *not* a requirement for out-of-the-box thinking and organizational change. Three longtime insiders who rose to the top of their organizations—Jack Welch at General Electric, Judy McGrath at MTV Networks Group, and Charlie Bell at McDonald's—demonstrated that understanding the existing culture and connecting to the founding mission of the company enabled them to transform business strategies and organizational performance.

No organization can rely entirely on outsiders, of course. To meet the challenge of developing internal leaders capable of transforming their organization, companies can systematically manage the careers and experiences of executives. Those experiences can provide individuals with the opportunity to learn new knowledge, attitudes, and behavior within the unique and special environment of the firm.

Building a Vocabulary of Change

Succession planning a formal process in which top executives regularly review all managers at or above a certain hierarchical level, looking at both performance and potential, and devise developmental plans for their most promising individuals.

Within organizations, career experiences are typically managed through a **succession planning** process in which top executives regularly review all managers at or above a certain hierarchical level, looking at both performance and potential, and devise developmental plans for their most promising individuals.

The implementation of succession planning is often flawed by inadequate—even nonexistent—follow-up. Said one executive of her company's succession planning system, "Our procedures are as good as any . . . The only problem is that people don't pay any attention to them."[11]

Lack of follow-up is not the only limitation. Succession planning can pay a great deal of attention to so-called fast-trackers, while ignoring the potential of others. The problem here is twofold. First, it is possible that those identified as non-fast-trackers have been held back less by their lack of potential than by contextual constraints imposed by the organization. Second, fast-trackers may be individuals who possess skills more associated with past successes than the future demands of change.[12]

Theory into Practice

Companies can manage the careers of executives in order to create a continuous stream of leaders from inside the organization capable of overseeing and leading effective change.

Career development can also help develop executives capable of adaptation and change. Effective change requires individuals who have learned, through a set of on-the-job activities, to be flexible and adaptive. Exhibit 5-2 offers a number of career development practices that can help organizations develop managers capable of moving out of their comfort zones, taking risks, and leading change.

PEOPLE ALIGNMENT

In his study of companies that transformed from "good" to "great"—companies such as Walgreens and Kimberly-Clark—Jim Collins noted that these successful transformations were built on getting "the right people on the bus"—that is, attracting, selecting, and retaining individuals whose skills and behavioral patterns aligned with the transformed requirement of outstanding performance—and getting "the wrong people off the bus."[13]

Structural and design changes	Delayering, increased span of control, matrix, or horizontal structures—all of these work to develop generalists far earlier in their careers and place a greater premium on interpersonal competencies.
Explicit international movement	Assigning managers to work in a non-native culture for a significant period of time develops cross-cultural awareness and skills that can be vital in a culturally diverse environment.
Career mazes	Explicit lateral movements replace rapid upward functional mobility with a far broader set of experiences. Functional blinders are removed, general management skills are enhanced, and commitment to the organization as a whole is enlarged.
Slower velocity to allow greater learning	So-called fast-track managers often fail to stay in one position long enough to deal with the consequences of their actions (and the reactions of employees). Learning about and dealing with the consequence of actions requires greater length of tenure in a position.

EXHIBIT 5-2   Practices for Developing Executives Capable of Adaptation and Leading Change. Based on James E. McElwain, "Succession Plans Designed to Manage Change," *HR Magazine* 36 (February 1991), pp. 67–71; T. Mullen and M. Lyles, "Toward Improving Management Development's Contribution to Organizational Learning," *Human Resource Planning* 16 (1993), pp. 35–49; P. Cappelli and A. Crocker-Hefter, "Distinctive Human Resources Are Firms' Core Competencies," *Organizational Dynamics* 3 (1996), pp. 7–22; Burack, Hochwarter, and Mathys, "The New Management Development Paradigm"; Edmund J. Metz, "Designing Succession Systems for New Competitive Realities," *Human Resource Planning* (1998), pp. 31–37.

The challenge of getting the right people on the bus and the wrong people off the bus lies at the core of Step 3. At this stage of implementation, leaders will have to ask and answer two key questions:

1. What does the organization mean by the "right" and "wrong" employee?
2. What are the most effective ways to manage this stage of the change process?

Let's start with the question of identifying and selecting the "right" employee in a situation of change.

Theory into Practice

People alignment—getting the right people on the bus and the wrong people off the bus—is a key to effective change implementation.

Selecting the "Right" Employees

Individuals are attracted to organizations for a number of reasons. Money, to be sure, as well as location, opportunity for advancement, prestige, and so on. There is also an attraction that derives from a perception of personal alignment. Potential employees may believe that the "personality" of an organization—its goals, structures ways of working, and so on—matches nicely with their own. Conversely, they may feel that there is too much of a discrepancy between them and the organization.[14]

"We're looking for personality," noted a recruiter for Disney World (known in the company as a "director of casting"). "We can train for skills."[15] Undoubtedly, organizations, especially those with strong corporate cultures such as Disney, take on personalities shaped by a combination of values and goals. Individuals, of course, have their own personalities with personal values and goals. During the joining-up process, individuals tend to seek out, and organizations tend to select for, a match between organizational values and individual personalities.

Theory into Practice

Employees attracted to and selected by the organization in an earlier phase are not necessarily the right employees for the newly defined strategies and goals of the changing organization.

The idea of attracting employees with a good personality fit is important to any organization. When an organization is attempting to implement change, the matter becomes even more complex. The personality of the organization is changing. Individuals attracted to and selected by the organization in an earlier phase are not necessarily the right employees for the newly defined strategies and goals of the changing organization.

Store managers at Grand Union, for instance, may have joined the company in part because of their perceptions of compatibility with the culture and its behavioral and performance expectations. When the company embarked on a new strategy, Bill Reffett recognized the requirement to change employee behaviors. In redefining the personality of their organizations, change leaders are, in essence, overturning the sense of personal alignment that existed in the past. They are changing what they are looking for in the "right" employee.

But what, exactly, is meant by the right employee? It is useful to introduce the concept of *fit*. The right employee means an employee who fits certain needs or requirements. Even that explanation does not tell us enough, because the question still remains: *what* needs or requirements? The requirements may be technical, behavioral, attitudinal, or some combination of the three.

We can leave the world of corporations and look at how a very different type of organization—a rock and roll band—dealt with the issue of selection and fit. The British rock band, The Rolling Stones—renowned for such 1960s mega-hits as "(I Can't Get No) Satisfaction" and "Time Is On My Side"—were in search of a new lead guitarist. This was 1975 and the band had already been through two guitarists.[16]

Now, the best known rock and roll band in the world faced a special challenge. Their strategy—and yes, a rock and roll band *can* have a business strategy—was changing. As the members aged and musical tastes changed, the Stones refocused their energies from studio recordings to live appearances. Given their renown, they had no difficulty attracting interested, immensely talented guitarists. Band members joked that they should charge a fee for the privilege of auditioning.

Early in the process, band member Keith Richards, a virtuoso rhythm guitarist, decided the band should not necessarily select the most talented musician available. Several of the hopefuls were incredibly proficient as players but were eliminated simply because they were American rather than English. "This is an English rock and roll band, after all, and that was basically the criterion," explained Richards.

Jeff Beck, who was widely thought to be the best guitar player to come out of Europe, made an impression on the entire band. Still, Richards hesitated. "It wasn't about who could play the sweetest notes" he said. Band members also looked at personality: the new guitarist would have to be someone they could "live with" on the road.

Theory into Practice

Hiring the most talented individual for a task may not be the best approach for an organization, especially if the organization is going through a change process.

Given the new emphasis on touring, Richards was insistent that the new lead guitarist be talented, yes, but also someone with whom the band could live with—literally as well as figuratively—for years to come. That individual turned out to be an old friend of Richards, Ron Wood. Neither Richards nor the rest of the group believed Jeff Beck would fit as comfortably into their touring life as would Wood.

In the case of the Stones, the hiring process worked well. The members understood both their changing strategy (from studio recording to touring) and how that shift impacted the selection criterion (from the best musician available to an excellent musician with whom current group members could live). That selection proved auspicious—to this day, Wood is a member and continues to tour with the Stones.

CRITERIA FOR SELECTION   To help clarify the choices an organization—Grand Union, the Rolling Stones, and others—faces in the selection process, it is useful to approach fit in two ways. The first involves fit with a specific job, and the second involves fit with the larger organizational culture and values.

Person-task fit is the most common approach organizations take to hiring employees. The organization has specific tasks that need to be done, so it hires individuals with the skills required of those tasks. Need an electrical engineer? Hire the most skilled electrical engineer available (keeping costs in mind, of course). Need a new guitarist? Hire the best musician available.

> **Building a Vocabulary of Change**
> *Person-task fit* screening and selecting individual employees based on their ability to perform certain tasks and fulfill specific jobs.

To help ensure that the organization hires people with the requisite skills, human resource specialists work in a structured way to define the key knowledge, skills, and abilities required in the performance of core organizational tasks. Individuals are sought, and often tested, to determine their competency levels to perform. The best-qualified individuals are then selected to fill the organization's job vacancies.

The second approach to selection involves what can be thought of as **person-organization fit.** Unlike the person-task approach, person-organization fit looks beyond the specific skill demands of a task, focusing instead of the values of an individual. Now, the organization asks: how do the values of potential hires fit with the values we are trying to promote? That is the criterion used by the Stones in hiring the guitar replacement.

> **Building a Vocabulary of Change**
> *Person-organization fit* screening and selecting employees based on congruence between patterns of organizational values and patterns of individual values.

Person-organization fit looks beyond specific jobs to the desired future state of the organization. What are the mind-set, the personality, and the competencies that the organization seeks through its change? What newly defined roles, responsibilities, and relationships are sought? Most importantly at this stage, what new competencies—both technical how-to competencies and interpersonal (creative problem solving, decision making, collaboration, communication, and so on) competencies—are required of this desired future state?

Aware of its changing strategy, the Rolling Stones recruited not the most talented lead guitarist, the individual who could play the "sweetest notes," but rather the individual with the personality to become part of the band. Talent is important, obviously, but fit with where the organization is headed is vital.

Determining who fits with the organization is a complex, even tricky business. Supervisors often make decisions about which employees fit or do not fit based implicitly, perhaps even subconsciously, on the goal of reproducing themselves. The question transforms from whether the employee behaves in ways consistent with the values and culture of the organization to whether the employee thinks and acts like the evaluating supervisor.

When supervisors seek—consciously or otherwise—to clone themselves, the effect can be damaging both to employees and to the organization. Employees may rightly wonder just how valid supervisory decisions are. Additionally, if organizations become homogeneous, they are in danger of weakening both diversity and creativity.[17]

That approach can be particularly harmful in periods of change. The supervisors' past successes may be the result of behaviors that no longer fit with the desired future strategy of the company. Additionally, the reproduction phenomenon risks eliminating diversity and promoting conformity within the organization. When change efforts are designed to enhance creativity and innovation, actions that drive out diversity, however inadvertently, will be detrimental. Finally, employees themselves may experience replacement less as a valid measure of ability to adopt new behaviors and more as a self-serving device that enhances supervisors' views of themselves.

An explicit and shared understanding of the new behaviors required of strategic renewal and outstanding performance can help to overcome the dangers of selective perception and reproduction.

An organization seeking higher levels of coordination and teamwork, for instance, might provide an explicit statement of the personal attributes and competencies required of managers in the future, including:[18]

- Inclination toward collaboration and the skills that go with it
- Competencies to engage in group problem solving
- Willingness and ability to confront conflict rather than to soothe or avoid
- Higher levels of interpersonal competence than are normally required

Once the requirements have been made explicit, managers are better able to make valid assumptions about whether individuals are displaying the required behaviors. Simultaneously, employees are more likely to accept the validity of those decisions.

SCREENING FOR FIT Particularly when an organization is attempting to implement change, there is an urgent need to attract employees whose behavior exemplifies the desired future state. But just how can organizations screen for person-organization fit?

Microsoft prides itself in screening potential hires for intelligence and creativity as much as—if not more than—depth of technical expertise. Even "technical" interviews for potential software developers focus more on "thought processes, problem-solving abilities, and work habits than on specific knowledge or experience." *How many times does the average person use the word "'the" in a day?* an interviewer might ask. The manner in which the individual organizes his thought processes and attacks the problem is the key, not providing any technically "right" answer.[19]

Microsoft considers creative problem solving to be a cornerstone of the company's culture and uses the screening process to find individuals who will fit with that desired culture.

Paying attention to the selection of new employees is a key to change implementation. Attracting and hiring employees who already possess both the motivation and competencies to enact the new culture will enhance the effectiveness of the desired change.

This is not to say that *all* issues of person-organization fit must be resolved in the selection process. Behaviorally focused training can help, while removing employees who cannot or will not adopt new behavioral patterns may be necessary. Getting it as right as possible in the selection phase certainly will reduce both the cost and time associated with training and minimize the difficulties—both emotional and financial—associated with removal and replacement.

Theory into Practice

Selecting the "right" employees—that is, employees who possess the values and competencies required of the change—will reduce time, cost, and other revenues required in later developmental interventions.

SELECTION TECHNIQUES   Companies can use any number of techniques to screen for the "right" employee, starting with what is anachronistically called **paper-and-pencil tests**: standardized, self-administered, and quantifiable tests. Whether using paper or interactive computer software, these tests assess any number of attributes, ranging from general intelligence and mental ability to mechanical aptitude and technical and industry-based knowledge.

When strategic renewal requires an alteration in the culture of the company, the most obvious paper-and-pencil instruments to call upon involve personality and psychological tests. These tests offer insight into whether an individual is open or defensive, extroverted or introverted, individualistic or team oriented, easygoing or reserved, suspicious or trusting, and so forth.

Using paper-and-pencil tests in the screening process offers some obvious advantages to a company in transition. The tests are relatively easy to administer and score. Quantifiable results are simple to compare. Most importantly, there is validity to the tests as predictors of on-the-job success as long as multiple tests are used in combination.

Paper-and-pencil tests are not without flaws. Opportunity for abuse and misuse of data are significant. Additionally, their use tends to produce a less diverse workforce in terms of race.[20] Differences in early cultural experiences and unfamiliarity with test-taking techniques on the part of applicants, especially when combined with unintended biases in the formulation of test questions, can produce undesired outcomes.[21] Minority job seekers often express deep suspicion of these tests and their

Building a Vocabulary of Change
Paper-and-pencil tests standardized, self-administered, and quantifiable tests used as part of a screening, selection, or assessment process.

use. Organizations desirous of seeking greater diversity within their workforce may find paper-and-pencil tests working against that goal.

Two mechanisms, both focusing explicitly on behaviors, offer supplements or alternatives to paper-and-pencil tests. **Behaviorally anchored interviews** ask potential hires to recount specific examples from their past experience to illustrate how they have responded to challenges and opportunities:

- Give me an example of a work-related problem that you had to deal with, and how you responded.
- Talk about a recent group experience you had at work and the role that you played.

When a group of employees participates in the interview, each asking questions and rating responses, the validity of the assessment increases. The goal is to increase the likelihood of achieving fit between new hires and the behavioral goals of the change without driving out diversity. Exhibit 5-3 offers examples of behaviorally anchored interview questions.

A selection process keen on exploring fit between a potential hire and the new behavioral demands might go beyond asking potential hires to recount past actions. A technique known as **behavioral simulation** asks applicants to *demonstrate* behaviors. An illustration of behavioral simulation in screening occurred at Cummins Engine Company's Jamestown, New York, plant.

Collaboration and teamwork were among the core values of plant management as they sought to create high employee commitment. As the diesel-engine plant grew beyond its original start-up levels, the management team realized that they would have to pay close attention to person-organization fit in the recruitment and selection process. The plant's high wage structure assured an abundant supply of applicants, but not just any employee would do. The management team focused the selection process on behaviors that matched the plant's culture and values.

Human resource specialists performed the initial screening. Soon, shop floor workers—team members in the parlance of the plant—entered the process. Teams did their own hiring in order to ensure fit with their particular orientation and set of expectations. In addition to conducting interviews, team members observed applicants

---

- Describe a time when you were placed on an ineffective work team and how you dealt with it.
- Tell me about a specific employee with whom you had difficulty managing and how you dealt with it.
- Describe how you handled going into a new work situation.
- Describe how you went about learning what was going on in a unit to which you were just moved.
- Tell me about a change process you were involved in and what role you played.
- Tell me about the best performing team you ever worked on and what your contribution was.

EXHIBIT 5-3 Behaviorally Anchored Interview Questions.

A group of individuals are assigned a complex problem to solve.
- Solving the problem requires multiple skills.
- The problem's solution is such that effective performance can be rated objectively.

Individuals are placed in teams and asked to solve the problem jointly.
- Afacilitator is on hand to offer behavioral observations.
- The joint problem-solving phase may be videotaped to allow participants to observe their behaviors.

A trained facilitator leads the team through a discussion of behaviors.

The solutions of the teams are measured, providing an effectiveness metric for each group.

Team members engage in a further discussion of behaviors based on their performance.

EXHIBIT 5-4   Components of a Behavioral Simulation.

in role-play situations—typically, team exercises (see Exhibit 5-4 for a description of a typical behavioral simulation). After conducting this kind of informal assessment, team members worked together to select future colleagues.

The techniques for person-organization fit screening (summarized in Exhibit 5-5) focus on personality and interpersonal behavior. Screening cannot ignore technical skills, although it is useful to remember that many technical skills can be learned relatively quickly. Interpersonal skills are often more difficult to develop. Organizations would do well to screen for traits that are both critical to performance success and the *most difficult to develop*. Attitude, values, and cultural fit are attributes that are difficult to develop within the context of organizational life yet vital to the sustained outstanding performance of a company.[22]

Patagonia, an outdoor clothing and gear company, bases its personnel selection decisions more on who applicants are than on what specific skills they possess. "This is a unique culture, extremely unique," said founder/owner Yvon Chouinard. "Not everyone fits in here." That is why the company places its greatest effort into looking for creative and committed "dirt bags," its term for outdoor types. "I've found that rather than bring in businessmen and teach them to be dirt bags," Chouinard observed, "it's easier to teach dirt bags to do business."[23]

Learning business skills, Chouinard insisted, is far easier than learning how to be a true dirt bag. Hiring individuals with the desired personality traits and behavioral competencies and then teaching required skills (rather than hiring for skills and attempting to teach personality and behavior) is far more likely to be successful.

Theory into Practice

It is far easier to teach new skills than to develop new values.

Mechanism	Description	Strengths	Weaknesses
Paper-and-pencil tests	Standardized, quantifiable, self-administered instruments	• Easy to administer and score • Inexpensive to use on large scales • Simple to compare • Valid job success predictors when used in combination with other mechanisms	• Produce homogeneous workforce • May be resisted/resented by applicants
Behaviorally anchored interviews	Applicants recount specific examples of past experiences	• Can focus on specific behaviors • Valid supplement to other screening mechanisms • Validity increases when multiple interviewers score results	• Deal with recounted rather than actual behaviors • Can be slow and expensive to administer
Behavioral simulation	Applicants engage in role-playing exercise while observed by screeners	• Focus on actual rather than recounted behaviors	• Can be slow and expensive to administer

EXHIBIT 5-5   Techniques for Person-Organization Fit Screening.

Removal and Replacement

In support of strategic renewal and change, a company may attempt to improve its mix of competencies rapidly by increasing the outflow of personnel through early retirement programs and/or layoffs. Early retirement increases the percentage of recently hired employees who may bring with them new skills, new values, or both. At the same time, personnel reductions allow for a rapid lowering of payroll costs, which will, it is hoped, improve profitability in the short term.

In the United States, this scenario has been used by companies in many industries as a response to rapid swings in either the particular competitive environment of the company or in general economic conditions. Pressured by quarterly earnings expectations, management has used workforce reductions as a strategy to maintain earnings and dividends expected by investors, stock analysts, and financial institutions.

Although the workforce reduction strategy may be popular, it has not been terribly effective in helping an organization transform itself into an outstanding performer. Given the short-term severance costs of large-scale reductions (a cost that is considerably higher in Europe than in the United States), the savings in compensation to the organization and subsequent impact on the bottom line are often minor.

One such study of the impact of workforce reductions, for instance, concluded that there is no conclusive, consistent evidence that downsizing leads to improved financial performance.[24] Layoffs are not, in other words, a quick fix for ailing performance.

A more broadly based turnaround involving the restructuring of assets through acquisition and divestiture, as well as significant changes in plant and equipment, could over time lead to improved performance.[25] Companies that simply reduce labor force in order to become "lean and mean," however, find little if any long-term performance improvement.

Theory into Practice

Don't count on workforce reductions and employee layoffs to produce the human resource competencies required to support strategic renewal and sustain outstanding performance.

Layoffs represent large-scale interventions designed mainly to improve short-term financial performance. **Removal and replacement** is a more specific, targeted tool for developing required new human resource competencies within the organization. Removal and replacement deals with individuals who cannot or will not develop new competencies and behaviors.

An optimistic view of human nature would suggest that many, perhaps even most, employees will be willing and able to learn the new competencies and enact the required behaviors of change. Some portion of past store managers at Grand Union, for instance, would be willing and able to operate in an interdependent, team-oriented culture. Training and development could help with the transition.

Although well-designed training programs can indeed be helpful in supporting new patterns of behavior, success will not be universal. Not all employees, after all, are capable of developing the new skills or enacting the new behaviors. Others might simply prefer not to alter their past behaviors.

IMPLEMENTING REMOVAL AND REPLACEMENT   When Asda, a large U.K.-based grocery store chain, sought to transform its failing business in the 1990s, removal and replacement became a vital part of the effort. A cross-functional renewal team started Asda's store-based change by designing a new set of roles and responsibilities for store employees at all levels. Team members realized that the targeted new behaviors—quite similar to the new behaviors articulated at Grand Union—would require store managers who were both willing and able to support the desired new culture.

After selecting three stores to pilot the "new" Asda—a store culture focused on value, offering customer responsiveness, with high levels of autonomy for individual department managers and strategic planning on behalf of store managers—the renewal team called on the corporate human resources department to evaluate current managers. In the terms Collins used, the team wanted to make sure they had "the right people on the bus" within the targeted stores. That review revealed that much of the challenge of change would focus on getting "the wrong people off the bus."

A sense of urgency required that the early change build on a store management team that displayed the potential for being able to make the required changes. Within the

Building a Vocabulary of Change
Removal and replacement a change tool that targets individuals who cannot or will not adopt behaviors required of the redesigned organization.

first three stores, about 40 percent of the existing managers were removed and replaced. Some were fired, others moved to other stores not immediately targeted for change. The renewal team brought in managers to the selected pilot stores who had been identified by the human resources staff as more likely to be effective in the new environment.

Removal and replacement does not necessarily involve firing individuals. When the general manager of Rubbermaid's Commercial Products division decided to re-design his operation around cross-functional business teams, it became clear that many employees were uncomfortable with the new approach. The vice president of marketing used a sports analogy to characterize the differences among employees in their reactions to the requirement for teamwork:

> When we first formed the business teams, we had a lot of tennis players and golfers on the team, not team players. They had good functional ex-pertise, but because they weren't team players we were getting into trou-ble. They didn't try to understand how what they were doing on their piece of the product was affecting other functions.[26]

Having the wrong people on the bus at Rubbermaid Commercial Products hurt team performance. A member of the upper-management operating team responsible for creating and supporting the various business teams in the division acknowledged the re-quirement to engage removal and replacement as a human resource development tool:

> When we have seen teams fail, the majority of the time, it was not due to lack of technical expertise. It was because there was a person on the team who was not a team player. We, as an operating team, have to recognize this, and insure that non-team players are relocated from the business team to another position which best complements their personality.[27]

Individuals who could not make the change were replaced and then carefully lo-cated in positions where their behaviors would not block or slow down the sought-after change to a team-based operation.

There will be situations in which replacement and removal is not an immediate option to change leaders. Collins described the change at a medical school where the in-stitution of tenure—essentially, guaranteed employment for professors—constrained the actions of the school's academic director. Because he could not remove tenured profes-sors, the director of academic medicine waited for openings to hire "the right people." By doing so, he created "an environment where the wrong people felt increasingly un-comfortable and eventually retired or decided to go elsewhere."[28] When leaders are clear about the behavioral implications of the desired new strategy, and employees are clear that behavioral change is required, individuals may elect to remove themselves.

GETTING THE SEQUENCE RIGHT: FAIR PROCESS

The change implementation model presented in Exhibit 2-7 separates sequentially the Help interventions from People Alignment. In that sequence, organizations offer em-ployees training in the new required skills and behaviors (Step 2) before decisions are made about moving employees (Step 3).

That sequence—first Help and *then* People Alignment—raises an interesting challenge. Why invest in training an employee if, in the very next step of the sequence, the organization may have to remove that same employee? The answer lies in the concept of fair process.

Fair process is a widely shared perception that decisions are being made based on valid criteria. Perceptions of unfair process lead to declining morale, increased turnover, and deteriorating commitment. Conversely, perceptions of fair process lead to higher levels of individual motivation and commitment to the organization and its changing goals.[29]

W. Chan Kim and Renée Mauborgne suggest that a fair process derives from three factors:

1. *Engagement*—involving individuals in decisions that impact them, both at the front end (collecting valid data) and the back end (allowing individuals to refute ideas and assumptions).
2. *Explanation*—making transparent the thinking that underlies decisions.
3. *Expectation clarity*—making clear the criteria that have been and will be used for decision making.[30]

Employee commitment will remain high even if employees disagree with the decision, Kim and Mauborgne conclude, "If they believe that the process the manager used to make the decision was fair."[31]

In terms of Step 3 decisions, fair process is, in large part, a function of validity. Are Talent Management decisions based on selective perception or on the requirements of the new strategy?

Perceptions of fairness can also be impacted by the degree to which an organization provides employees with due process and appeal mechanisms. What avenues are available to employees who believe that they have been treated by human resource development decisions such as evaluation, promotion, or even firing?

Union contracts typically offer grievance and appeal avenues with union officials advocating for members. In nonunion settings, employers may provide their own grievance and appeal mechanisms—panels of managers and employees; trained fact finders, mediators, or arbitrators—that can either make suggestions or overturn decisions if they find an employee has been treated unfairly.

Theory into Practice

Unless Talent Management decisions are viewed by employees as being fair in process, valid in content, and appropriate in sequence, the decisions can undermine commitment to change implementation.

Finally, perceptions of fairness will be based on the timing of People Alignment decisions. Perceived fairness will be enhanced by a sequence of actions that has already included:

- A shared diagnosis that has surfaced the relationship between past behavioral patterns and current performance shortcomings
- A redesign process that has identified new patterns of behavior required for sustained outstanding performance

Building a Vocabulary of Change

Fair process a widely shared perception that decisions are being made on the basis of valid criteria.

- Training and development that have been offered to employees as a way of gaining and demonstrating required new behaviors

At this stage, individuals have been offered the opportunity to alter their behaviors, those who cannot or will not make the required changes have been identified, and People Alignment decisions—promotion, removal and replacement—can be seen as conforming to the imperatives of outstanding performance rather than to the selective perception of individual supervisors.

Conclusion

By its nature, strategic renewal and organizational change demand new behaviors from employees. Patterns of behavior that have sustained a company in the past will need to be altered in response to the dynamics of the competitive environment. The diagnostic stage of change has surfaced a misfit between current behaviors and competitive realities. Global customers, for example, may be expecting greater coordination between a company's various units, local customers may be expecting greater employee responsiveness to their specific and special needs, and increasing competition may be demanding faster innovation and greater speed to market with new products and offerings.

In the redesign stage (Step 1), employees create a behavioral model for how the business will respond to those shifts in order to achieve and maintain outstanding performance. At this stage, leaders face a new challenge. Employees who have succeeded in the past may not possess the skills required to excel in the future. Companies may do an assessment to analyze "old" and "new" patterns of behavior and identify the gap that exists within their current human resource.

Now is the time in the change implementation process for leaders to turn their attention to human resource development, an explicit and systematic effort to develop among organizational employees the competencies to enact desired new behaviors. Organizations first seek to help (Step 2) employees acquire the necessary competencies and skills. Training programs can be helpful at this stage, especially experiential training that offers employees an opportunity to learn new behaviors. The danger of experiential training, however, is that unless the work environment to which participants return supports and even demands that participants enact those newly learned behaviors, the impact of learning will quickly fade out and employees will retreat to their old ways. That is why training is most effective and impactful when it *follows* redesign to ensure that employees leave training and find a newly altered work context to support and reinforce their new behaviors.

In Step 3, leaders seek to align people with the strategic requirements of outstanding performance in a number of different ways. The selection process becomes a key element of that process. Attracting and hiring individuals already in possession of the desired skills—especially those competencies that are difficult to develop—will infuse the organization with employees capable of enacting the desired future model.

Not all employees can or will make the required transition. Once the performance requirements of the future model have been articulated through a process of mutual engagement (Step 1), and employees have been offered an opportunity to develop the required new competencies (Step 2), organizations will be able to identify individuals whose behaviors do promote or replace (Step 3). When Step 3, people alignment decisions are viewed by employees as being both fair and valid, those decisions will support the change effort.

Now at the final stage (Step 4), organizational leaders can seek to reinforce behavioral patterns. For that purpose, they turn to new structures and systems. That will be the subject of Chapter 6.

Discussion Questions

1. What specific suggestions would you have made to Bill Reffett at Grand Union in order to develop the required human resource competencies to support the firm's new strategy?
2. Is the increasing diversity of the workforce—in terms of race, gender, national origins, health status, cultural values, and so on—a positive or negative in terms of helping organizations make successful transformations? Explain your answer.
3. What are the main differences between hiring for task and hiring for organizational fit? Why is hiring for organizational fit so difficult to do? What techniques might an organization use?
4. What specific recommendations would you make to an organization seeking to avoid training fade-out?
5. The author sees removal and replacement as a key element of devolving human resource competencies. Do you agree or disagree? Why?

Case Discussion

Read "'Employee First, Customer Second': Vineet Nayar Transforms HCL Technologies" and prepare answer to the following questions:

1. Explain how—or *if*—Vineet Nayar's new strategy for the company and his approach to human resource development reinforce each other.
2. Do you see potential problems implementing Nayar's human resource initiatives within India?
3. Are Nayar's ideas about human resource development transferable to other industries and other countries?

"Employee First, Customer Second": Vineet Nayar Transforms HCL Technologies

Headquartered in Noida, a suburb of New Delhi, HCL Technologies competed in India's hyperdynamic information technology (IT) sector.[32] Founded in 1976, HCL defined itself as "one of India's original IT garage startups." For its first 25 years, HCL found success offering IT hardware. However, as the global IT industry shifted from hardware to software and to offering infrastructure services, HCL proved to be less than nimble.

In April 2005, the company looked within and promoted Vineet Nayar to the position of president. Nayar immediately set his goal for HCL: transformational change within the company in order to position HCL as a global leader in transformational outsourcing services "working with clients in areas that impact and redefine the core of their business."

Strategic Renewal

Strategic renewal at HCL would involve, Nayar announced, a movement away from "small time engagements" and toward high value-added integrated service consulting and outsourcing. In order to turn that vision into reality, Nayar would oversee transformational change at his $1.5 billion, 46,600-employee company. (HCL had operations in 11 countries, including the United States, France, Germany, China, and Japan, with 96 percent of its employees worldwide being Indian.)

His first strategic goal was to pay a great deal more attention to internal operating efficiencies than HCL had in the past, while simultaneously emphasizing innovative offerings. Nayar would, he promised, "put our house in order by rejuvenating employees and improving operating efficiencies."

From his past management experience, Nayar (who had spent seven years as an HCL engineer before taking the assignment of running an internally developed start-up company) had come to believe that employees rather than leaders would be the source of improvement and innovation.

India's traditional hierarchical culture led executives to take a "dictatorial" approach to management. Studies of national culture have found that India ranks high on two dimensions: power distance and long-term orientation. High power distance suggests greater acceptance of hierarchical authority and a greater capacity to follow than lead. A high score on the long-term orientation index suggests a preference for thrift, perseverance, and predictability.[33]

If HCL was to compete successfully against larger Indian competitors such as Infosys, Nayar wanted to "invert the pyramid," he said, explaining his meaning in blunt terms. For most companies, "it's the employee who sucks up to the boss." Nayar's goal for HCL was to create a culture where "as much as possible, [we] get the manager to suck up to the employee."

Rejuvenating Employees

Three months after assuming the president's position, Nayar announced two initiatives designed to rejuvenate employees and unleash their creative potential. Both initiatives, he also admitted, were intended to be "shocks" to the system and signal a shaking up of the old culture.

"Employee First, Customer Second"

In July 2005, Nayar introduced his "Employee First, Customer Second" initiative in order to "invert the pyramid." That initiative, explained Dilip Kumar Srivastava, head of corporate human resources, had four strategic objectives:

1. to provide a unique employee environment
2. to drive an inverted organizational structure
3. to create transparency and accountability in the organization
4. to encourage a value-driven culture.

Added Nayar, "I wanted value focused employees that were willing and able to drive an innovative, sophisticated experience for customers. From the start, though, I was clear: Employee First was not about free lunch, free buses, and subsidies. It was about setting clear priorities, investing in employees' development, and unleashing their potential to produce bottom-line results."

360° Performance Evaluations

Simultaneously with announcing the Employee First, Customer Second philosophy, Nayar introduced 360° performance evaluations. Initially, the evaluations were performed on Nayar and his top 20 managers. That was not the shock however; rather, it was Nayar's directive that the results of that evaluation be posted in the company's intranet for any employee to see.

Executives report to feelings of unease at the airing of those results. Said R. Srikrishna, head of the U.S. infrastructure services division, "There was this whole picture of me that [emerged] as a heavy taskmaster. It was very unsettling the first time."

For Nayar, the publication of 360° results signaled that HCL was serious about his Employee First philosophy. Nayar expanded the system so that employees can see the results for their managers as well as their peers. Nayar assured them that the ratings would *not* be used to determine bonuses or promotions. Instead, they would allow the individuals to work with the company's human resources department to create developmental programs for them.

Nayar appreciated that the idea of posting results would be shocking, at first, to employees. He referred to this as disruptive thinking. "When I put my 360° evaluation in the Intranet within my first 90 days of taking charge at HCL Technologies, it showed that the CEO was willing to put his neck on the line. It is a simple gesture that galvanizes others into thinking on similar lines. We [India] claim to be the world's largest democracy, but while running our businesses we are dictatorial toward our employees."

Additional Human Resource Initiatives

Some additional initiatives started by Nayar include:

- Employees could pose questions directly for Nayar on the company's intranet. He then spent about seven hours answering the 50 or so weekly questions and posted those answers for everyone to see.
- HCL's training program was renamed "Talent Transformation and Intrapreneurship Development."[34] "We did not just want to have swanky off-site development programs, then have employees return to work and go back to status quo," explained Anand Pillai, who headed the program. Instead, HCL rotated employees through multiple projects and jobs and then helped them "understand the work of their operation at both the tactical and strategic level."
- HCL created a "smart service desk" where employees can post "tickets" of complaints about the food, the temperature at which the air conditioner is set, or the size of their bonus. Under Nayar's rules, only the poster himself can close the ticket when they feel their issue has been resolved.
- HCL abandoned performance-based bonuses and adopted, instead, what was called "trust pay." Aimed most especially at junior engineers, pay would be fixed at the beginning of the year. That represented a dramatic break from the industry standard of having variable pay account for up to 30 percent of total compensation. "It increased our cost base," admitted Nayar, but the idea was, we'd pay you fully, but we trusted that you would deliver. It was intended to reduce transaction volume and increase trust."

Further Challenges

By 2007, Nayar could point to some impressive improvements. Under his leadership, HCL has achieved the highest level of organic growth—defined as growth achieved through internal development rather than by acquisitions and mergers—among India's

IT sector. Employee retention had been a particular problem for HCL. In 2005, the company's attrition rate—the percentage of total employees who leave a company in a year—was 20.4 percent, among the highest in the industry. In 2007 that figure dropped to 17.2 percent (still higher than many competitors). At the same time, competition remained unrelenting and was becoming more global. IBM announced plans to invest $6 billion in India in the upcoming three years, up from $2 billion in the previous three years.

Endnotes

1. Information on Grand Union and its human resource strategy comes from Randall S. Schuler, "Strategic Human Resource Management: Linking the People with the Strategic Needs of the Business," *Organizational Dynamics* 21 (Summer 1992), pp. 18–33.

2. This definition of HRD is from G. J. Bergenhenegouwen, E. A. M. Moorijiman, and H. H. Tillema as cited in A. A. M. Wognum and M. M. Mulder, "Strategic HRD Within Companies," *International Journal of Training and Development* 3 (1999), p. 2.

3. George Bohlander and Kathy McCarty, "How to Get the Most from Team Training," *National Productivity Review* (Autumn 1996), pp. 25–35.

4. Raymond A. Noe, *Employee Training and Development* (Boston: McGraw-Hill Irwin, 2002), pp. 150–175. These conclusions were confirmed empirically in Dian L. Seyler, Elwood F. Holton III, Reid A. Bates, Michael F. Burnett, and Manuel A. S. Carvalho, "Factors Affecting Motivation to Transfer Training," *International Journal of Training and Development* 2 (1998), pp. 2–16.

5. This research is reviewed in Herbert M. Meyer, "A Solution to the Performance Appraisal Feedback Enigma," *Academy of Management Executive* 5 (1991), pp. 68–76.

6. Gary P. Latham and Kenneth N. Wexley, *Increasing Productivity Through Performance Appraisal* (Reading, MA: Addison-Wesley, 1981); David B. Balkin and Luis Gomez-Mejia, *New Perspectives on Compensation* (New Jersey: Prentice Hall, 1987); C. Longenecker, H. Sims, and D. Gioia, "Behind the Mask: The Politics of Employee Appraisal," *Academy of Management Executive* 1 (1987), pp. 183–191; George T. Milkovich and John W. Bourdeau, *Human Resource Management* (Homewood, IL: Irwin, 1991); Donald J. Campbell, Kathleen M. Campbell, and Ho-Beng Chia, "Merit Pay, Performance Appraisal, and Individual Motivation: An Analysis and Alternative," *Human Resource Management* 37 (Summer 1998), pp. 131–146.

7. Tracy Maylett and Juan Riboldi, "Using 360° Feedback to Predict Performance," *Training and Development* (September 2007), pp. 48–52.

8. M. M. Greller, "Subordinate Participation and Reactions to the Appraisal Interview," *Journal of Applied Psychology* 6 (1975), pp. 544–549; R. J. Burke, W. Weitzel, and T. Weir, "Characteristics of Effective Performance Review and Development Interviews: Replication and Extension," *Personnel Psychology* 31 (1978), pp. 903–919; Charles C. Manz and Henry P. Sims, Jr., "Self-Management As a Substitute for Leadership: A Social Learning Perspective," *Academy of Management Review* (1980), pp. 361–367; R. L. Dipboye and R. de Pontbriand, "Correlates of Employee Reactions to Performance Appraisal and Appraisal Systems," *Journal of Applied Psychology* (1981), pp. 248–251; J. M. Ivancevich and J. T. McMahon, "The Effects of Goal Setting, External Feedback, and Self-Generated Feedback on Outcome Variables: A Field Experiment," *Academy of Management Journal* (1982), pp. 359–372; D. M. Herold, R. C. Liden, and M. L. Leatherwood, "Using Multiple Attributes to Assess Sources of Performance Feedback," *Academy of Management Journal* (1987), pp. 826–835.

9. Richard E. Boyatzis, *The Competent Manager: A Model for Effective Performance* (New York: Wiley, 1992); and Richard E. Boyatzis, Scott S. Cowen, David A. Kold, and associates, *Innovation in Professional Education: Steps on a Journey from Teaching to Learning* (San Francisco: Jossey-Bass, 1995).

10. Research has demonstrated that lagging organizational performance is one of the key reasons for turning to outside leadership. See Donald C. Hambrick

and Phyllis A. Mason, "Upper Echelons: The Organization As a Reflection of Top Managers," *Academy of Management Review* 9 (1984), pp. 193–206; Rajeswararao Chaganti and Rakesh Sambharya, "Strategic Orientation and Characteristics of Upper Management," *Strategic Management Journal* 8 (1987), pp. 393–401; James P. Guthrie and Judy D. Olian, "Does Context Affect Staffing Decisions? The Case of General Managers," *Personnel Psychology* 44 (1991), pp. 263–292.

11. Quoted in Douglas T. Hall, "Dilemmas in Linking Succession Planning to Individual Learning," *Human Resource Management* 25 (Summer 1986), p. 237.

12. Anil K. Gupta, "Matching Managers to Strategies: Point and Counterpoint," *Human Resource Management* 25 (Summer 1986), pp. 215–234.

13. Jim Collins, *Good to Great: Why Some Companies Make the Leap and Others Don't* (New York: Harper Business, 2001).

14. The notion of "personality fit" between individuals and organizations is explored in Benjamin Schneider, Harold W. Goldstein, and D. Brent Smith, "The ASA Framework: An Update," *Personnel Psychology* 48 (1995), p. 749.

15. Disney recruiter quoted in Ronald Henkoff, "Finding, Training, and Keeping the Best Service Workers," *Fortune*, October 3, 1994, p. 114. For research on personalities and the attraction/selection process, see Chris Argyris, "Some Problems in Conceptualizing Organizational Climate: A Case Study of a Bank," *Administrative Science Quarterly* 2 (1957), pp. 501–520; Benjamin Schneider, "The People Make the Place," *Personnel Psychology* 40 (1987), pp. 437–454; Benjamin Schneider, Harold W. Goldstein, and D. Brent Smith, "The ASA Framework: An Update," *Personnel Psychology* 48 (1995), pp. 747–773.

16. See Victor Bockeris, *Keith Richards: The Biography* (New York: Poseidon Press, 1992) and Mick Jagger, Keith Richards, Charlie Watts, and Ronnie Wood, *According to the Rolling Stones* (San Francisco: Chronicle Books, 2003).

17. Benjamin Schneider, D. Brent Smith, Sylvester Taylor, and John Flannor, "Personality and Organizations: A Test of Homogeneity of Personality Hypothesis," *Journal of Applied Psychology* 83 (June 1998), pp. 462–470.

18. Collins, *Good to Great*, p. 217.

19. Quotes from Christopher A. Bartlett and Meg Wozny, *Microsoft: Competing on Talent* (Boston: Harvard Business School Publishing, 2000), p. 2.

20. Neal Schmitt, "Employee Selection: How Simulations Change the Picture for Minority Groups," *Cornell Hotel and Restaurant Administration Quarterly* 44 (February 2003), pp. 25–33.

21. William C. Byham, "Recruitment, Screening, and Selection," in William R. Tracey, ed., *Human Resources Management and Development Handbook* (New York: AMACOM, 1994), p. 197.

22. Donald Bowen, Gerald E. Ledford, Jr., and B. Nathan, "Hiring for the Organization, Not the Job," *Academy of Management Executive* 5 (1991), pp. 35–51; Randy W. Boxx and Randall Odom, "Organizational Values and Value Congruency and Their Impact on Satisfaction, Commitment, and Cohesion," *Public Personnel Management* 20 (1991), pp. 195–205; Jennifer Chatman, "Matching People and Organizations: Selection and Socialization in Public Accounting Firms," *Administrative Science Quarterly* 36 (1991), pp. 459–484; Charles A. O'Reilly, Jennifer Chatman, and David F. Caldwell, "People and Organizational Culture: A Profile Comparison Approach to Assessing Person-Organization Fit," *Academy of Management Journal* 34 (1991), pp. 487–516; and Elizabeth F. Cabrera and Jaime Bonache, "An Expert HR System for Aligning Organizational Culture and Strategy," *Human Resource Planning* 22 (1999), pp. 51–60.

23. Chouinard quoted in Edward O. Wells, "Lost in Patagonia," *Inc.* (August 1992), p. 54.

24. John W. Slocum, James R. Morris, Wayne F. Cascio, and Clifford E. Young, "Downsizing After All These Years," *Organizational Dynamics* 27 (Winter 1999), pp. 84–85.

25. Harlan P. Platt, *Principles of Corporate Renewal* (Ann Arbor: University of Michigan Press, 1998).

26. Teresa Amabile and Dean Whitney, *Business Teams at Rubbermaid Inc.* (Boston: Harvard Business School Publishing, 1997), p. 14.

27. *Ibid.*

28. Collins, *Good to Great*, p. 41.

29. The topic of fair process—and the related subject, organizational justice—has received a great deal of attention of late. See, for example, Kees Van Den Bos, Henk Wilke, E. Allen Lind, and Riël Vermunt, "Evaluating Outcomes by Means of the Fair Process Effect: Evidence for Different Processes in Fairness and Satisfaction Judgments," *Journal of Personality and Social Psychology* 74 (June 1998), pp. 1493–1503; Kees Van Den Bos, "Assimilation and Contrast in Organizational Justice: The Role of Primed Mindsets in the Psychology of the Fair

Process Effect," *Organizational Behavior and Human Decision Processes* 89 (September 2002), pp. 866–881; W. Chan Kim and Renée Mauborgne, "Fair Process: Managing in the Knowledge Economy," *Harvard Business Review* 81 (January 2003), pp. 127–136; and Kwok Leung, Kwok-Kit Tong, and Lind E. Allan, "Realpolitik Versus Fair Process: Moderating Effects of Group Identification on Acceptance of Political Decisions," *Journal of Personality and Social Psychology* 92 (March 2007), pp. 476–489.

30. Kim and Mauborgne, "Fair Process," p. 132.

31. *Ibid.*, p. 127.

32. This case is based on information from the following sources: www.hcltech.com; "Wanted: Employees Ready for a Challenge," *Business India Intelligence*, June 21, 2006, p. 8; Linda A. Hill, Farun Khanna, and Emily A. Stecker, *HCL Technologies (A-B) Abridged* (Boston: Harvard Business School Publishing, 2007); "Hungry Tiger, Dancing Elephant," *The Economist*, April 7, 2007, pp. 67–69; "Vineet Nayar's Inverted Pyramid," *CNN Money*, July 12, 2007; "How Vineet Nayar Transformed HCL Tech," *Rediff India Abroad: India as it Happens*, November 7, 2007; Jena McGregor, "The Employee is Always Right," *Business Week* November 19, 2007, pp. 80–82.

33. Judith C. Simon, Charles J. Campbell, Judith C. Brown, and Sandra Richardson, "Can Employees' Personality and Cultural Characteristics Be Used to Predict their Best Fit with Software Testing Job Tasks?" *Proceedings of the Workshop on Advances and Innovations in Systems Testing*, Memphis, TN, May 6–8, 2007.

34. Intrapreneurship is defined as the application of entrepreneurial approaches within a company.

CHAPTER 6

Reinforcing New Behaviors

Effective change implementation proceeds in an unfolding sequence of interventions. A dynamic competitive environment triggers the requirement for change.

Diagnosis sets the stage for effective change implementation by surfacing any misalignment that may exist between patterns of internal behavior and a desired new strategy.

In Step 1, redesign considers alternative patterns of behavior that will help the organization create and sustain outstanding performance. Out of the diagnostic process comes a shared understanding of the roles and responsibilities that employees must enact and the relationships that employees must create both among themselves and with key external stakeholders.

In Step 2, training and development helps employees acquire the required new skills and behaviors.

In Step 3, people alignment decisions ensure that the organization has employees with the needed competencies and behaviors.

Now, at Step 4, organizational leaders reinforce the new behaviors through what might be thought of as the "hardwiring" of the organization: structures, systems, and technologies. This chapter will explore the choices available in terms of hardwiring and analyze the importance of placing structural, system, and technology changes at the back end of a change process rather than leading with those interventions.

In particular, this chapter will:

- Identify the major structural choices faced by organizational leaders and the behavioral implications of those choices
- Consider the requirement of aligning financial measures with the strategic goals of the firm
- Appreciate the role of compensation in shaping desired behaviors
- Analyze the role of information technology (IT) in impacting employee behaviors

Before doing so, we will examine an attempt by a CEO to drive a desired strategic renewal into his organization's global structure.

GLOBAL STRUCTURE AT IBM

When Lou Gerstner took the reins of an ailing IBM, he made a strategic decision: derive competitive advantage from the size and scope of his global operation.[1] Rejecting suggestions that he spin IBM off into a number of smaller companies, he sought instead to create an integrated global organization.

Gerstner's initial challenge in pursuit of that strategy was to integrate IBM's overseas operations with the base of the company. What was often known within IBM as a "religion of decentralization" had led to highly autonomous country general managers who reported to powerful regional executives. The head of IBM-France, say, ran what amounted to a largely independent operation.

IBM's decentralized structure worked wonders for the company. Country managers could focus on their own regions and grow the business based on local responsiveness. But if local responsiveness was the benefit of decentralized structures, the cost was low collaboration. Employees in non-U.S. operations had come to think of themselves as working in and for their own home country company. *I work for IBM France, not IBM*. Little connection existed between the country-based operations and the corporate entity.

IBM customers provided the trigger for change. Global customers such as American Express complained about interacting with what seemed like different mini-IBMs in each country rather than one IBM with a global presence. Give us one face for IBM globally, they said, not many faces for each IBM national operation.

Gerstner agreed that the lack of global interaction posed a problem: "Each country had its own independent system. In Europe alone we had 142 different financial systems." The status quo simply did not allow for the seamless global responsiveness that Gerstner's new strategy and IBM's global customers demanded. "Customer data could not be tracked across the company. Employees belonged to their geography first, while IBM took a distant second place." This, Gerstner believed, *had* to change and change fast if his strategy of global integration was to succeed.

As a former employee at the global consulting firm McKinsey & Company, Gerstner had experienced what he believed to have been an effective approach to globalization. Customer-focused global teams transcended national borders, allowing seamless responsiveness to global customers. To help IBM achieve that same global seamlessness, Gerstner turned to Ned Lautenbach, head of non-U.S. sales. Gerstner and Lautenbach would pursue their strategy with a globally focused, customer-centered organization.

Gerstner announced a new structure. Twelve customer groups (such as banking, government, and insurance) and one small- and medium-size company group would take over all IBM accounts, including responsibility for budgets and personnel. The restructuring reassigned most employees in non-U.S. operations to a specific group; they would now report to the global leaders of their industry group rather than to their country general manager.

The response from country general managers was overwhelmingly negative. *It will never work* and *You will destroy the company* were statements that expressed their resistance. Some country general managers responded by simply ignoring the new structure. One regional executive unilaterally decided to block all communications between Gerstner and the field.

It took three years of what Gerstner called a "painful and sometimes tumultuous process" before the new global strategy could be driven into IBM's multinational structure. "Regional heads clung to the old system," reflects Gerstner, "sometimes out of mutiny, but more often out of tradition." Only after "massive" shifts in resources, systems, and processes—not to mention the removal and replacement of numerous country managers who could not or would not make the transition—did the new structure take hold.

SELECTING THE APPROPRIATE ORGANIZATIONAL FOCUS

In Step 1, effective change implementation focuses on the process of reshaping informal arrangements to change employee behavior. Informal redesign addresses questions of coordination, decision-making authority, and flexibility and control. Mutual engagement in the process of redesign builds motivation to change, while the Help stage (Step 2) builds needed competencies. People alignment (Step 3) gets the right people in the right position. Now, in Step 4, more formal aspects of redesign, which include rewards, performance measurements, and reporting relationships, can be called upon to reinforce desired behaviors.

The fierce resistance that greeted Gerstner's attempt to realign IBM's global structure with its new strategy was, in part, a predictable response to his calling on the restructuring lever too early in the change process. Instead of working through the implementation sequence, Gerstner jumped to Step 4. We can address the relationship between sequencing restructuring and behavioral response later in the chapter. For now, let us look at the structural options available to organizational leaders.

Choices of Organizational Structure

Often, in a change process, organizational leaders attempt to reshape the structure of their organizations. **Organizational structure** refers to the formal manner in which employees are subdivided into units and divisions as a way of focusing their efforts on the required tasks of the company.

Structures impact behaviors by defining the context for work. The change implementation question, therefore, becomes twofold:

1. *What* structures to use?
2. *How* and *when* do we change structures?

Let's examine the *what* question first: what are the structural options available to leaders?

A quick look at an organizational chart reveals the choices leaders have made concerning structure. A chart may show, for instance, functional units such as manufacturing, marketing, and engineering. Another chart might include product-oriented divisions, such as General Motors' Chevrolet, Buick, Cadillac, Hummer, Opel, Pontiac, Saturn, Saab, and Vauxhall divisions. Far more complex charts might find lines of responsibility crisscrossing both horizontally and vertically, linking functions with product lines and perhaps even geographic regions.

Building a Vocabulary of Change
Organizational structure the manner in which employees are subdivided into units and divisions as a way of focusing efforts on the required activities of the company.

Although structure is often thought of in terms of boxes and lines—who holds what title and who reports to whom—the key question is really one of focus. In all organizations, the activities of employees need to be focused on two separate issues:

1. The *functional* or technical activities required to achieve the desired outcomes of the organization
2. Responsiveness to the external *marketplace* (customers, suppliers, competitors, regulators, and so on) in which the organization has elected to compete

No organization can select one focus to the exclusion of the other; the focus of employees must be simultaneous. Nonetheless, organizational leaders may choose to emphasize one over the other, and that emphasis is likely to change over time in response to the dynamism of the competitive environment and the strategic choices of the organization. It is important, therefore, that leaders understand the impact that various structural choices will have on the focus of employees and, consequently, on their behavior.

Theory into Practice

Organization structure is more than just boxes and lines; it is a way to focus the activities of employees.

FOCUS ON FUNCTIONAL EXCELLENCE   In their earliest founding stages, organizations typically exist in a prestructural state. When Open Markets, Inc. (OMI), a software tools and development business, started, for instance, 12 employees shared office space in a Cambridge, Massachusetts, basement. They had no job titles and only the most general definition of individual responsibilities. The tasks that needed to be accomplished were simply shared.[2]

At some point, as organizations evolve, leaders adopt a more formal structure to add greater order, stability, and focus. "As we've grown," noted an OMI employee, "some people feel it is difficult not knowing who your boss is, who will evaluate your performance, where to go for help. As we get larger, we need a little more structure."[3] At OMI, employees naturally assumed responsibilities for the various functional activities of their organization: software development, of course, but also marketing, sales, vendor relationships, finance, and administration.

Theory into Practice

As organizations move beyond the small, start-up stage, they are likely to adopt a simple functional structure: people with similar skills performing related activities are placed in functional departments.

Building a Vocabulary of Change
Functional structure an organizational design choice that groups people together in units based on common tasks and specialized skills.

Over time, as an organization continues to grow, individuals with like-minded interests, inclinations, and competencies find a home among one or another of these functional activities. In doing so, they adopt a **functional structure**: a structure meant to focus activities on the functional or technical tasks of the organization. Exhibit 6-1 depicts a prototypical functional organization chart for an Internet portal provider.

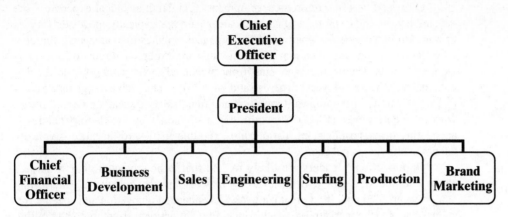

EXHIBIT 6-1 Functional Organizational Chart.

Clear focus on functional activities brings discipline and efficiency to an operation. Functional structures help the organization achieve efficiencies of operation and standardization of offerings. Functionally structured organizations are in a position to fine-tune the product and service offerings, making sure the customer, "gets the most for the least."[4]

Theory into Practice

Use functional structures to shape the development of technical skills and expert knowledge on the part of employees.

No matter how functionally oriented an organization might be, there must also be some simultaneous capacity to respond to the marketplace. Functional structures attempt to achieve that responsiveness through a well-ordered sequential process.

In a functionally structured manufacturing firm, for example, we can follow the sequence:

1. Ideas from the marketplace enter the organization through the marketing department.
2. Engineers translate those ideas into designs.
3. Production transforms designs from concept to reality.
4. Products are delivered to customers via the sales department.
5. The financial department attends to such matters as profit margin and return on investment.

It is the responsibility of the general manager who sits atop the functional structure—sometimes a CEO, a senior vice president, or a managing director—to assure that the appropriate level of coordination among these sequential functional activities is achieved.

Because leaders call upon structures to focus employee behaviors, it is important to ask: Just what kind of employee behaviors can functional structures be expected to reinforce?

Let's start with the rigorous development of in-depth technical expertise. That development is enhanced by a functional career path that typically moves employees upward through a specific department. The organization hires individuals who enter at a low level of a function, then move vertically upward through that function as performance warrants. The organization gains from functional career pathing by developing and retaining their employees' expertise and knowledge. The individual gains clear career expectations, speedy upward mobility, and rapid salary escalation. Organizations whose success depends heavily on the depth of their technical competencies—accounting firms, hospitals, law partnerships, and universities, for instance—typically adhere to this functional pattern.

Organizational leaders are likely to find that although functional structures shape a number of desirable behaviors, they may also prompt behavioral patterns that can prove problematic. If an organization seeks enhanced innovation and speedier responsiveness to the marketplace, leaders may find a functional structure to be limiting and inhibiting. By focusing employees on achieving efficiencies and incremental improvements in existing products and services, functional structures may render employees less likely to be able to respond quickly with new and innovative offerings.

Much of the behavioral problem inherent in functional structures relates to low levels of coordination among employees, especially employees across different functional units. Functionally trained and developed individuals may find coordinated efforts with individuals from other departments to be difficult. Over time, insulated units tend to develop their own ways of thinking; unique patterns of working, of speaking, of conceptualizing time, even of defining effectiveness.[5]

In functional structures, employees have little opportunity to develop the competencies required of working together across departmental boundaries. At its worst, a kind of "us against them" mentality can evolve as employees battle each other across functions rather than uniting against common (external) competitors. The skills of the general manager may not be sufficient to overcome these structural barriers and achieve the required coordination.

Theory into Practice

Organizations seeking to create seamless coordination across functions may find that the silos erected through functional structures get in the way.

Organizational change efforts may seek to deal with the challenges raised by a functional structure. The particular challenge is to enhance marketplace responsiveness. One of the most common ways of achieving that focus is to adopt a divisional structure.

Building a Vocabulary of Change
Divisional structure an organizational design choice that groups people together in units based on common products, services, or customers.

FOCUS ON MARKETPLACE RESPONSIVENESS   As organizations grow in both size and complexity, they often seek greater external focus. Most typically, they turn to a **divisional structure** as a way of reinforcing behaviors that respond to the marketplace.

All activities associated with a particular product or families of products are brought together in a divisional unit. A general manager, often a senior vice president, divisional president, or managing director, sits atop each unit. That structure is depicted in Exhibit 6-2 for a prototypical software developer.

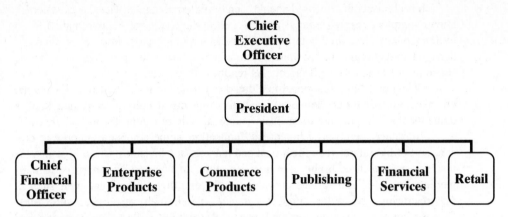

EXHIBIT 6-2   Divisional Organization Chart.

Greater organizational complexity might compel an organization to further sub-divide into multiple strategic business units (SBUs), which bring together multiple product divisions into large, strategic groupings. Siemens, for instance, maintains SBUs in such diverse industries as power, transportation, and lighting, each with its own set of autonomous divisions.

Another divisional option, particularly for multinationals, is to adopt a geo-graphically focused structure. To reinforce geographic responsiveness, a fast-food chain, which is essentially a single-product operation, can create separate geo-graphic divisions. McDonald's non-U.S. operations are subdivided into four regions: Asia/Pacific/Middle East/Africa, Canada, Europe, and Latin America. The company does so based on the assumption that important differences exist in these multiple regions—in customer tastes and expectations, in supplier relationships, in government regulations, and in financial and labor markets—that require a differen-tiated response.

All, or at least most, of the functions required to deliver that product will be located within each of the geographic areas. A multiproduct corporation such as IBM can also call upon highly autonomous geographic divisions to maximize responsiveness to local conditions, the status quo that greeted Lou Gerstner when he became CEO.

Theory into Practice

Divisional structures enhance coordinated focus on the marketplace but make integration across highly autonomous divisional units difficult to achieve.

The object of the divisional structure, whether it is based on products, customer groups, or geographic locations, is to reinforce a market focus. Product divisions and SBUs pay close attention to the expectations and needs of customers for their particu-lar offerings, while geographic divisions can attend to the special requirements and habits of the customers in their regions.

It is precisely that focused attention on the external marketplace that, it is hoped, allows companies organized divisionally to meet the challenge of coordination faced by functionally structured companies. By concentrating on a clearly defined and understood market segment, divisions seek to win by offering new products and services. Rapid responsiveness to shifting market realities is the goal.

Changing from a functional to a divisional structure is not cost free. Functional organizations seek the economies of scale; divisional organizations can be thought of as doing the opposite. In pure form, each functional activity is repeated in each division.

To reduce the costs of functional duplication, some companies choose to create a sort of hybrid between functional and marketplace divisions. Cisco Systems, for instance, mixed three highly autonomous "lines of business"—enterprise, small/medium business, and service provider—with centralized functional areas such as manufacturing, customer support, finance, IT, human resources, and sales. Engineering and marketing, on the other hand, were left within each division.[6] But caution is required. Organizations electing to centralize functions for the sake of efficiencies must take care not to allow centralization to interfere with marketplace responsiveness.

Theory into Practice

Centralizing some functions, such as finance or marketing, may make sense economically, but organizations need to be careful that centralizing does not interfere with the goal of market place responsiveness.

Adopting a divisional structure is meant to shape market-focused behaviors. It is not, in and of itself, any guarantee of true responsiveness. Remember, each product division is a self-contained functional organization. The problems often associated with functional organizations—internal focus, poor coordination, sluggish response time—can accrue over time in a product division. In multidivisional organizations, problems of coordination may arise across and between divisions. In order to respond to such problems, organizational leaders may now seek a kind of collaborative balance between functional and product divisions.

Theory into Practice

Functional silos can exist within divisional structures.

DUAL FOCUS Leaders opt for a functional structure in order to emphasize efficiencies and depth of technical know-how and experience. A shift to divisional structures helps reinforce external focus on the marketplace. However, many organizations cannot make an either/or choice between internal and external focus. As the external environment becomes increasingly complex, organizational leaders need to consider increasing the complexity of their internal structures.

One choice available to organizations is the **matrix structure**. Exhibit 6-3 depicts one type of matrix structure. In that organization, both divisional and functional structures exist in an overlapping fashion, allowing for dual focus.

Building a Vocabulary of Change
Matrix structure an organizational design choice that groups people by both function and product or product and geographical region.

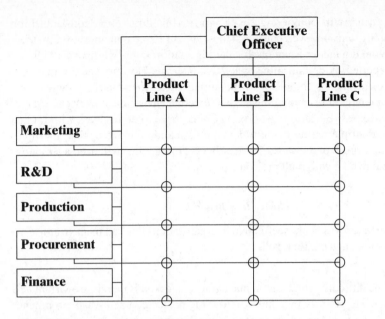

EXHIBIT 6-3   Matrix Organizational Chart.

The requirement for dual focus might also arise from geographic demands. ABB built a geographic matrix through three regional groupings—Europe/Middle East/Africa, the Americas, and Asia—while simultaneously seeking segment focus through power, transmission and distribution, and industry and building systems divisions. Strategic focus again lies at the heart of the organization's challenge. While functional and product divisions prioritize their focus, matrix structures seek dual focus, attempting to move both quickly and efficiently.

Theory into Practice

Organizations can move to a matrix structure to help support dual focus—on technical expertise and marketplace responsiveness.

The most striking—and for many people the most troubling—feature of the matrix is the dual reporting relationship.* Consider the matrix structure depicted in Exhibit 6-3. Assume you are a market analyst housed in product line C. Who is your boss: the manager of product line C or the head of marketing? The answer, of course, is: both. In order to achieve the desired complexity of focus, you will be reporting to and expected to be responsive to both simultaneously.

The notion of dual reporting relationships violates one of people's most deeply held assumptions about the desirability of a clear and unified chain of command in organizations. By breaking that clear chain of command, matrix structures require

*It could be more than two, although two is the most typical.

employees to deal with competing, even conflicting directions from multiple bosses. Ambiguity, tension, even conflict—these are all likely outcomes of a matrix. That likelihood undoubtedly accounts for the high failure rate—perhaps as high as 70 percent—reported by organizations who have attempted to implement a matrix.[7]

Despite their obvious complexities and ambiguities, when matrix organizations reflect the complexities and ambiguities in their external environment, they can enable greater responsiveness. Because most organizations "have to do business with multiple customers, multiple partners, multiple suppliers, and compete against multiple rivals can multiple areas of the world," writes Jay Galbraith, they will need a structure that allows them to deal with multiple constituencies.[8]

Theory into Practice

Matrix structures will be most effective in organizations that can manage ambiguity, tension, and conflict well.

Despite the difficulties inherent in managing a matrix, it is therefore a virtual necessity to compete effectively in today's highly fragmented competitive environment. Organizations that are able to make a matrix function effectively will enjoy a great competitive advantage.

FOCUS ON THE VALUE CHAIN   The advent of sophisticated IT and the geographic dispersion of technological excellence and knowledge have encouraged organizations to focus on their value chain. Organizations develop competitive advantage and create shareholder wealth through an interdependent sequence of activities known as the value chain.

The value chain can be defined as "the separate activities, functions, and business processes that are performed in designing, producing, marketing, delivering, and supporting a product or service."[9] **Horizontally linked structures** focus employees on the interrelated activities of the value chain.

Horizontally linked structures usually supplement rather than replace existing functional or product structure in an organization. Dell Computers, a pioneer in value chain linkages, relies on what founder Michael Dell calls "virtual integration." Dell focuses its attention on "how we can coordinate our activities to create the most value for customers."[10] Companies as varied as Zara, Wal-Mart, Southwest Airlines, and Shouldice Hospital call upon horizontally linked structures to coordinate value chain activities in order to provide customers with a unique experience and their companies with a unique competitive advantage.

Zara, a fashion chain owned by Spain-based Inditex (which also owns and operates Pull & Bear, Massimo, and Dutti, among other retail formats), has succeeded by organizing activities around its value chain. Starting with a clearly stated strategy—a focus on the ever-changing tastes of trendy young shoppers—Zara created raw material and design teams that could deliver their newly designed products into Zara retail stores within 3 to 15 days.[11] An organization chart for Zara is presented in Exhibit 6-4.

More traditionally structured apparel companies, where activities in the value chain are separate and unlinked, often take up to a year to move from design to sale.

Building a Vocabulary of Change
Horizontally linked structure an organizational design choice that groups people along the value chain activities and processes that produce, market, deliver, and service the firm's offerings.

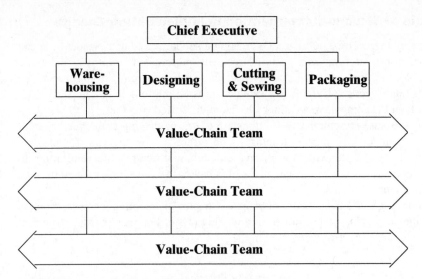

EXHIBIT 6-4   Horizontally Linked Structure at Zara.

Given the dynamic tastes of the rather fickle consumer base for fashion, slowness often leads to unused inventory, price-slashing sales, and waste.

Theory into Practice

Organizations can use cross-functional teams to achieve linkages across the various and interdependent activities of their value chain.

Organizations that have pioneered horizontally linked structures typically started with a clear strategic focus on their value chain. It has been far more difficult for older, traditionally organized companies to respond. Delta's effort to create its own low-cost airline, Song, to compete with Southwest Airlines fell flat. Marks & Spencer tried and failed to compete with Zara for the young, fashion-trendy customer. Kmart has repeatedly slashed prices to compete with Wal-Mart while undermining its own profitability. Compaq and Hewlett-Packard have been unable to mount an effective response to Dell.

The difficulty seems to lie not in any formal structural change but in the organizational context that supports and reinforces the structure. Long-standing functional arrangements have cemented patterns of employee behavior that remain unchanged despite efforts to create horizontally linked activities.

Horizontally linked structures alone do not guarantee coordinated, interdependent value chain activities. The key to successful implementation is to embed the supply chain interactions deep into the organization. That, said Michael Dell, is his company's "secret": a supply chain DNA that has developed over years to reinforce linkages.[12]

No structure, whether it is horizontally linked, matrixed, or divided into divisions or functions can, in and of itself, provide an organization with distinctive competitive advantage for the simple reason that structures are not and cannot be distinctive.

The Role of Structural Intervention in Implementing Change

After articulating a strategic focus and creating a supportive context, leaders can call upon structural interventions to reinforce new patterns of employee behavior. Organizations seeking greater customer responsiveness may move from a functional to a divisional function. If the firm's value chain is failing to deliver competitive advantage, then the company may adopt a horizontally linked structure.

Just because structural interventions are useful in shaping employee behavior does not mean that changing structure is an effective opening tool for change. Effective change implementation, in fact, calls upon structural intervention not to *drive* change but to *reinforce* new patterns of behavior that have been created through earlier-stage interventions.

Returning to Lewin's theory of change (Chapter 2), adopting a new structure is part of the refreezing stage, not the unfreezing stage. For that reason, structural changes are most effective when used in Step 4.

Theory into Practice

Think of structural change in terms of Lewin's refreezing, not in terms of unfreezing.

To understand the power of appropriate sequencing of interventions in impacting effective implementation, we can return to Lou Gerstner's attempt, described at the opening of this chapter, to achieve heightened levels of global cooperation.

IBM's highly decentralized divisional structure allowed responsiveness to multiple national markets served by this giant corporation. Global customers such as American Express now demanded greater coordination across national boundaries. *We're a global company*, customers were telling IBM. *We expect* you *to be a global supplier. We don't want to be dealing with multiple national mini-IBMs with little capacity to provide consistent and seamless service.*

Gerstner's new strategy for IBM counted on taking advantage of the company's depth and scope. He drove that renewed strategy by creating a global matrix structure: customer-based groups laid over a geographically divisionalized organization.

Gerstner's reasoning seemed solid: Global responsiveness could be coordinated by global customer-group executives. That was the approach that Gerstner had experienced at McKinsey. It worked well there, so why not at IBM as well?

The problem Gerstner ran into had far less to do with the efficacy of the idea than the implementation process he called upon to introduce that idea. The structural change occurred early in the process of transforming IBM. Gerstner had failed to unfreeze attitudes by creating dissatisfaction with the status quo. Used to a high level of autonomy, country managers resisted. That resistance grew, in part, from their own habits, competencies, and preferences. It also grew from the process used to introduce change.

The country managers themselves had not been part of the diagnosis that led to the change; nor had the country and industry group managers worked collaboratively to develop well-defined roles, responsibilities, and relationships among the two groups; nor had IBM provided training on how to enact these new, complex roles.

In essence, Gerstner jumped from a diagnosis formulated by a handful of corporate executives—mainly him and Ned Lautenbach—to a new structure.

Faced with fierce resistance on the part of country managers, he removed and replaced a number of them. Despite all his formal authority and the power of his vision for a truly global IBM, it took three years of what Gerstner himself called pain and tumult before the desired new behaviors began to take hold in the organization.

This is not to say that pain and tumult can be avoided entirely in implementation. The point, rather, is that the approach of using structural change as a driver rather than a reinforcer helps create heightened levels of resistance, some of which might have been avoided.

Structural change typically unfolds as a top-down intervention. It is the task of leadership, after all, to design the architecture of the organization in order to enable outstanding performance. However, if structural change takes place late in the change process, restructuring will not be experienced as a unilateral imposition from above.

Remember the old adage: People don't resist change; they resist being changed. If structural change occurs early in the process, it will be experienced by employees as being changed. If new structures are used to reinforce new behaviors, employees are more likely to support the change.

Theory into Practice

When structural change occurs early in a change process, employees can be confused by its purpose, unsure of what new competencies are being required, and unwilling—or unable—to make appropriate alterations in behavioral patterns.

ALIGNING FINANCIAL MEASURES WITH NEW BEHAVIORS

The way organizations assign monetary value to specific activities and objects (costs) and measure the benefits received (revenues) powerfully influences how employees make decisions and behave.[13] Accounting systems designed to measure costs and benefits, then, become what is often called the "language of business." Effective change implementation will, in Step 4, seek alignment between desired new behaviors and financial measures.

Traditional accounting systems typically function as reporting mechanisms, allowing managers and investors to assess quarterly and annual performance. That reporting function, as vital as it may be, can work against the goals of change in two ways:

1. By focusing employee attention inward rather than outward
2. By blurring the distinction between value-added and non-value-added costs

The inward-focused problem arises because traditional reporting systems are typically built around annual budgets and operating plans. Adherence to plan is rewarded; variance from plan is discouraged.

Jack Welch experienced that effect early in his effort to transform General Electric.[14] He discovered that many plant managers were shutting down their factories temporarily before the end of the year. That shutdown occurred even in the face of strong customer demand and even stronger competition. How could plant managers behave in such an apparently irrational way?

The answer had to do with how GE accounted for performance. The emphasis was on meeting budget, with bad performance being defined by exceeding plan. When plant managers reached the limits of their annual budgets, often four to six weeks prior to the end of the year, they simply (and, from their point of view at least, rationally) shut down their facilities. That was their way of keeping annual expenditures from going over budget. That's what GE's accounting system measured and rewarded: staying under budget.

Traditional accounting reporting systems such as the one Welch encountered focus employee efforts internally.[15] The impact, as Welch is purported to have said, turns employee faces inward toward corporate headquarters and their backsides outward toward the customer.

Particularly when significant rewards are tightly linked to the achievement of measured goals, employees are likely, said H. Thomas Johnson, "to manipulate processes in order to achieve accounting results."[16] Leaders seeking to transform employee behaviors will want to make sure that accounting systems work to reinforce rather than undermine their strategic goals.

Some specific performance measures—market share, speed to market, rate of innovation, customer and employee satisfaction—can better reflect marketplace-focused performance. When they do, measures can direct employee effort appropriately, which is to say strategically, while allowing the organization to review and improve performance.

Theory into Practice

In the later stages of change implementation, organizations can develop a set of measurements that place financial performance within a broader strategic context that looks at outcomes from the perspective of multiple stakeholders and takes into account long-term outstanding performance.

Activity-Based Management

In addition to focusing employee attention on internal reporting requirements rather than external responsiveness, traditional accounting reporting systems tend to ignore the distinction between value-added and non-value-added costs. Stanley Grubel, CEO of MiCRUS, a joint venture between IBM's microelectronics division and Cirrus Logic Corporation, ran into that problem as he attempted to realign his company's strategy. As MiCRUS sought to attract non-IBM customers for its fabricated memory and logic-integrated circuit wafers, Grubel realized that intense global competition would require a new strategy. Only by combining aggressive cost cutting with high-quality standards could MiCRUS succeed. But how and where to cut costs in a way that would not compromise quality—that was the question.

MiCRUS adopted an accounting system known as **activity-based management (ABM)**. Activity-based management works to offer decision makers a more robust picture of the performance of an operation.[17] Under ABM, cost drivers—the activities and materials that lead to increases or decreases in the cost of products or

Building a Vocabulary of Change

Activity-based management (ABM) a financial tool that helps managers make decisions by separating the costs of activities that add value to a product or service line from those costs that do not add value.

services—are separated from allocated costs that are not influenceable (and directly traceable) costs for various product and service lines. By understanding the real costs of an offering—not the costs with overhead allocated via some arbitrary formula (who pays for corporate headquarters, the company jet, and the CEO's salary)—managers can make better-informed decisions. Which of our products and services are actually profitable? How much cost will be recovered if we eliminate a product or service?

Within MiCRUS, cross-functional department teams worked to sort out those costs that added value to the final product from those that were unnecessary in producing quality product. Said Laura Stearns, a team leader:

> The activity-based management information gave us a new actionable perspective on how costs related to the activities we performed. Previously we only saw costs classified by our traditional accounts [cost objects for which the unit would write checks such as support departments]. Activity-based management also helped us understand how our behavior influenced costs.[18]

MiCRUS paired an alteration in its accounting systems with a new openness concerning performance measures. Said CFO Ron Gallaway, "We stopped doling out information by the 'thimble-full' as was the finance function's custom."[19] A far more performance-oriented atmosphere helped MiCRUS achieve its strategic goals.

Theory into Practice

Organizations can use ABM to help insure decisions that are made as part of the change process are based on an accurate financial picture of their operations.

Balanced Scorecard

Activity-based management provides managers with more accurate information about the profitability of particular products or services. That allows decision making, especially when deciding how to manage firm assets during periods of change, to be more precise and helpful. It still leaves some important strategic questions unanswered, however. Are we creating real value for our multiple stakeholders: customers, employees, and investors? Are our activities aligned with the goals and strategies of the organization?

A number of companies—Canon, Aquafin, Mobistar, and SAS among them—have turned to the **balanced scorecard (BSC)** as a way of focusing employee attention on shareholders and customers.

The premise for the BSC (depicted in Exhibit 6-5) is that financial returns need to be understood as one among several vital outcome measures. Financial measures of performance, wrote Robert Kaplan and David Norton, "are lag indicators that report on the outcomes from past actions. Exclusive reliance on financial

Building a Vocabulary of Change
Balanced scorecard (BSC) a tool for measuring multiple outcomes—financial performance, customer satisfaction, internal process excellence, and employee learning and growth—and the connection of those outcomes to the vision and strategy of the organization.

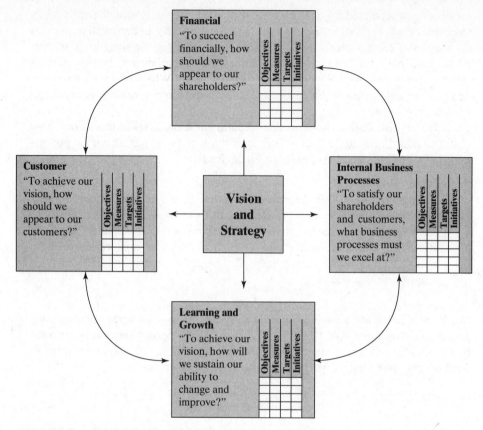

EXHIBIT 6-5 Balanced Scorecard.

indicators could promote behavior that sacrifices long-term value creation for short-term performance."[20]

The scorecard balances financial measures with three additional metrics:

1. Customer—To achieve our vision, how should we appear to our customers?
2. Internal Business Processes—To satisfy our shareholders and customers, what business processes must we excel at?
3. Learning and Growth—To achieve our vision, how will we sustain our ability to change and improve?[21]

If tools such as ABM are used to evaluate financial performance, the BSC can help guide managerial decisions concerning which customers to target and which product and service offerings provide desired returns.[22]

By focusing on multiple outcomes—customers, internal processes, and learning—the BSC can help managers escape the exclusive focus on a single outcome—mostly financial—and help ensure that their change interventions are having the intended results on the other key activities of their firm.

Theory into Practice

BSC is a tool for measuring the effectiveness of change efforts on multiple dimensions.

At the core of the BSC lies a clearly stated and widely understood vision and strategy for the organization. The vision and strategy determined in the earlier phases of change can now be used to drive *all* performance measures, financial measures included. Each perspective can be evaluated only in terms of objectives, measures, targets, and initiatives when that vision and strategy are clear and widely shared.

As a measurement tool, the BSC will be more effective in supporting change when introduced at a later stage in the process. When leaders introduce a tool such as the BSC early in the implementation process, they run the risk of undermining the effectiveness of their effort. Unless and until employees have learned themselves that the status quo—including their own behaviors—must be changed in order to meet the new strategic realities of the competitive environment, their motivation to engage in such difficult change will be low.

Financial controls can *drive* new behaviors but mainly as a form of compliance. Managers will behave in ways that are being measured and rewarded. But their commitment to long-term behavioral change, to bringing innovation and discretionary effort to the goals of change, will be low.

Theory into Practice

Use financial controls to reinforce and assess desired change rather than to drive change.

Financial controls have a more important—and useful—role to play in reinforcing behavioral change. When existing controls work as a barrier to change—when teams find their effectiveness undercut by individually based measures, when efforts to improve profitability of a unit are blurred by cost allocation decisions, when value chain integration is hindered by measures that concentrate on the individual activities rather than the entire process—that is the time when employees will accept, even demand, alterations in financial control systems.

USING INCENTIVES TO SUPPORT NEW BEHAVIORS

Compensation represents one of the strongest, perhaps most immediate tools that can be called upon to impact patterns of employee behavior. Do we need a more performance-driven culture? Let's place employees on a pay-for-performance incentive. Need to attract young, highly skilled employees to our start-up business? Let's dangle huge stock offerings. Having trouble implementing activity chain process teams? Let's try team-based performance bonuses.

Organizations expend a huge amount of resources on pay—time, energy, not to mention money (anywhere from 40 percent to 70 percent of sales revenues). What value are they gaining in return for that expenditure? How successful are monetary incentives in shaping and altering employee behaviors?

The answer may seem obvious: *Of course* money can shape and alter behaviors. The real question, however, relates to long-term effectiveness. What role can compensation play in efforts to implement organizational change? To answer that question, we need to understand both the nature of pay's impact on behavior as well as the choices available to organizational leaders.

Focusing Pay on Performance

As the competitive business environment increasingly pressures organizations to achieve ever-improving performance, companies have rushed to adopt some sort of pay-for-performance plan. **Pay for performance** devotes at least some portion of an individual's pay (ranging anywhere from 3 percent to multiples of 100 percent) to measurable performance outcomes.

Pay for performance can take one of two forms: *merit pay*, which raises base salary based on performance, and *incentive bonuses*, which offer regular but onetime payouts on the basis of performance. Bonuses do not alter base salary. They are considered onetime payments because they are not guaranteed. Substandard performance the following year can reduce or eliminate the bonus.

Virtually every organization in the United States claims to have some kind of a merit pay system already in place. Incentive bonuses have become more popular over the past two decades. As a percentage of total payroll costs, bonuses rose from 4 percent in 1991 to 9 percent in 2000.[23]

Most organizations select a mix of performance pay in order to shape employee behavior. GE, for example, calls for a blend of different bonuses to motivate executives, as indicated in the following company statement:

- Salary and Bonus—We pay salaries that are designed to attract and retain superior leaders, and we pay annual bonuses to reward exceptional performance.
- Stock Options and Stock Appreciation Rights—We award these to provide incentives for superior long-term performance and to retain top executives because the awards are fortified if the executive leaves before they become fully exercisable five years after grant.
- Restricted Stock Units—We grant RSUs to more closely align executives' interests with investors' long-term interests, to retain top executives because the awards are paid out only to executives who remain with the company for extended periods.
- Long-Term Performance Awards—We use these to provide a strong incentive for achieving specific performance measurements over multiyear periods.[24]

Organizations seek a mix of rewards in order to help ensure alignment between employee behaviors and their strategic goals.

One question to be raised in introducing or redesigning a pay-for-performance plan relates to level of aggregation: At what level of outcome should a pay-for-performance incentive be targeted: the individual, the group or team, or the organization? Pay for *individual* performance dominates the design of compensation in the United States. Exhibit 6-6 summarizes the various forms of individual pay-for-performance plans.

Piece rate	Employee earns all or part of a wage based on number of units produced
Commission	Salesperson earns all or part of a wage based on number of units sold
Merit pay	Employee earns raise to base wage based on performance evaluation
Bonus	Employee earns extra payment based on performance

EXHIBIT 6-6   Forms of Individual Pay-for-Performance Plans.

Theory into Practice

Individual incentives will be most effective in shaping behavior when the individual controls the outcomes being measured and rewarded, when the outcomes are tied to improved performance, when the evaluation of an employee's contribution is perceived as being valid, and when the difference between rewards for high and low performance is significant.

Although individual pay-for-performance incentives seem to hold great potential for shaping behavior, a number of challenges constrict that potential impact. The first question that can be raised about a pay-for-performance plan relates to the degree to which individuals have *control* over the outcomes that are being measured and rewarded. Without a significant and clear relationship between individual effort and outcome, a pay-for-performance incentive can drain the system of its full behavioral impact.

A second question relates to whether the incentive system has targeted appropriate *measures of performance* on which to base the reward. Failure to include *all* outcomes that are important for outstanding performance can lead to dysfunctional consequences. The more effectively the system impacts behavior, in fact, the more likely it will be that singling out one aspect of performance for measurement will give that aspect disproportionate attention.

For an individual pay-for-performance plan to impact behavior, the pay increment tied to outstanding performance must be perceived as being *significant*. To have a behavioral impact, the additional reward for that behavior should be 10 percent to 20 percent higher than the reward received absent the behavior. Raises, however, often amount to a relatively small amount of total compensation, making their potential to impact behavior weak. The "significance range" can be reduced considerably—down to 3 percent to 5 percent—if raises are accompanied by public recognition and praise.[25] Concerns over secrecy and confidentiality, however, often blunt an organization's willingness and ability to accompany merit raises with public acknowledgment.

Finally, in order to be effective, pay for performance must be based on *valid judgments* about individual performance. Distortions often creep into the evaluation process, leading participants to question the validity of resulting assessments. That lack of trust in the evaluation process presents itself as one of the key reasons U.S. employees report high levels of dissatisfaction with the implementation of their companies' pay-for-performance

Performance appraisals are inherently subjective, with supervisors evaluating subordinates according to their own preconceived biases

Emphasize individual rather than group goals that may lead to dysfunction conflict in the organization

Encourage a short-term orientation (the performance period being evaluated) at the expense of long-term goals

Merit pay raises become an annuity on which employees continue to draw regardless of future performance

The often lengthy time lag between actual performance and reward undermines perceived connection between the two

Many jobs cannot be individually isolated and precisely measured without taking into account complex interdependencies

Pay differentials between performance levels tend to be relatively small and therefore of questionable behavioral value

Actual payout of program often determined by organizational factors beyond the control of individual employees and only indirectly related to actual performance

EXHIBIT 6-7 Factors that May Undermine Effectiveness of Individual Pay-for-Performance Plans.

Based on Luis R. Gomez-Mejia, David B. Balkin, and Robert L. Cardy, *Managing Human Resources* (Englewood Cliffs, NJ: Prentice-Hall, 1995), p. 404 and Edward E. Lawler III, "Pay Strategy: New Thinking for the New Millennium," *Compensation and Benefits Review* 32 (January–February 2000), pp. 7–12.

plans. Less than one-third of surveyed U.S. employees believe a direct link exists between pay and performance, despite company claims of a merit pay plan.[26]

Despite the numerous questions that can be raised about the limitations of individual pay-for-performance incentives (summarized in Exhibit 6-7), such plans are nonetheless becoming more popular. Although there is evidence that managers in non-U.S. countries are far more skeptical of the positive arguments U.S. managers make concerning the performance benefits of discretionary bonuses, such bonuses are becoming increasingly popular around the world.[27]

Team-based pay-for-performance plans are becoming more popular in direct relationship to the rising reliance on team effort. Among performance incentives aimed at nonexecutive employees, in fact, team-based plans have become the most popular.[28] Under such a plan, teams can share a performance bonus equally or allocate to individual members based on an evaluation of their contribution. Team-based bonuses enhance team performance, although the effect is relatively weak.[29] A caveat is in order, however. Team-level bonuses can hurt collaboration *among* and *between* teams.

Theory into Practice

Organizations call upon team-based performance bonuses to enhance the effectiveness of teams, but the bonus may undermine collaboration between teams.

Because strategic renewal focuses on organizational performance, *organization-level* incentives often supplement or replace individual bonuses. Traditionally, organizations have offered organization-wide incentive bonuses only to executives and upper management on the assumption that their actions are more closely tied to overall organizational performance than employees at lower levels. However, some organizations have adopted a different perspective. Part of Archie Norman's strategic renewal at Asda was to offer an organization-level performance bonus to all employees, encouraging everyone to keep focused on the same measures of overall effectiveness.[30]

Theory into Practice

Bonuses based on the overall performance of the organization make a symbolic statement recognizing the shared purpose and responsibility of all employees and organizational units.

Stock options are intended to tie the total compensation package of individuals to the performance of their organization.[31] The goal, as articulated by the board of directors of eBay, is to "align the interests of directors and executives with the interests of stockholders."[32] Favorable tax laws have made these plans more popular in the United States than elsewhere, although a number of multinational firms—PepsiCo, Bristol-Myers Squibb, DuPont, and Merck among them—have offered stock options to virtually all of their employees worldwide.[33]

The actual effectiveness of these various organization-level performance bonuses is unclear. Some sort of incentive tied to organization-level performance is a frequent characteristic of high-performance companies.[34] What is less certain is whether the organization-level performance bonus results *in* or *from* outstanding performance. The cause-and-effect relationship between specific behaviors and organizational outcomes may be far too vague, especially in large organizations, to create a powerful incentive on the part of individual employees.

Undoubtedly, the degree to which organization-wide bonuses are accompanied by communication and feedback on firm performance, as well as the empowerment of employees to impact performance, will enhance the plan's motivational impact. Tying all employees' pay packages in some significant way to the same organizational-level outcomes may help in both a symbolic and real way to communicate a mutuality of interests and concerns.

Intrinsic and Extrinsic Rewards

Incentive pay, regardless of the specific design, is an **extrinsic reward**: a reward external to the individual and provided by the organization. Money is the most obvious and prevalent example of an extrinsic reward. Motivational theory tells us that extrinsic rewards, although powerful, may not be terribly effective in driving long-term behavioral change.

Building a Vocabulary of Change
Extrinsic reward rewards (pay, promotion, praise, and so forth) provided by the organization to employees.

Theory into Practice

By relying heavily on extrinsic rewards to shape employee behavior, organizations risk driving out the intrinsic rewards that might be associated with the work; as a result curiosity, creativity, and problem-solving behaviors may be lessened.

Building a Vocabulary of Change
Intrinsic reward rewards (feelings of pride, satisfaction, and self-esteem) that accrue to the individual based on the performance of a task.

Commitment to adopt new behaviors comes from *within* individuals. If the goal of change is to create motivation—as internalized desire on the part of employees—to adopt new behaviors, then organizational leaders need to consider intrinsic rewards as well. An **intrinsic reward** is a positive outcome naturally associated with a behavior.

Intrinsic rewards—a sense of accomplishment, learning, and growth, for example—are provided in a constant and ongoing way as individuals interact with their environments. Intrinsic rewards, according to Edward Deci, motivate exploration, play, curiosity, and puzzle solving.[35] For that reason, intrinsic rewards can be more helpful in building commitment to new behaviors, especially when the desired new behaviors are based on creativity and problem-solving activities.

No organization can rely solely on either extrinsic or intrinsic rewards to support new patterns of behavior. The challenge is that the two approaches to shaping behavior do not easily coexist. Overreliance on extrinsic rewards, pay in particular, can actually *dampen* internal motivation.[36] Employees may, and often do, find themselves behaving in a certain way *because* of the money attached to the behavior rather than an internalized desire to undertake the behavior. And the more attractive the reward is to that employee, the more likely it is to drive out internal motivation.

Not all extrinsic rewards work against internal motivation and creativity. Praise, which is an extrinsic reward, can enhance motivation by helping individuals feel competent and self-determining. Even pay can be used in ways that do not drive out motivation: When pay is used to *attract* individuals to an organization, it does not have a negative impact on motivation.

Rewards such as bonuses that are *not* tied a priori to specific outcomes but are presented after the fact in recognition of particularly creative effort are likely to lead to higher creativity in the future. The creativity benefit of such after-the-fact bonuses is enhanced when those bonuses are coupled with constructive feedback and tied to creative outcomes rather than any particular or specific methodology for achieving those outcomes.[37] Even so, intrinsic rewards are the primary factors contributing to creativity; extrinsic rewards more typically encourage routine behavior.

Theory into Practice

Bonuses provided "after the fact"—without being announced or promised before hand—can be used to reinforce desired new behaviors.

The opportunity as well as the challenge for a manager is to provide motivation that is, in essence, internal to employees. Design decisions that allow employees to participate in decision making enhance the developmental opportunities of work, thus providing a key intrinsic motivation. Providing employees with autonomy and performance feedback enhances employees' sense of self-efficacy and ego satisfaction. In these cases, the organization is creating an environment where employees are more likely to find intrinsic motivation in their work.

Building a Vocabulary of Change
Pay equity a perception by employees that their pay is fair and equitable in relationship to others: peers inside the organization and out as well as subordinates and superiors in the hierarchy.

Pay equity is also vital to the achievement of intrinsic motivation. Only employees who believe that their pay level is fair and equitable—compared to peers both inside and outside the organization, to subordinates, and to superiors—will be intrinsically motivated by the desire to learn, to develop, and to grow.[38] Job evaluation plans endeavor to create a sense of internal equity, and regular salary surveys can help achieve external equity. Just as importantly, organizations that supply employees with regular and candid feedback about performance and contribution can help ensure congruence between pay levels and perceptions of fairness.

Theory into Practice

Organizations will not be able to call on intrinsic motivation unless employees feel that they are being paid equitably.

Sequencing the Introduction of Incentives

The temptation to introduce a new incentive plan early in change implementation is powerful but potentially harmful. Some brief examples of unintended consequences include:

- A community bank introduces a sales bonus designed to encourage more aggressive revenue generation on the part of employees. Customer service representatives now ignore the complaints of, and even occasionally hang up on customers once those customers have expressed a lack of interest in purchasing additional bank services or product offerings.
- After introducing a new executive bonus based on divisional performance, an organization finds its executives withdrawing shared resources from other divisions in order to maximize their own performance.
- A Silicon Valley–based software developer, which had relied heavily on stock options to attract employees, reels when its stock price drops sharply; high turnover deteriorates performance, which leads to even lower stock prices and leaves management with little to offer new employees by way of attraction.
- A plant manager halts a team-based incentive plan because of increasing rivalry among teams.
- A school system finds its "Teacher of the Year" bonus award designed to enhance performance instead leads to dissension and distrust among its formerly collegial faculty.

When applied early, new pay incentives can either fail to alter long-standing patterns of behavior or, even more troubling, change patterns of behavior in an unintended, even unwelcome way.

In the above examples, new incentives were put into place before a thorough diagnosis of the existent patterns of behavior in the organization; before a carefully, strategically guided, and participative effort was made to redesign roles, responsibilities, and relationships among employees; and before human resource development worked to imbue the organization with required new competencies. Management turned to incentives as a quick fix: an intervention that would immediately shape employee behavior. That is exactly what they did, of course, but not in a desired way.

Theory into Practice

Introducing new incentives early in a change implementation process risks negative consequences.

When it comes to integrating new incentives into change implementation, leaders face two types of choices: *what* and *when*.

What choices relate to decisions concerning the design of their incentives:

- At what level of performance will incentives be set?
- How large will potential incentive earnings be in relationship to base salary?
- To what extent will the incentives emphasize short-term or long-term performance or some blend of the two?
- How far up and down the hierarchy will incentives be offered?

The goal of the *what* questions is to make design choices that reinforce the behaviors sought of the strategic renewal and organizational change.

The *when* question relates to when incentives will be introduced in a sequence of transformational interventions. Michael Beer has suggested that pay changes be thought of as a "lag" intervention: one that follows other interventions and is not called upon to drive new behaviors.[39] Failure to diagnose and redesign first increases the likelihood that the new incentives will misfire, leading to unintended and perhaps negative consequences.

TECHNOLOGY AND BEHAVIOR CHANGE

Most employees, whether in high- or low-tech companies, in manufacturing or services, or in small or large organizations, have experienced the impact of new technology. Advances in computers and connectivity, in particular, have revolutionized the use of information.

Building a Vocabulary of Change
Technology the processes, mechanics, and interactions of human behavior required to convert raw material into finished offerings.

Technology refers not just to the actual hardware but also to the processes and interactions of human behavior required to convert raw material into finished offerings, to turn raw data into actionable information that can guide behaviors. Although the technology itself may be stunningly innovative, the use to which that technology is put does not always alter patterns of employee behavior; it may simply automate existing patterns of behavior.

Making a Choice

Richard Walton articulated what he referred to as the choice inherent in the introduction of new technology into a work setting.[40] One of the most fundamental choices managers face when introducing new technology, he noted, is whether to apply that technology in a way that merely automates existing processes or in a manner that transforms those processes.[41]

Using new technology to automate existing processes essentially leaves the status quo in place. *I used to get information through paper memos*, a manager in an automated workplace might say. *Now I get the same information over our network.* Or, *When it comes to introducing and supporting new products, those guys in Japan never got on board before we had SAP, and they still don't know even though we now have SAP*. One company—a state-run mass transit operation—forbid employees from sending e-mails, regardless of their contents, to anyone in other departments or functions without going through their boss. Functional silos remained intact.

Theory into Practice

When introducing new technology, organizational leaders face a choice: to use that technology to automate existing processes or to use new technology to support transformed behaviors.

The second option for introducing new technology is one that applies technology in such a way that supports transformed behaviors, that upgrades rather than downgrades skill requirements, that opens up new opportunities for individual and shared contribution, that increases cohesion between employee and customers, and that allows for greater decentralization of control and autonomy of effort.

Some executives resist the transforming strategy for fear of losing control and disrupting required discipline. "There has been a fear of letting it out of our hands," said one corporate vice president in reflecting a widespread resistance to the use of IT to share performance data up and down the company. "That is why information is so carefully guarded . . . Traditionally, we have thought that such data can only be managed by certain people with certain accountabilities and, I hesitate to say, endowed with certain skills or capabilities."[42] But other leaders, including the chief of staff of the U.S. Army, see the transforming strategy as a way of supporting the end of "business as usual" and the institutionalization of new behaviors.

Sequencing New Technology in Change Implementation

No one questions that new technology can have a powerful, transformative impact on the manner in which work is conducted, becoming a vital contributor to outstanding performance. However, as with other "hardwiring" interventions, organizational leaders must deal not just with the *what* question—what new technologies can we call on—but the *how* and *when* questions as well. How will the new technologies be introduced and when will they be added to the mix? Effective change implementation calls on new technology to enable and reinforce new behaviors.

Theory into Practice

New technologies can be introduced as a way to support desired behavioral changes.

Conclusion

Leaders find interventions designed to alter the hard-wiring of their organization—structures, systems, and technologies—especially appealing. That appeal flows from the well-reasoned theory that structure and systems impact behavior. Because behavior must be altered as part of the change effort, the thinking goes, why not call upon new structures and systems early in the implementation effort to drive that change?

Time and time again, such interventions end up in disappointment. Instead of encouraging new behaviors, structural change can provoke resistance, even sabotage. (Lou Gerstner ran into both at IBM.) Any change, when imposed from above, risks energizing resistance from the very employees whose behavior needs to change.

The impact of incentive and technology changes coming too early in the implementation process runs an even greater risk. Leaders run the risk not just of failing to alter long-term patterns of behavior but of altering patterns of behavior in an unintended, even unwelcome way. That risk is enhanced when implementation starts from an inadequate and non-inclusive diagnosis or from inadequate training to ensure employees are capable of exercising the new behaviors.

When formal structures are changed in Step 4 of the implementation process, they are experienced as reinforcers of new behaviors. Desired patterns of new behavior are now recognized and supported, and become built into the new hardwiring of the organization.

Discussion Questions

1. In realigning IBM's global organization with his new strategy, what options did Lou Gerstner have other than restructuring?
2. It has been said that, given the growing complexity and dynamism of the world of business, *all* organizations will have to adopt some type of a matrix structure. Do you agree or disagree with that argument? Explain.
3. What is it about incentive systems that makes them so attractive to leaders attempting to implement organization change? Can you think of examples when it would be useful to create new incentives early in a transformation process?
4. Can you think of examples from your own experience—at work or in the classroom—where the manner in which your performance was being measured worked *against* the goals you were trying to achieve?

Case Discussion

Read "Making the Problem Worse" and prepare answer to the following discussion questions:

1. What went wrong? How can you explain how the technology actually led to more rather than fewer mistakes?
2. What theories of change implementation would have helped the administrators at the Complex General Hospital solve the problem of medication mistakes?
3. How might you have gone about solving the problem at Complex General? To what extent, if any, would new technology have been helpful?

Making the Problem Worse

The chief administrators at the Complex General Hospital (a disguised name), a large urban teaching hospital, were determined to use technology to solve a nagging and disturbing problem: medication mistakes.[43]

Prescribing errors, confusion over drugs with similar names, inadequate attention to the synergistic effects of multiple drugs and patient allergies—those and other related errors that are lumped together under the label "adverse drug event"—kill or injure more than 770,000 patients annually in U.S. hospitals. In added health care costs alone, adverse drug events add several hundred billion dollars a year. And the most common type of error—the simplest to understand and, seemingly, to correct—is "handwriting identification": poor or illegible handwriting by the prescribing physician.

Administrators at Complex General called upon a computerized physician order entry (CPOE) system to solve the problem. CPOE worked to ensure safety and accuracy by the following steps:

- All physician prescriptions for medicine and treatment would be entered into the hospital's IT network.
- Those computer entries would be available to all hospital staff, including both treatment and pharmacy staff.
- The system would catch all prescription errors: incorrect dosages, duplicate requisitions, patient allergies, and even adverse impact statements of multiple medications being prescribed to a patient.
- The system also displays the patient's complete medical history as well as the latest clinical guidelines for treatment.

Ample evidence exists that CPOE can and has been used to reduce both errors and costs.

Surprisingly, the results at Complex General were stunningly disappointing. Not only did the CPOE system not eliminate errors, it actually *increased* adverse drug events.

A subsequent study identified a number of problems:

- Incorrect Dosage Information—"House staff often rely on CPOE displays to determine minimal effective or usual doses. The dosages listed in the CPOE display, however, are based on the pharmacy's warehousing and purchasing decisions, not clinical guidelines. For example, if usual dosages are 20 or 30 mg, the pharmacy might stock only 10-mg doses, so 10-mg units are displayed on the CPOE screen. Consequently, some house staff order 10-mg doses as the usual or 'minimally effective' dose."
- Discontinuation Failures—"Ordering new or modifying existing medications is usually a separate process from canceling (discontinuing) an existing medication . . . medication-canceling ambiguities are exacerbated by the computer interface and multiple-screen displays of medications . . . viewing one patient's medications may require 20 screens."
- Patient Confusion—"It is easy to select the wrong patient file because names and drugs are close together, the font is small, and, most critical here, patients' names do not appear on all screens. Different CPOE computer screens offer differing colors and typefaces for the same information, enhancing misinterpretation as physicians switch among screens. Patients' names are grouped alphabetically rather than by house staff teams or rooms. Thus, similar names (combined with small fonts, hectic workstations, and interruptions) are easily confused."

How could this have happened?

Endnotes

1. Based on Louis V. Gerstner, Jr., *Who Says Elephants Can't Dance? Inside IBM's Historic Turnaround* (New York: Harper Business, 2002), pp. 86–87.
2. Janis L. Gogan and Lynda M. Applegate, *Open Market, Inc.: Managing In a Turbulent Environment* (Boston: Harvard Business School Publishing, 1996).
3. *Ibid.*, p. 13.
4. Quoted from Raymond E. Miles and Charles C. Snow, *Fit, Failure, and the Hall of Fame: How Companies Succeed and Fail* (New York: Free Press, 1994), p. 14.
5. Paul R. Lawrence and Jay W. Lorsch, *Organization and Environment: Managing Differentiation and Integration* (Boston: Harvard Graduate School of Business Administration Division of Research, 1967).
6. Steven C. Wheelwright, Charles A. Holloway, Nicole Tempest, and Christian G. Kasper, *Cisco Systems, Inc.: Acquisition Integration for Manufacturing (A)* (Boston: Harvard Business School Publishing, 1999), p. 3.
7. Jay R. Galbraith, *Competing with Flexible Lateral Organizations* (Reading, MA: Addison-Wesley, 1994), pp. 101–102.
8. *Ibid.*, p. 13.
9. Arthur A. Thompson, Jr., and A. J. Strickland III, *Strategic Management: Concepts and Cases*, 13th ed. (Boston: McGraw-Hill Irwin, 2003), p. 129.
10. Dell is quoted in Joan Magretta, "The Power of Virtual Integration: An Interview with Dell Computer's Michael Dell," *Harvard Business Review* (March–April 1998), p. 75.
11. Ludo Van der Heyden, *Marks & Spencer and Zara: Process Competition in the Textile Apparel Industry* (France: INSEAD, 2002).
12. Thomas A. Stewart and Louise O'Brien, "Execution without Excuses: An Interview with Michael Dell and Kevin Rollins," *Harvard Business Review* (March 2005), p. 105.
13. William J. Bruns, Jr., "Accounting Information and Decision-Making: Some Behavioral Hypotheses," *Accounting Review* 43 (1968), pp. 469–480.
14. This example is cited in Noel M. Tichy and Stratford Sherman, *Control Your Own Destiny or Someone Else Will* (New York: Doubleday, 1993), p. 38.
15. This point is elaborated upon in H. Thomas Johnson, *Relevance Regained: From Top-Down Control to Bottom-Up Empowerment* (New York: Free Press, 1992).
16. *Ibid.*, p. 115.
17. Gary Cokins, *Activity-Based Cost Management: An Executive's Guide* (San Francisco: Wiley, 2001).
18. Quoted in Jonathan Schiff and Stanley Abraham, *MiCRUS: Activity-Based Management for Business Turnaround* (Boston: Harvard Business School Publishing, 2001), p. 7.
19. *Ibid.*, p. 8.
20. Robert S. Kaplan and David P. Norton, "Transforming the Balanced Scorecard from Performance Measurement to Strategic Management: Part I," *Accounting Horizons* 15 (March 2001), p. 87.
21. Robert S. Kaplan and David P. Norton, "Using the Balanced Scorecard as a Strategic Management System," *Harvard Business Review* (January–February 1996), p. 3.
22. Robert S. Kaplan and David P. Norton, "Integrating Shareholder Value and Activity-Based Costing with the Balanced Scorecard," *In Context* (Boston: Harvard Business School Publishing, 2001), p. 4.
23. Michelle Conlin and Peter Coy, "The Wild New Work Force," *Business Week*, December 6, 1999, pp. 39–41.
24. Quoted in V. G. Narayanan and Lisa Brem, *Executive Compensation at General Electric* (Boston: Harvard Business School Publishing, 2004), p. 8.
25. Thomas B. Wilson, *Innovative Reward Systems for the Changing Workplace* (New York: McGraw-Hill, 1993), p. 49.
26. Peter V. LeBlanc and Paul W. Mulvey, "How American Workers See the Rewards of Work," *Compensation and Benefits Review* 30 (January–February 1998), pp. 24–28; Jamie Hale and George Bailey, "Seven Dimensions of Successful Reward Plans," *Compensation and Benefits Review* 30 (July–August 1998), pp. 72–73.
27. *Compensation and Benefits Review* 29 (March–April 1997), p. 7; *Compensation and Benefits Review* 29 (November–December 1997), p. 18. The Hewitt Associates survey results are reported in Kenan S. Abosch, "Variable Pay: Do We Have the Basics in Place?" *Compensation and Benefits Review* 30 (July–August 1998), pp. 12–22. A comparison of executive attitudes toward bonuses in the United States, France, and the Netherlands can be found in Johannes M. Pennings, "Executive Reward Systems: A Cross-National Comparison," *Journal of Management Studies* 30 (March 1993), pp. 261–273.
28. *Compensation and Benefits Review* 29 (November–December 1997), p. 18.
29. This was the conclusion of a study of cross-functional process teams in the U.S. electronics manufacturing

industry. See Ann Majchrzak and Qianwei Wang, "Breaking the Functional Mind-Set in Functional Organizations," *Harvard Business Review* (September–October 1996), pp. 93–99.

30. The percentage and amount differed based on hierarchical level.
31. For a good summary of the many stock option plans available, see David G. Strege, "Employee Strategies for Stock Based Compensation," *Compensation and Benefits Review* 31 (November–December 1999), pp. 41–54.
32. "Stock Ownership Guidelines for Directors and Executive Officers," eBay Investor Relations.
33. Calvin Reynolds, "Global Compensation and Benefits in Transition," *Compensation and Benefits Review* 32 (January–February 2000), p. 29.
34. Jeffrey Pfeffer, *The Human Equation: Building Profits by Putting People First* (Boston: Harvard Business School Press, 1998), pp. 80–85.
35. Edward L. Deci, "The Hidden Costs of Rewards," *Organizational Dynamics* 4 (Winter 1976), p. 62.
36. Edward L. Deci, "Effects of Externally Mediated Rewards on Intrinsic Motivation," *Journal of Personality and Social Psychology* 18 (1971), pp. 105–115, and "Intrinsic Motivation, Extrinsic Reinforcement, and Equity," *Journal of Personality and Social Psychology* 22 (1972), pp. 113–120.
37. Teresa M. Amabile, *Creativity in Context* (Boulder, CO: Westview Press, 1996).
38. This is a conclusion based on equity theory. See George C. Homans, *The Human Group* (New York: Harcourt, Brace, 1950); Leonard R. Sayles, *Behavior of Industrial Work Groups: Prediction and Control* (New York: Wiley, 1958); Elliott Jacques, *Equitable Payment* (New York: Wiley, 1961); George C. Homans, *Social Behavior: Its Elementary Forms* (New York: Harcourt, Brace, 1961); J. Stacy Adams, "Toward An Understanding of Inequity," *Journal of Abnormal and Social Psychology* 67 (1963), pp. 422–436; J. Stacy Adams, "Inequity in Social Exchange," in Leonard Berkowitz, ed., *Advances in Experimental Social Psychology,* Vol. 2 (New York: Academic Press, 1965).

39. Tom Ehrendfeld, Maggie Coil, Donald Berwick, Tom Nyberg, and Michael Beer, "The Case of the Unpopular Pay Plan," *Harvard Business Review* 70 (January–February 1992), p. 22.
40. Richard E. Walton, "Social Choice in the Development of Advanced Information Technology," *Human Relations* 35 (1982), pp. 1073–1083.
41. Shoshona Zuboff, *In the Age of the Smart Machine: The Future of Work and Power* (New York: Basic Books, 1984).
42. Quoted in Zuboff, *In the Age of the Smart Machine,* p. 239.
43. This case study is based on research published in Ross Koppel, Joshua P. Metlay, Abigail Cohen, Brian Abaluck, A. Russell Localio, Stephen E. Kimmel, and Brian L. Storm, "Role of Computerized Physician Order Entry Systems in Facilitating Medication Errors," *Journal of the American Medical Association* 293 (2005), pp. 1197–1203. The hospital is not identified in the article.

CHAPTER **7**

Organizational Culture and Change

Eager to implement organizational change, leaders might leap into change implementation fueled by enthusiasm, offering real and symbolic support, and demanding results. There is a factor, however, too important to overlook: the organization's culture. Culture might serve as an enabler of change, but it might also erect barriers.

For that reason, this chapter will examine organizational culture and its role in hindering and implementing change. In particular, this chapter will:

- Define organizational culture as an emergent phenomenon in organizations
- Analyze the relationship between culture and organizational change
- Delineate the six cultural traits most associated with organizational adaptation and change
- Suggest how organizations can go about assessing their culture
- Discuss actions that organizational leaders can take to reshape culture

Before doing that, we will examine how attempts by a progression of CEOs intent on change at what once was a premier American company faced a strong, resistant organizational culture.

CULTURE AND CHANGE AT XEROX

In some ways, Xerox represented American business at its best.[1] In 1960 when the company issued its 914 copier, no one understood just how significant that launch would be. Five years later, Xerox's flagship product generated revenues of over $390 million; it went on to be the most profitable product in the history of the United States. The brand was so popular and ubiquitous that the name itself became iconic: people didn't "copy" documents, they "Xeroxed" them.

But Xerox became one of the most extraordinary stories of corporate decline as well. As the company gained a near monopoly over the centralized office copier market, employees' attitudes and behaviors became increasingly insular. Personal aggrandizement, turf protection, and career advancement directed employee behaviors away from the marketplace. The cultural values which pervaded the company in the 1960s and 1970s became "somewhat intolerant of initiatives and leadership from the ranks.

Decision making was often centralized. Experimentation was often discouraged, and error was not tolerated well."[2]

The company failed to commercialize many of its own internally developed breakthrough technologies: the personal computer created at Xerox's Palo Alto Research Center being only the most famous example. The looming threat of high quality/low cost Japanese competitors—Canon would revolutionize the copy market through smaller, decentralized machines that could now be placed in each office—blindsided Xerox executives.

Perhaps most troubling was a culture that treated customers with a contempt bordering on arrogance. One story, small though it might be, captures the prevailing attitude. It used to be that Xerox users were unable to write in blue ink; Xerox machines simply did not reproduce blue very well. Customers wondered why Xerox could not fix the "problem." When they complained, the company's response was simple and straightforward: use another color ink! If our processes don't meet your needs, they were saying, why, you'll just have to adjust your needs. After all, *we* set the standards, *we* will decide how to define effective performance on the part of our products, and our products are high quality because we say they are high quality.

An attempt at strategic renewal—from producing copier machines to providing all-purpose document management for the office space—did nothing to halt Xerox's slide. The company failed to take advantage of low cost, high quality ink jet printing, allowing Hewlett-Packard to build a printer division that soon dwarfed all of Xerox.

An attempt to compete head-on with IBM in computing generated only huge losses. Finally, Xerox's board went outside the company for the first time in its history to bring in a leader from IBM. G. Richard (Rick) Thoman worked for 13 months, attempting to instill a new culture of customer focus and aggressiveness. Then he was fired, replaced by his own predecessor, Paul Allaire. "What I see," said a senior sales executive, "is a retreat back into the comfort zone of the way things used to be before Rick Thoman." What followed was a decade of severe retrenchment, a battle with bankruptcy, and a return, eventually, as a much diminished company under new CEO Ann Mulcahy.

CULTURE AND BEHAVIOR

Xerox's culture diminished the company's ability to respond effectively to a dynamic competitive environment. A series of CEOs failed to transform Xerox into an agile, customer-focused company. Numerous business organizations have faced the same challenge. General Motors and Xerox, for example, have struggled against entrenched culture as they attempted to respond to a dynamic competitive environment.

On the other hand, there are many companies—think of Google, Nucor Steel, Southwest Airlines, General Electric, and Starbucks, for example—where leaders proudly proclaim their culture to be supportive of adaptability and sustained outstanding performance. "We're profitable *because* of the value system of our company," proclaimed Starbuck's Howard Schultz. "I truly believe that Nucor's success," claimed the steel company's chairman, Ken Iverson, "has been 70 percent culture and 30 percent technology." Louis Gerstner, who spent 25 years as a senior executive at

Building a Vocabulary of Change
Organizational culture the common and shared values and assumptions that help shape employee behavior and are typically passed down from current to future employees.

three companies, including IBM, came to see "that culture isn't just one aspect of the game—it *is* the game."

Organizational culture refers to the common and shared values that help shape employee behavior and are typically passed down from current to future employees. Culture serves as the glue that binds an organization or, in the words of Terrence Deal and Allan Kennedy, "the way we do things around here."[3]

In the early days of an organization's life, founders embed their personal values in the structures, systems, even the strategies of their companies. When two Stanford graduate students, Larry Page and Sergey Brim, created their first algorithm for delivering relevant Internet searches, they simultaneously created the culture for what would soon become Google. The company's culture, in fact, practically mirrored the personalities of its founders.[4]

There were three cornerstones to their beliefs:

1. Don't be evil (never compromise search results but put a sense of individual ethics into advertisements*).
2. Technology matters (the two were, after all engineers).
3. We make our own rules (particularly in terms of earnings reports and earnings guidance reported to analysis).

When outsider Eric Schmidt joined the company in 2001 as CEO, he was shocked to hear the phrase "don't be evil" come up during company policy meetings.

Theory into Practice

An organization's culture is composed of the shared values of its members and the resulting patterns of employee behavior.

Page and Brim are just part of a long list of founders—individuals such as William Procter and James Gamble (Procter & Gamble), Bill Hewlett and David Packard (Hewlett-Packard), Bill Gates (Microsoft), Mark Zuckerman (Facebook) and the trio of Steve Chen, Chad Hurley, and Jawed Karim (YouTube)—whose values become part of the shared DNA of the organization, what Geert Hofstede calls the "software of the mind," that determines how employees ought to behave.[5]

When deviations occur, they are quickly criticized based on the values. Shortly after joining Google, Eric Schmidt was faced with an engineer arguing that an idea linking an advertising system into the company's search was evil. "It was as if he said there was a murderer in the room. The whole conversation stopped, but then people challenged his assumptions." In the end, Schmidt and the group rejected the idea because, said Schmidt, "it *was* evil."[6]

Employees do not have to wait for procedures to be enforced, for bosses to tell them what to do and how to do it; they define and debate acceptable behavior based on organizational culture. But just what is this phenomenon called culture?

---

*The company turned down ads for hard liquor and guns based on the personal values of Page and Brim.

Values and Culture

Culture consists of an interaction between predominant values and patterns of behavior. **Values** refer to the beliefs and assumptions that individuals bring with them into the workplace. They are deeply held beliefs concerning such fundamental matters as the nature of people and relationships, how to deal with conflict and solving problems, as well as the goals and purpose of the organization.

Values are not so much rules or codes of behavior as they are what Andrew Pettigrew refers to as the logics of action and the invisible rules of an organization.[7] When a cohesive set of values becomes predominant in a group or organization, those shared values come to shape patterns of behavior. These are the "social habits" that Lewin addressed (see Chapter 2)—behaviors shaped by values. Now we have an organizational culture: a relatively homogeneous collection of values and the behavioral patterns that emerge as a result.

Culture as an Emergent Phenomenon

Founders embed their values, their beliefs and assumptions about people, about the organization, and about the world. But even they cannot impose a culture. As an organization grows and ages (especially after founders cease to be active), culture emerges from a complex interaction among numerous factors (Exhibit 7-1).

Founder values affect choices made by the next generation of leaders. Past founders and future leaders shape managerial practices and the organizational design of the company: how behaviors will be controlled and rewarded, how decisions will be made, and so on. What emerges from that interaction is the organization's culture.

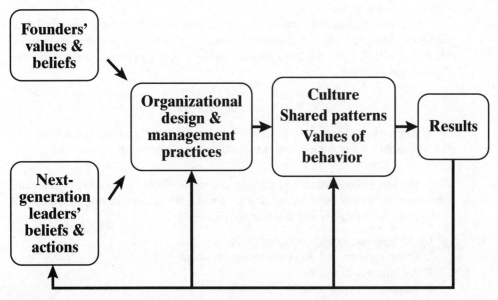

EXHIBIT 7-1   Culture as an Emergent Organizational Phenomenon.

CULTURE AND CHANGE

Culture shapes behaviors, behaviors produce results, and results reinforce culture. Particularly when outcomes are positive, an organization's culture becomes increasingly entrenched and robust. A robust culture, in fact, is a necessary component of adaptation and sustained outstanding performance.[8] **Robust cultures**—those with widely and deeply shared values—bring with them cohesiveness and shared commitment while simultaneously offering channels of communication and coordination.[9]

Building a Vocabulary of Change
Robust cultures cultures in which a common set of values and assumptions are deeply and widely held.

Strong, robust organizational cultures enhance organizational performance in three ways:

1. Culture makes an appeal to the "higher ideals and values" of employees, and in doing so provides energy, identity, commitment, and meaning.[10]
2. A strong, robust culture enhances coordination by focusing employee attention on strategic priorities without restricting autonomy and imposing unnecessary controls.
3. A strong, robust culture can help change implementation.

Culture, in other words supports outstanding performance by building commitment and coordination among employees.

That does not mean, however, that all strong, robust cultures are equally suitable to *sustained* outstanding performance. Culture, as Xerox discovered, may also hinder adaptiveness and change, a problem that can be particularly debilitating in a dynamic external environment. Strong cultures can turn the attention of employees inward as they attempt to preserve old, traditional ways of doing things without responding to the new for new approaches. Cultures that focus attention exclusively on the past while sacrificing the need to respond to the future can be said to be nonadaptive.

Building a Vocabulary of Change
Adaptive cultures cultures that encourage responsiveness and change as part of their core values.

In contrast, **adaptive cultures** encourage adaptation and enable the implementation of change as part of their core values.[11] Nordstrom, Southwest Airlines, Microsoft, and Google all rely on robust, adaptive cultures to remain competitive in a dynamic environment.

Theory into Practice

Strong, internally consistent cultures may resist change; adaptive cultures will embrace, encourage, and enable change implementation.

The adaptiveness of an organization's culture—its ability to support change implementation in response to a dynamic environment—resides in seven separate but interrelated sets of values and assumptions concerning:

1. The legitimacy of multiple stakeholders
2. The motivation and developmental potential of people
3. Performance expectations
4. Employee participation
5. Learning

6. Diversity

7. A global mindset

We can examine each to analyze how culture can support or hinder change.

Valuing Multiple Shareholders

Turnaround champion Al Dunlop took the view that organizations are accountable only to investors. "Shareholders are the number one constituency," he said. "Show me an annual report that lists six or seven constituencies, and I'll show you a mismanaged company."[12]

Whatever else might be said about Dunlop's philosophy and turnaround efforts, he failed to create adaptive organizations capable of transforming themselves in response to external environmental and competitive changes. Most of his "turned-around" companies, in fact, ceased to exist.

Organizations capable of adaptation and change do not emphasize a single stakeholder, whether it is shareholders, employees, or even customers. In the end, organizations whose leaders value the perspectives of multiple stakeholders—with particular emphasis on customers, employees, and shareholders—outperform those that focus on one or two.[13]

A key source of adaptation is the willingness of organizational leaders to commit time, energy, and resources to tending to the interests of multiple stakeholders; most especially, to shareholders, to customers, and to employees.

- By paying attention to *customers*, companies remain responsive to external markets.
- By paying attention to *employees*, companies are able to recruit and retain the people who serve customers.
- By taking care of *shareholders*, companies strive to perform well financially over time.[14]

Adaptation and change is not only made possible by attention to these multiple stakeholders; it is driven by responsiveness to their legitimate interests.

Valuing the Developmental Potential of Employees

Organizational leaders seek to motivate employees to change. But just what do they mean by motivation? Will they achieve motivation through rewards and punishments? Or will they seek to create the conditions to achieve self-motivation?

Nearly half a century ago, MIT's Douglas McGregor articulated a simple but powerful distinction between these two distinct approaches to motivation.[15] At their base, the two views represent alternative belief systems about people. The assumptions managers make about the ability and desire of employees to develop motivation consistent with the goals of objectives of the organization can be delineated into two theories: Theory X and Theory Y (Exhibit 7-2).

When pervasive attitudes support what McGregor called Theory X beliefs, managers seek to impose change down through their organization. When pervasive attitudes support Theory Y beliefs, managers approach change by working to unleash creativity, energy, and drive among employees.

Theory X	Theory Y
The average person has an inherent dislike for work and will avoid it if possible.	People will exercise self-direction and self-control in the service of objectives to which they are committed.
Because of this inherent dislike of work, most people must be coerced, controlled, directed, and/or threatened with punishment to get them to put forward adequate effort toward the achievement of organizational objectives.	The average person learns, under the proper conditions, not only to accept but to seek responsibility.
The average person prefers to be directed, wishes to avoid responsibility, has relatively little ambition, and wants security above all.	The capacity to exercise a relatively high degree of imagination, ingenuity, and creativity in the solution of organizational problems is widely, not narrowly, distributed.

EXHIBIT 7-2   Contrasting Managerial Assumptions about People.
Based on Douglas McGregor, *The Human Enterprise* (New York: McGraw-Hill, 1960).

"Above all," McGregor wrote, "the assumptions of Theory Y point up the fact that the limits on human collaboration in the organizational setting are not limits of human nature but of management's ingenuity in discovering how to realize the potential represented by its human resources."[16] Since effective change implementation rests on the desire to motivate employees to adopt new patterns of behavior, a culture based on Theory Y values supports the belief that employees can be motivated to change their behaviors in order to act on behalf of the organization.

Theory into Practice

When the pervasive values of an organization hold that most employees will exercise self-direction and self-control in the service of objectives to which they are committed, the organization's culture will be more welcoming to the implementation of behavioral change.

Building a Vocabulary of Change
Self-sealing value loop a self-fulfilling prophecy in which values lead to behaviors on the part of managers that, in turn, lead to responsive behaviors on the part of employees that, in turn, reinforce the original values held by managers.

When attitudes become pervasive in a culture, they tend to be reinforced. An individual's own on-the-job experience helps shape and reinforce values because of the feedback loop that exists between the assumptions of managers and the resultant behaviors of employees. Exhibit 7-3 illustrates what might be considered a **self–sealing value loop**, the phenomenon that acts like a self-fulfilling prophecy. Values lead to behaviors on the part of managers that, in turn, lead to reactions on the part of employees. The manner in which employees react, in turn, reinforces the original values held by managers.

Theory into Practice

Values tend to be self reinforcing; managers create an environment where employees behave in ways that confirm those managers' beliefs.

A manager believes that most employees dislike work and will avoid it whenever possible.

Because of that belief, the manager imposes tight control on work, closely supervises performance, and relies heavily on carrot-and-stick differentiation of individual effort.

With little trust and less autonomy coming from the manager, employees respond by working within rules, by performing up to expected levels but not endeavoring to exceed those levels, by offering little if any insight into how to innovate or improve, and by doing whatever is required to maximize rewards (the carrot) and avoid punishment (the stick).

Seeing employees bringing little by way of dedication, commitment, or imagination to their job performance, the manager concludes that his/her initial assumptions were correct and becomes even less trusting and more controlling of employees.

"See. I was *right*; my own experience *proves* it."

EXHIBIT 7-3 Dynamics of a Self-Sealing Value Loop.

Valuing Outstanding Performance

Effective change implementation aims to alter behaviors in order to support renewed strategies and achieve outstanding performance. The most effective change leaders are driven to produce not modest or incremental performance improvements but *outstanding* results. Cultures that demand outstanding performance from their employees—and support their efforts to achieve high performance levels—will enable appropriate behavioral change.

It is the interconnection between performance goals and employee commitment that forms the basis of this core value. It is the conviction that, given high performance goals—coupled with the requisite levels of autonomy and resources—employees will constantly work to meet those goals as well as to seek improvement in their own performance and the performance of the organization. When change occurs within an organization that values outstanding performance, that change will be aligned with the strategic goals of the organization.

Valuing Employee Participation

Decades of research and experience have confirmed and broadened an understanding of the positive performance impact of employee participation. **Participation** refers to the ability of employees at all levels to influence decisions concerning the planning and execution of key tasks.

Allowing for employee participation can support change implementation for a number of reasons:[17]

- Participation can improve decision-making quality by involving lower-level employees who have access to important information and by encouraging diverse opinions.
- Participation enhances the commitment of participants to the chosen course of action.
- Participation enhances motivation to achieve performance goals.
- Participation opens avenues of communication and builds coordination among involved employees.
- Participation encourages employees to become self-supervising.
- Participation can improve employee-management relations.
- Participation allows employees to learn and use new skills while enabling an organization to identify individuals with leadership potential.

When employees participate in the identification of a problem as well as the design of a solution, they will be more motivated to achieve the new goals. Additionally, the participation of employees brings forth points of view and information that might trigger the recognition that change is required. By their closeness to customers, especially in service organizations, and their direct involvement in work processes, employees can provide vital knowledge concerning the need for adaptation and change.

Focus of Concern	Can Be Expressed Through the Question
Control	What if employees make decisions with which I am uncomfortable/in disagreement?
Competency	Do employees have the competencies—analytic, strategic, communication, and so on—required to make valid decisions?
Knowledge	Do employees know enough—about the organization, its strategy, products, and services, and the competitive environment—to make informed decisions?
Motivation	Do employees really want to be involved in decision making, or would they prefer to cede that responsibility to management?
Responsibility	Even if employees want to be involved in decision making and are capable of doing just that, isn't decision making my job?

EXHIBIT 7-4   Values That Inhibit Allowing Employee Participation.

Although managers may claim to accept the performance benefits of participation, some may hold beliefs that work against allowing for employee involvement in decision making. Those contrary values can be expressed in a number of concerns summarized in Exhibit 7-4. Managers who harbor such reservations will hesitate to invest decision-making authority in employees. Managers who value participation harbor no such reservations. They believe that the competencies of employees and the quality of decision making will increase, as well as the commitment to the implementation of those decisions.

Valuing Learning

Learning is the process by which individuals receive data from the external environment, analyze that data, and adjust their thinking and behaviors accordingly. A learning culture has both individual and organizational components to it. At the individual level, a learning culture depends on a willingness to admit limitations and vulnerability— *I don't know everything I need to know*. Admitting vulnerability opens the individual to the possibility of transforming input from others.

Individual learning is central to effective change. When learning occurs, writes David Garvin, employees become "skilled at creating, acquiring, and transferring knowledge, and at modifying [their] behavior to reflect new knowledge and insights."[18] Learning becomes transformative when it encourages individuals not just to acquire and process new knowledge but also to change their behaviors as a result. When the pervasive values of an organization's culture nurture learning, change implementation is more likely to be effective.

Building a Vocabulary of Change

Learning the process by which individuals receive data from the external environment, analyze that data, and adjust their thinking and behaviors based on that analysis.

Theory into Practice

Individuals and organizations learn by receiving and analyzing valid information, then altering thinking and acting as appropriate.

Valuing Diversity

Diversity refers to the willingness and ability of an organization to bring together people of different perspectives who have been shaped by their varied backgrounds and experiences. When coupled with participation and learning, diversity can contribute to effective change implementation.

David Thomas and Robin Ely offer the example of a small public-interest law firm to demonstrate how their valuing of diversity supported strategic renewal. In the mid-1980s, the firm's all-white legal staff became concerned that the women they represented in employment-related disputes were exclusively white. The firm hired a Hispanic female attorney, thinking she would expand the firm's client base to include other Hispanic women.

The change brought by the attorney's inclusion was far more sweeping than anticipated. In particular, the new attorney argued that the firm's strategy—focusing on traditional affirmative action cases—should be broadened to include employment issues relating to English-only work policies.

The firm, wrote Thomas and Ely, now recognized "a link between English-only policies and employment issues for a large group of women—primarily recent immigrants—whom it had previously failed to serve adequately."[19] The willingness of partners to value diversity of ideas as well as diversity of ethnic background allowed the organization to incorporate new perspectives in pursuit of strategic aims. Diversity brought with it new approaches and greater effectiveness.

Theory into Practice

Valuing diversity offers the opportunity for creativity within an organization by encouraging collaboration among people with different perspectives derived from varied backgrounds and experiences.

Valuing a Global Mindset

Back in the early 1990s, Yves Doz, José Santos, and Peter Williamson tell us, Nokia leaders realized that their home base in Finland would not provide them with the needed technology, innovation, and skills to gain dominance in the telephone business.[20] With research expertise in the United Kingdom, advanced technologies and global marketing know-how from the United States, cutting edge electronics capabilities in Japan, and management knowledge specific to low-cost manufacturing and low-margin business in Southeast Asia, Nokia could succeed only by thinking globally.

While Nokia accepted, even embraced, a global mindset, their main competitor remained focused on its domestic know-how. Motorola had every intention, of course, of selling their cellular technology globally. Nonetheless, the company continued to develop its technologies and products based on the capabilities available in its own U.S. backyard.

Motorola was among the first to mass-product mobile telephones and had been leading the world market by projecting from the original cellular technology home. The company lost ground, however, by remaining too parochial: thinking the future could be invented within the United States. Motorola missed the shift to digital mobile telephony and the Global System for Mobile (GSM) standard—an outcome of European cooperation that would be the choice of many countries around the world, even in Asia.

Both Nokia and Motorola intended to complete in a global marketplace, but only one company valued a global mindset.[21] **Global mindset** can be defined as a positive openness to the complexities and opportunities of multiple environments. Because "differences still matter in the world," organizations that value a global mindset will be better able to cross national borders.[22]

Building a Vocabulary of Change
Global mindset a positive openness to the complexities and opportunities of multiple environments.

Valuing a global mindset will be an especially significant cornerstone for organizations attempting to compete across national borders. Percy Barnevik, the founding CEO of ABB, suggested why valuing a global mindset would be so critical to managers in an increasingly complex world: "Global managers have exceptionally open minds. They respect how different countries do things, and they have the imagination to appreciate why they do them that way." But a global mindset involves more than the simple acceptance of difference. Managers with a global mindset, added Barnevik, "are also incisive; they push the limits of the culture . . . They sort through the debris of cultural excuses and find opportunities to innovate."[23]

If an organization values a global mindset, it will be able to move beyond parochialism without abandoning local responsiveness. A global mindset allowed Nokia to outpace its competition because it was able first to identify centers of excellence and opportunity within nonhome operations and then integrate those opportunities into a company strategy.

ASSESSING CULTURE

Each of the seven values (summarized in Exhibit 7-5) reflects a dimension of corporate culture that impacts the organization's capacity to change. Whether they are printed on cards, posted on wall plaques, chanted at company gatherings, or proclaimed on banners, values are expressed through words.

- 3M claims innovation ("Thou shalt not kill a new product idea").
- American Express claims, "Heroic customer service and worldwide reliability of service."
- Merck Pharmaceuticals claims, "We are in the business of preserving and improving human life."
- Sony claims as its core values, "To experience the sheer joy that comes from the advancement, application, and innovation of technology that benefits the general public" as well as "To elevate the Japanese culture and national status."[24]

These words represent the espoused values of the organization.

It is useful to remember, however, that culture translates values into action. Employees may claim to hold one set of values; their behaviors, however, might be quite different. Kenneth Lay, the CEO of Enron, hung banners in the Houston corporate lobby proclaiming four core values: communication, respect, integrity, and excellence. "I was always in the forefront of making sure that our people did in fact live and honor those values . . . Integrity and character are incredibly important to me."[25] There is overwhelming evidence that those words did little to shape behaviors of Enron employees.

Cultural Values	Impact Ability to Implement Change
Valuing the legitimacy of multiple stakeholders	Assuming that shareholders, employees, and customers are legitimate stakeholders in organizational outcomes leads management to adapt to shifts in customer exceptions and employees needs while aligning their actions with outstanding performance.
Valuing motivation and developmental potential	Assuming that employees are internally motivated to contribute to outstanding performance and to adapt and change as required leads management to create conditions that motivate altered behaviors.
Valuing high performance expectations	Assuming that high performance goals motivate and energize keeps change efforts aligned with requirements of outstanding performance.
Valuing employee participation	Assuming that employees are capable and motivated to be involved in decision-making processes helps build commitment to required new behaviors.
Valuing learning	Assuming that individuals at all organizational levels need to place themselves in path of learning leads organization to create mechanisms for problem solving and innovation.
Valuing diversity	Assuming that diversity of opinions and insights are required for innovation and outstanding performance makes employees feel valued while encouraging learning, experimentation and adaptation.
Valuing a global mindset	Assuming the complexities of a diversified world offer positive opportunities for learning opens the organization to cross-national collaboration.

EXHIBIT 7-5   Values of Adaptive Cultures.

The leaders at Enron were espousing one set of values but living or enacting another. Gary Hamel noted that the sole responsibility of Enron traders "was simply to find ways to make money."[26] The real rules of the organization ignored the banners in the headquarters' lobby and followed the logic of doing whatever needed to be done to make money. **Espoused values** are the values called upon by individuals to explain or justify their course of action or pattern of behavior. **Enacted values** are the values that are implicit in that course of action or pattern of behavior.[27]

Building a Vocabulary of Change
Espoused values the set of values called upon by individuals to explain or justify their course of action or pattern of behavior.

Building a Vocabulary of Change
Enacted values the set of values that are implicit in that course of action or pattern of behavior.

Theory into Practice

Culture is determined by enacted rather than espoused values; but when those two are out of alignment, cynicism and frustration will drain energy away from outstanding performance.

Managers can find themselves tripping over that difference. Aligning enacted with espoused values requires aligning behavior with words. When the words call for a new approach to management, old habits must be changed. When espoused and enacted values contradict themselves, frustration and cynicism can erode employee motivation and undermine effective implementation.

To avoid that erosion of energy, leaders can assess the alignment between words and deeds. Assessment starts with the question: Do our current values and principles align with the requirements of our renewed strategy? No values, regardless of how lofty, appealing, or sincere they may be, are sustainable if they do not support outstanding performance.

The next question to be asked is: Are the behaviors of employees at all levels of the organization largely consistent with our stated values and principles? The degree to which a gap exists between espoused and enacted values can be particularly debilitating to an organization in that it is likely to engender frustration or cynicism. But how does an organization go about assessing the state of its values and especially the consistency between espoused and enacted values?

Ed Schein urges organizational leaders to start with a cultural audit that surfaces the enacted values and principles in their organization.[28] That cultural audit starts not with the culture itself but with an analysis of a real business problem. A business-problem audit would identify patterns of behavior—the role of authority, the process of decision making, patterns of communication, the management of disagreement and conflict, and so forth—and resulting performance outcomes, then explore the underlying values and principles that shaped the behavior. In that way, the audit accesses culture not directly but through patterns of behavior. The focus is placed on enacted rather than espoused values.

The process of articulating values can, in and of itself, be advantageous for an organization. The articulation of values can, and inevitably will, draw attention to inconsistencies between those espoused values and the values enacted by employees—most particularly top management—in their day-to-day behaviors.

Some managers may wish to avoid the discomfort, self-revelation, even potential turmoil that will result from shining a light on these inconsistencies. But organizations that embrace learning will welcome the opportunity to act upon these inconsistencies. Additionally, the explicitness of values can guide the recruitment and development of employees. The point is to achieve a high degree of alignment between the values of individual employees and those of the organization.

LEADERS SHAPE CULTURE

Reflecting on his 13-year effort to transform Siemens, Heinrich von Pierer recalled his early attention to changing the company's culture. "Some people told me when I started, 'It's nice to talk about culture change, but how long do you think it will take until you really achieve something?'

"I said, 'Well, two years.'

'Young friend,' they laughed, 'it will take 10 years.' Unfortunately, they were right."[29]

Von Pierer's reflection captures the difficulty and challenge of altering an organization's culture. The actions of leaders can shape culture in powerful ways.

Leaders desirous of shaping their organization's culture to support a renewed strategy for achieving outstanding performance need to appreciate the degree to which their own decisions and actions resonate throughout the company. Leaders can examine four sets of behaviors that Schein says help create and embed culture in an organization.[30]

First, *leaders make choices about what to pay attention to, what to measure, control, and reward*. Is it the quality of the product or service or the profit margin? Is it the needs and concerns of shareholders or of multiple stakeholders? Is it the innovativeness of the firm's offerings or the stability of old, dependable lines? These are not either/or choices or options. But they do represent choices in organizational focus and resource allocation that, over time, become embedded as cultural values.

A second set of leader behaviors that helps shape the organization's culture relates to *reactions to critical incidents and crises*. Contrast, for instance, the reaction of executives at Source Perrier with those at Johnson & Johnson to crises. When traces of the carcinogen benzene, a petroleum by-product, turned up in Perrier water, the company labeled the incident as isolated, recalling a small number of bottles distributed in the United States. It was only when similar contamination was found in European bottles and it became clear that the problem had existed for months that executives issued a worldwide recall.

At Johnson & Johnson, cyanide-laced Tylenol capsules killed seven people in Chicago in 1982. The company immediately alerted the public and then issued a worldwide recall for over 31 million bottles. Johnson & Johnson chairman James Burke not only salvaged the brand name but embedded, in ways that words or banners could not, the company's 40-year-old credo to first meet the needs of "the doctors, nurses, and patients, to mothers and fathers and all others who use our products and services."

A third set of behaviors that leaders call upon to shape their organization's culture involves the *"observed criteria" by which they allocate scarce resources*.[31] A CEO who extols the virtue of marketplace responsiveness but slices marketing budgets in order to meet short-term financial goals sends a signal about what the company values. The same can be said of a supervisor who repeats her company's espoused commitment to quality and then urges employees to just "ship it" as monthly deadlines loom. A managing director who refuses to cut training budgets during a downturn emphasizes the extent to which the company values human resources. Making tough choices about resource allocation helps shape the values and resulting culture of an organization.

Finally, leaders choose to *emphasize certain criteria in their recruitment, selection, and promotion of employees and future leaders*. Remember General Motor's Livonia plant (see Chapter 1)? Hoping to instill a culture of teamwork and collaborative problem solving, the company and the union applied certain criteria to their selection process. They placed less emphasis in their search on the technical skills of job applicants and far more on their interpersonal competencies. Willingness and ability to commit to overall company goals, to work cooperatively with fellow employees, and to take initiative all became vital screens in the selection process.

Top executives are the most visible embodiment of their organization's culture. Their behaviors are apparent to both external stakeholders—customers, suppliers, labor markets, and the host community—and to employees. What leaders *say* matters; what leaders *do* matters even more. Key choices and decisions, more than speeches and documents posted on walls, embed values and spread culture.

Conclusion

Organizational culture—the values and assumptions that individuals bring with them to the workplace and the resulting behavioral patterns—has a powerful impact on the ability of organizations to implement change. Culture derives mainly from the values of founders as passed on through future generations of leaders. These leaders make decisions about focus and emphasis, about how to respond to a crisis, about which employees to hire and which to promote. That is why culture is an emergent phenomenon: It emerges from those values and the management policies and practices that reflect the values.

Robust cultures—that is, cultures in which a consistent set of values is widely and deeply shared within the organization—can promote outstanding performance by motivating employees to behave in a coordinated manner toward a common strategy. Some robust cultures, however, provide barriers to adaptation and change implementation. Employees seek the comfortable and familiar even as the external environment is demanding new and significantly altered patterns of behavior.

Cultural values that promote adaptation and change include valuing the legitimate perspective of multiple stakeholders, especially employees, customers, and shareholders; valuing the potential of most employees to develop a commitment to achieving the performance goals of the organization; valuing high expectations that encourage employees to stretch their aspirations; valuing widespread employee participation in decision-making processes; valuing learning at both an individual and organizational level; and valuing diversity of perspectives, experience, and background. These cultural traits will help an organization change patterns of behavior in response to the dynamism of the firm's competitive environment.

A cultural audit can surface the enacted values of an organization. Because the diagnostic process has allowed employees to determine the gap between the status quo of the organization—the existing patterns of employee behavior and the values that underlie those behaviors—and the requirements of the organization's strategic response to the competitive environment, change implementation can now move to the next stage: redesigning the roles, responsibilities, and relationships of employees.

Discussion Questions

1. How can a culture such as the one at Xerox be so successful in supporting outstanding performance and at the same time be resistant to adaptation and change?
2. It has been argued that while a strong organizational culture is a necessary component of outstanding performance, it is not sufficient. Do you agree? Explain your position.

3. Why are organizations with multiple stakeholder values likely to be more adaptive than organizations that value just one stakeholder?
4. Referring to Exhibit 7–3, how might the self-sealing value loop work for a manager who holds Theory Y values?
5. If the value of employee participation in creating motivation for change is so widely recognized, why is it that managers might still resist the idea?

Case Discussion

Read "Balancing Culture and Growth At Starbucks" and prepare answers to the following questions:

1. How does the culture of Starbucks support its strategy?
2. Does rapid growth inevitably undermine a company's culture? Did it at Starbucks?

3. What steps can Starbucks take to maintain its culture while achieving desirable levels of growth?

Balancing Culture and Growth at Starbucks

Howard Schultz built Starbucks into one of the most successful companies in the United States.[32] Indeed, Starbucks has joined such other iconic American corporations as Disney and McDonald's in spreading its brand across the globe. Indeed, Schultz has come to symbolize a new breed of high successful entrepreneurs. His 2000 memoir, *Pour Your Heart into It: How Starbucks Built a Company One Cup at a Time*, became an instant best-seller. People can be forgiven if they believe Schultz was the company's founder, but this is not the case.

Starbucks, in fact, was founded in 1971. It was already a thriving, albeit small, coffee bean market in Seattle's Pike Place Market when Schultz first dropped in. At the time, he was selling kitchenware for a Swedish manufacturer. It was, he claims, love at first smell. In 1982, he moved to Seattle and joined the company as director of retail operations. A visit to an espresso bar in Milan convinced him that he had stumbled onto a viable business model that could be brought back to the Unites States. "There was nothing like this in America. It was an extension of people's front porch. It was an emotional experience. I believed intuitively we could do it. I felt it in my bones." Current Starbucks' owners resisted Schultz's urgings to expand from the bean business, so he left the company. After opening his own espresso bar, Schultz raised $3.8 million to buy the company. Starbucks was now his, and he was ready to expand, first beyond a coffee bean market and then beyond Seattle.

Under Schultz's leadership, Starbucks became "the fastest-growing retail story of all time. 'It has grown faster than McDonald's ever did.'" From nine stores in 1987, Starbucks grew to over 10,000 stores in 30 countries by 2006. In 2005, revenues reached $6.4 billion. Growth, in fact, became a particular passion of Schultz's. He expressed concern that if Starbucks did not grow rapidly, it risked being cannibalized by another chain. Revenues from his stores climbed above 20 percent annually with same store sales growing at over 10 percent. International expansion began in 1996 in Japan and has continued through Europe. By 2004, the green, familiar Starbucks' logo could be seen in over 7,500 stores worldwide. It is considered to be "possibly the most dynamic new brand and retailer to be conceived over the past two decades."

Schultz pursued a number of brand extensions as part of his strategy of growth. Some—Starbucks' branded premium coffee ice cream, bottled coffee beverages (in partnership with PepsiCo), a Starbucks Visa credit card, and a CD music label (by purchasing Hear Music)—provided quite successful. Others—a magazine named Joe published with Time and a carbonated coffee drink—proved far less so. As the company grew to $1 billion in sales, Schultz brought in professional management from Wal-Mart, Dell, and PepsiCo. "I wanted to bring in people who had experience working at $10 billion companies," he explained. Schultz's vision is to grow to 25,000 stores worldwide (McDonald's has 30,000). The stock market rewarded Starbucks' growth in spectacular fashion: Between 1992, when Starbucks' stock went public, and 2007, the stock price rose 5,000 percent.

In 2005, Jim Donald became CEO after spending 3 years as president of North America. Donald grew up in the supermarket business, having worked closely with Sam Walton to develop Wal-Mart's supermarket expansion. Schultz had first ceded the CEO position to Orin Smith in 2000 so he could focus his own energies on global strategy. Donald announced his goal as "building stores, adding emerging growth drivers, and adding to the product pipeline. We'll always be attempting to do things that are new. And if we stop doing that, then the whole entrepreneurial culture and spirit fails." Donald established a long-term goal of 30,000 stores, compared to 9,200 in April 2005. "We're going to open 1,500 this year. We're looking at top line growth of 20 percent annually in the next three to five years—and bottom line 23 to 25 percent."

In November 2006, Schultz told a CNBC reporter, "We're headed to 40,000 stores." Where will the growth occur? "We're just now getting to smaller cities. And there are 165,000 miles of U.S. roadway that haven't been tapped. I just got back from a four-market tour: Spain, Germany, Amsterdam, and Zurich. We're just scratching the surface in China. We have 1,590 stores and the potential for more than 2,000 there. We're not in India, but we're looking at it. We'd love to be in Wal-Mart parking lots with company-operated stores."

The "Third Place"

"We're profitable because of the value system of our company," insists Schultz. "American companies have failed to realize that there's tremendous value in inspiring people to share a common purpose of self-esteem, self-respect and appreciation." His stated goal was to create a culture that created a kind of partnership between employees and customers. The cozy environment of each Starbucks was meant to create what Schultz called a third place. "The first place is home," he said. "The second place is work. We are the place in between. It's a place to feel comfort. A place to feel safe. A place to feel like you belong." And, of course, to buy coffee, pastries, books, and music.

To make sure the Starbucks' culture was being maintained, the company conducted regular audits. Every 18 months, employees are asked to fill out a Partner View survey. Participation, which is voluntary, runs as high as 90 percent, because employees fill out survey on-line during company time. Plus, says the president of Starbucks Canada, "People have seen tangible results from providing us feedback."

The Tensions of Growth

Donald recognized the inherent tension between rapid growth and maintaining the culture that had been so instrumental to Starbucks' success. "I want to grow big and stay small at the same time. We want to run the company just like we did when we were one store in Pike Place Market in Seattle." A February 14, 2007 internal memo titled "The Commoditization of the Starbucks Experience" written by Howard Schultz appeared on the Starbucks Gossip blog [the memo can be found in Exhibit 7-6]. The trade-off between growth and culture, Schultz worried, had tilted too far toward growth. "Over the past ten years, in order to achieve the growth, development, and scale necessary to go from less than 1,000 stores to 13,000 stores and beyond, we have had to make a series of decisions that, in retrospect, have lead to the watering down of the Starbucks experience, and, what some might call the commoditization of our brand."

Schultz was especially concerned with the lack of in-store coffee scent and the cookie-cutter feel of the stores. Automatic espresso machines "solved a major problem in terms of speed and service," but "eliminated the smell of beans being ground." Those decisions, all of which had been approved by Schultz himself, were giving Starbucks the feel of a chain store rather than a third place. Schultz concluded with a

From: Howard Schultz

Sent: Wednesday, February 14, 2007 10:39 AM Pacific Standard Time

To: Jim Donald

Cc: Anne Saunders; Dave Pace; Dorothy Kim; Gerry Lopez; Jim Alling; Ken Lombard; Martin Coles; Michael Casey; Michelle Gass; Paula Boggs; Sandra Taylor

Subject: The Commoditization of the Starbucks Experience

As you prepare for the FY 08 strategic planning process, I want to share some of my thoughts with you.

Over the past ten years, in order to achieve the growth, development, and scale necessary to go from less than 1,000 stores to 13,000 stores and beyond, we have had to make a series of decisions that, in retrospect, have lead to the watering down of the Starbucks experience, and, what some might call the commoditization of our brand.

Many of these decisions were probably right at the time, and on their own merit would not have created the dilution of the experience; but in this case, the sum is much greater and, unfortunately, much more damaging than the individual pieces. For example, when we went to automatic espresso machines, we solved a major problem in terms of speed of service and efficiency. At the same time, we overlooked the fact that we would remove much of the romance and theatre that was in play with the use of the La Marzocca machines. This specific decision became even more damaging when the height of the machines, which are now in thousands of stores, blocked the visual sight line the customer previously had to watch the drink being made, and for the intimate experience with the barista. This, coupled with the need for fresh roasted coffee in every North America city and every international market, moved us toward the decision and the need for flavor locked packaging. Again, the right decision at the right time, and once again I believe we overlooked the cause and the affect of flavor lock in our stores. We achieved fresh roasted bagged coffee, but at what cost? The loss of aroma—perhaps the most powerful non-verbal signal we had in our stores; the loss of our people scooping fresh coffee from the bins and grinding it fresh in front of the customer, and once again stripping the store of tradition and our heritage? Then we moved to store design. Clearly we have had to streamline store design to gain efficiencies of scale and to make sure we had the ROI on sales to investment ratios that would satisfy the financial side of our business. However, one of the results has been stores that no longer have the soul of the past and reflect a chain of stores vs. the warm feeling of a neighborhood store. Some people even call our stores sterile, cookie cutter, no longer reflecting the passion our partners feel about our coffee. In fact, I am not sure people today even know we are roasting coffee. You certainly can't get the message from being in our stores. The merchandise, more art than science, is far removed from being the merchant that I believe we can be and certainly at a minimum should support the foundation of our coffee heritage. Some stores don't have coffee grinders, French presses from Bodum, or even coffee filters.

Now that I have provided you with a list of some of the underlying issues that I believe we need to solve, let me say at the outset that we have all been part of these decisions. I take full responsibility myself, but we desperately need to look into the mirror and realize it's time to get back to the core and make the changes necessary to evoke the heritage, the tradition, and the passion that we all have for the true Starbucks experience. While the current state of affairs for the most part is self induced, that has lead to competitors of all kinds, small and large coffee companies, fast food operators, and mom and pops, to position themselves in a way that creates awareness, trial and loyalty of people who previously have been Starbucks customers. This must be eradicated.

I have said for 20 years that our success is not an entitlement and now it's proving to be a reality. Let's be smarter about how we are spending our time, money and resources. Let's get back to the core. Push for innovation and do the things necessary to once again differentiate Starbucks from all others. We source and buy the highest quality coffee. We have built the most trusted brand in coffee in the world, and we have an enormous responsibility to both the people who have come before us and the 150,000 partners and their families who are relying on our stewardship.

Finally, I would like to acknowledge all that you do for Starbucks. Without your passion and commitment, we would not be where we are today. Onward . . .

EXHIBIT 7-6   Valentine's Day Memo.

call for Starbucks to "get back to the core. Push for innovation and do the things necessary to once again differentiate Starbucks from all others."

Throughout 2007 Starbucks' stock plummeted (from $36.29 in January 2007 to 18.38 in January 2008). Coffee competition from both McDonald's and Dunkin' Donuts ate into same store sales. In January 2008, conceding that "we lost the focus that we once had, and that is the customer," Schultz removed James Donald and placed himself in the CEO role. He would slow down domestic growth, Schultz promised, shift resources to international expansion. "Starbucks is not a broken company," he said. "Just as we created this problem, we can fix it."

In his first month, Schultz took a number of specific steps: closing 100 underperforming stores, scaling back on domestic expansion plans, and eliminating the sale of heated breakfast sandwiches whose aroma overpowered the smell of the coffee itself. His most dramatic step came in February 2008 when all 7,100 U.S. stores closed simultaneously for three hours to conduct an in-store training session for employees. Employees first watched a video massage from Schultz. "This is not about training," he said. "This is about the love and compassion and commitment that we all need to have for our customers." Employees then talked about new approaches to improve taste and texture and to improve the customer's experience. One store manager commented immediately after the session, "It's really inspiring to talk about the quality of our expresso when we're here all in the same room."

Rival Dunkin' Donuts took advantage of the well-publicized shutdown of all Starbucks stores by offering $1 lattes during the same three-hour period.

Endnotes

1. This case is based on information from Douglas K. Smith and Robert C. Alexander, *Fumbling the Future: How Xerox Invented, Then Ignored, the First Personal Computer* (New York: Morrow, 1988); John P. Kotter and James L. Heskett, *Corporate Culture and Performance* (New York: Free Press, 1992); Bert Spector, *Taking Charge and Letting Go: A Breakthrough Strategy for Creating and Managing the Horizontal Company* (New York: Free Press, 1995); and Anthony Bianco and Pamela L. Moore, "Xerox: The Downfall," *BusinessWeek Online*, March 5, 2001, p. 2.

2. Kotter and Heskett, *Corporate Culture and Performance*, pp. 76–77.

3. Terrence E. Deal and Allan A. Kennedy, *Corporate Cultures: The Rites and Rituals of Corporate Life* (Reading, MA: Addison-Wesley, 1982), p. 4.

4. John Battele, *The Search: How Google and Its Rivals Rewrote the Rules of Business and Transformed Our Culture* (New York: Penguin Books, 2005); David Vise and Mark Malseed, *The Google Story* (New York: Delacortte Press, 2005); and Thomas R. Eisenmann and Kerry Herman, *Google, Inc.* (Boston: Harvard Business School Publishing, 2005).

5. Geert Hofstede, *Cultures and Organizations: Software of the Mind* (New York: McGraw-Hill, 1991).

6. John Battele, "The 70 Percent Solution," *Business 2.0*, December 2005, p. 134.

7. Andrew Pettigrew, *The Awakening Giant: Continuity and Change in Imperial Chemical Industries* (Oxford: Blackwell, 1985).

8. Kotter and Heskett, *Corporate Culture and Performance*.

9. Daniel R. Denison, *Corporate Culture and Organizational Effectiveness* (New York: Wiley, 1990), p. 2.

10. Jennifer A. Chatman and Sandra Eunyoung Cha, "Leading by Leveraging Culture," *California Management Review* 45 (Summer 2003), p. 21.

11. This finding is documented in Kotter and Heskett, *Corporate Culture and Performance*.

12. Quoted in Ross Petty, Virginia Soyberl, Phyllis Schlesinger, and Al Anderson, *Albert Dunlop and Corporate Transformation* (A) (Boston: Babson College, 1999), p. 6.

13. Kotter and Heskett, *Corporate Culture and Performance*.

14. *Ibid.*, p. 46.

15. Douglas McGregor, *The Human Side of Enterprise* (New York: McGraw-Hill, 1960).

16. *Ibid.*, p. 48.

17. Frank Heller, Eugen Pusic, George Strauss, and Bernhard Wilpert, *Organizational Participation: Myth and Reality* (New York: Oxford University Press, 1998), p. 10.

18. David A. Garvin, "Building a Learning Organization," *Harvard Business Review* (July–August 1993), p. 80.

19. David A. Thomas and Robin J Ely, "Making Differences Matter: A New Paradigm for Managing Diversity," *Harvard Business Review* (September–October 1996), p. 85.

20. Information on Nokia is from Yves Doz, José Santos, and Peter Williamson, *From Global to Metanational: How Companies Win in the Knowledge Economy* (Boston: Harvard Business School Press, 2001).

21. The notion of global mindset is explored in Anil K. Gupta and Vijay Govindarajan, "Cultivating a Global Mindset," *Academy of Management Executive* 16 (2002), pp. 116–126; Thomas M. Begley and David P. Boyd, "The Need for a Corporate Global Mind-Set," *Sloan Management Review* 44 (Winter 2003), pp. 25–32; Nina Nummela, Sami Saarenketo, and Kaisu Puumalainen, "A Global Mindset—A Prerequisite for Successful Internationalization?" *Canadian Journal of Administrative Sciences* 21 (March 2004), pp. 51–64; John O'Connell, "Global Mindset," *Blackwell Encyclopedia of International Management* (2005), p. 179; and Catherine Bolgar, "Corporations Need a Global Mindset to Succeed in Today's Multipolar Business World," *Wall Street Journal*, June 18, 2007.

22. That phrase is from Panda Getaway, *Redefining Global Strategy: Crossing Borders in a World Where Differences Still Matter* (Boston: Harvard Business School Press, 2007).

23. Quoted in William E. Taylor, "The Logic of Global Business: An Interview with ABB's Percy Barnevik," *Harvard Business Review* 69 (March–April 1991), p. 94.

24. Quoted from Collins and Porras, *Built to Last*, pp. 88–90.

25. Brian Gruley and Russ Smith, "Keys to Success Left Kenneth Lay Open to Disaster," *Wall Street Journal*, April 26, 2002, p. A5.

26. Gary Hamel, *Leading the Revolution* (Boston: Harvard Business School Press, 2000), p. 213.

27. Chris Argyris and Donald A. Schön, *Organizational Learning II: Theory, Method, Practice* (Reading, MA: Addison-Wesley, 1996), p. 13.

28. Edgar H. Schein, *The Corporate Culture Survival Guide: Sense and Nonsense About Culture Change* (San Francisco: Jossey-Bass Publishers, 1999).

29. Thomas A. Stewart and Louise O'Brien, "Transforming an Industrial Giant: An Interview with Heinrich von Pierer," *Harvard Business Review* (February 2005), p. 117.

30. *Ibid.*, pp. 97–99.

31. *Ibid.*, p. 98.

32. This case is based on the following publications: Naomi Weiss, "How Starbucks Impassions Workers to Drive Growth," *Workforce* 77 (August 1998); Kate Bonamici, "Hot Starbucks to Go," *Fortune*, January 26, 2004; Kristen Millares Bolt, "Jim Donald Brings New Energy to Starbucks CEO Post," *Seattle Post-Intelligencer Reporter*, March 31, 2005; Calvin Leung, "Culture Club," *Canadian Business*, October 9, 2006; Matthew Creamer, "Starbucks Wakes Up and Smells the Death of Its Brand Experience," *Advertising Age*, February 26, 2007; Joe Nocera, "Talking Business: A Double Shot of Nostalgia for Starbucks," *New York Times*, March 3, 2007; and Michael M. Grynbaum and Andrew Martin, "Starbucks Takes a 3-Hour Coffee Break," *New York Times*, February 27, 2008, p. C1.

CHAPTER 8

Leading Change

At every stage of organizational change, leaders intervene to oversee and orchestrate implementation. That reliance on the effective orchestration by leaders in a change process is true not just for top executives but also for leaders throughout the organization. Implementation depends not just on oversight and orchestration by individual leaders. Effective change demands the coordinated efforts of multiple leaders.

Although the role of leaders in implementation underlies much of what has appeared earlier, this chapter will offer more focused attention on the enactment of that leadership role. In particular, the chapter will:

- Define effective leadership
- Explore the difficulty of enacting effective leadership
- Delineate the tasks associated with leading change
- Analyze the requirements for developing future leaders in an organization

First, we will examine the difficulties faced by a leader whose personality and style appeared to be at odds with his attempt to implement strategic renewal and organizational change.

ROBERT HORTON AT BRITISH PETROLEUM

The appointment of Robert Horton as CEO of British Petroleum (BP) sent shock waves through that conservative, many said stuffy, British company.[1] Not that Horton's rise to the top was such a surprise. He had been with BP since leaving university, moving frequently and with apparent success through a number of operations.

When he landed in the United States, Horton assumed control of one of the company's largest subsidiaries, Standard Oil (soon renamed BP America). During his years in the States, Horton became an outspoken champion of the "American Way": a hard-driving, high visibility, performance-oriented leadership style. Perhaps that was the source of the shock: the fact that Horton vowed on his return to the United Kingdom to "Americanize" the ailing British giant.

There was little doubt that BP needed renewal when Horton took control. The company was mired in poor performance, not just in its core businesses such as oil and chemicals, but also in unrelated businesses—detergents and animal feed, for example— into which they had recently ventured. Internal attitude surveys of executives and non-executives alike revealed deep confusion and uncertainty about the future (more than half of the respondents at all levels could not say what the company's strategy was or where it was headed) and frustration over the lack of flexibility and low levels of co-ordination within and across the organization.

Horton vowed to lead BP through a change process that would replace what he described as a distrustful, power hoarding "civil service" culture with an attitude of "open thinking, personal impact, empowering, and networking." He was determined, he said, "to make this organization a damned sight quicker and smarter than the opposition." And to do that, he said, he would release "the ingenuity of our people."

At the same time, employees worried. Horton's past aggressiveness in workforce reduction had earned him the nickname, "Horton the Hatchet." Were words like "open thinking" and "empowering" and vows to work through his people meant to gloss over the hard realities of massive layoffs and centralized control? Or did they reflect deeply held convictions that would allow Horton to remake BP into a collaborative, high commitment organization capable of sustained outstanding performance? This was the debate that pervaded BP as employees looked for actions to back up the words.

Horton began by slashing half the jobs at corporate headquarters (moving from 2,400 to 1,200), then eliminating 80 of the 86 corporate committees used to run BP's complex international matrix structure. Virtually all employees were ordered to attend two- or three-day training workshops focused on problem solving and change management.

During this time, corporate performance continued to plunge: profits fell by 85 percent. Attributing BP's performance woes to an ever-deepening and lingering national recession, Horton undertook another round of job cuts.

Employee surveys taken a year after Horton's arrival surfaced deep skepticism about the CEO's true beliefs and the degree to which his actions and words aligned. Horton, in the view of the majority of employees, imposed rather than fostered change. He spoke of openness while hoarding power and centralizing control.

Horton gave an interview to the American magazine *Forbes* which seemed to galvanize their worries. The article concluded with the following paragraph:

> There are moments, Horton confesses, when he wishes he could deal with some of his problems more quickly, rather than waiting for his subordinates to deal with them on their own. But that, he recognizes, would be self-defeating to his goal of producing an efficient and responsive organization. "Because I am blessed with my good brain I tend to get to the right answer rather quicker and more often than most people. That will sound frightfully arrogant, but it's true. So I have to rein in my impatience."[2]

Many observers took those words, which were widely reported across the United Kingdom, as a tacit admission on Horton's part that his heart was not in the direction of the renewal he had been promoting for the past two years.

Less than four months after the interview appeared, BP's board asked for and received Horton's resignation. Board members had become convinced, they admitted, that Horton's personality led him to concentrate power in his own hands to the detriment of the entire organization.

UNDERSTANDING LEADERSHIP

When he became CEO of British Petroleum, Robert Horton appeared to be positioned perfectly to lead change. He was strong, firm, and decisive, in possession of an impressive résumé. The board lined up solidly behind him. Yet none of that seemed to help.

Horton's intention to transform the company butted up against the manner in which he intervened. Desirous of building an atmosphere of trust based on power sharing, he took actions that instead created suspicion and cynicism. Horton's attempt to be an effective change leader, in other words, floundered on his difficulty in exercising effective change leadership.

The distinction between the formal job of *leader* and the act of exercising *leadership* is an important one to understand. To be a **formal leader** requires some legitimate grant of authority to an individual. In that role, the formal leader makes decisions vital to the future of the company. To see that role played out, we can revisit Xerox, described in Chapter 7 as a company in severe decline. After a great deal of turmoil at the top of the organization, Ann Mulcahy led the company back from near bankruptcy and financial scandal. While reducing head count from 90,000 to 30,000, she maintained spending on research and development. By 2005, two-thirds of the company's revenues came from new products developed internally.[3]

Deciding how and where to allocate resources is only one of the key roles played by formal leaders. They also represent the organization to multiple internal and external constituencies, embody the culture and values of the company, mediate internal disputes and conflicts, even occasionally serve as marketing symbols (such as Dave Thomas of Wendy's or Frank Purdue of Purdue Farms).

Building a Vocabulary of Change
Formal leader an individual who is granted authority, usually based on hierarchical position, in an organization.

Theory into Practice

Formal leaders have important roles to play as decision-makers, resource-allocators, and occasionally even company symbols.

Leadership is something different from that formal role, as important as it is. Leadership involves specific interventions aimed at motivating behavioral change among employees. Formal leaders can exercise leadership, of course. Individuals who reside elsewhere in the organization can also undertake interventions to implement change. At whatever level, effective **leadership** can be understood as a set of activities or behaviors that mobilize adaptive behavior on the part of members of the organization.[4]

Building a Vocabulary of Change
Leadership actions that mobilize adaptive behavior within an organization

---

Theory into Practice

Think of leadership as an intervention into the organization designed to impact the behaviors of others.

Thinking of change leadership as an intervention designed to mobilize adaptive behaviors focuses attention away from the particular individuals who reside at the head of an organizational hierarchy. Instead of examining the traits or personalities of individual leaders, change leadership involves actions and behaviors. The effectiveness of change leadership will be judged not by personalities and traits but by the impact those actions and behaviors exert on the change process.

Theory into Practice

Effective leadership can be exercised at all levels of an organization.

Effective leadership can be found in three separate but interrelated notions. First, effective change leadership affects the *behaviors* of others in the organization. No matter how talented an individual may be or what personal traits that individual may possess, she alone will be unable to create and sustain outstanding performance. How employees react in response to the actions of leaders will determine the effectiveness of leadership. No individual is an effective leader unless and until employees behave in effective ways. In terms of change leadership, the behavior of leaders is meant to impact changes in the behavior of followers.

Theory into Practice

Effective change leadership mobilizes adaptive behavior on the part of organizational members.

Second, the term *mobilize* implies that the mechanism used to help shape behavior will be internalized motivation. Leader actions that result in compliant reactions on the part of employees—following orders and adhering to rules in order to achieve extrinsic rewards and/or to avoid negative consequences—fail that definition of effectiveness. Mobilizing employees involves affecting an internalized commitment to the achievement of mutual goals. Leadership behavior that creates dependency or alienation on the part of employees undermines mobilization; by definition, then, it is ineffective. Effective leadership motivates, organizes, orients, and focuses attention on the achievement of organizational goals.[5]

The third aspect of effective leadership—mobilizing *adaptive* behavior— suggests that not all behaviors resulting from the actions of leaders are equally desirable. The distinction is between effective leadership and the effective exercise of power. Formal leaders may exert a powerful influence over followers without exercising effective leadership. Influential individuals can induce followers to take actions that may be, literally, self-destructive (e.g., Jim Jones and the members of the People's Temple) or destructive to the continued efficacy of the organization (e.g., Kenneth Lay, Jeffrey Skilling, and the employees of Enron). As powerful and influential as these individuals were, they were not exercising effective leadership. Effectiveness is determined by the degree to which employee behavior is adaptive; moving people in a direction that is in the long-term best interests of employees and the organization.[6]

THE TASKS OF LEADERSHIP

Dissatisfied and demanding leaders often attempt to impose change on their organization. Think of the examples we have run into already:

- Morgan Smith, president of the Concord Bookshop, imposed a new management structure as a way of reducing costs and meeting competitive pressures from online booksellers (Chapter 1).
- Bob Nardelli arrived at Home Depot and brought with him the operating efficiencies that had worked for him at General Electric (Chapter 3).
- Louis Gerstner created a global matrix in order to integrate IBM's highly autonomous national operations (Chapter 6).
- Robert Horton told BP employees that concepts such as "open thinking" and "empowerment" would drive a needed cultural transformation (this chapter).

The results, as we have also seen, were disappointing and frustrating. Effective leadership is not about imposing new directions and demanding new behaviors. Instead, effective change leaders energize an organization for change, build commitment to new directions, and then put into place a process that will translate such commitment into action.[7]

Theory into Practice

Strong, demanding leaders don't always succeed at leading change.

Although all organizations and circumstances differ, it is possible to suggest there are five core tasks that lie at the heart of effective change leadership. Those tasks, summarized in Exhibit 8-1, place greater emphasis on what the leader does rather than who the leader is.

Develop and Communicate Purpose

Building a Vocabulary of Change
Organizational purpose a clearly articulated and well defined ambition for the organization

Leadership starts by identifying and articulating organizational purpose. **Organizational purpose** is something broader and less specifically operational than strategy, less connected to the vagaries of the shifting competitive environment. Worldwide Pants, a television production company founded by late-night host David Letterman, has a clear purpose: *whatever makes Dave laugh*.[8]

Develop and articulate *clear and consistent sense of purpose and direction* for the organization

Establish *demanding performance* expectations

Enable *upward communication*

Forge an *emotional bond* between employees and the organization

Develop *future change leaders*

EXHIBIT 8-1 Core Tasks of Change Leadership.

The Internet-based social networking giant MySpace, owned now by Rupert Murdoch's News Corporation, served the purpose of Tom Anderson's "intimate, primal" interests of linking with "cool" people and promoting "cool" projects.[9] That drive for "cool" created a business model that opened MySpace up to far more creativity and its more constrained rival, Facebook. As MySpace grew and came under the ownership of a large media conglomerate, outsiders worried that the sight would lose its strategic hold on cool social networking. Co-founder Chris DeWolfe insisted that the openness of the culture would protect it from such commoditizing. "We're not deciding what's cool," he insisted, "our users are. MySpace is about letting people be what they want to be."[10] That clear and consistent sense of propose supported MySpace's strategic dominance of the social networking community.

Purpose involves a "clearly articulated, well-defined ambition" for the organization, an ambition that engenders "strong, enduring emotional attachments" among employees and remains constant over time.[11] By articulating a clear and consistent purpose, leaders enhance the effectiveness of change implementation in a number of ways:

- A common sense of direction and goals allows decentralized decision making and greater autonomy over enacting that purpose.
- Autonomy places decision-making authority in the hands of employees who are best able to respond, and respond quickly, to a dynamic environment.
- Additionally, common purpose enhances the ability of an organization to achieve required levels of coordination and teamwork.
- Leaders at operational levels can formulate strategy to help advance that purpose and then change the strategy in response to or anticipation of a dynamic environment.

Organizational purpose provides a steady framework that helps shape strategic responsiveness (summarized in Exhibit 8-2).

Theory into Practice

A widespread and common understanding of organizational purpose allows employees to exercise greater autonomy in moving the change effort in its desired direction.

Supports decentralized decision making	Common sense of direction and goals allows employees at multiple levels to make decisions that further overall purpose of organization
Supports enhanced autonomy	Employees at all levels understand purpose and goals and can respond quickly and effectively to dynamic environment
Supports coordination	Employees working toward a common goal better able to coordinate their efforts

EXHIBIT 8-2 Shared Purpose Helps Change Implementation.

Establish Demanding Performance Goals

In his study of the most effective U.S. CEOs in terms of leading their companies through a leap from "good to great," Collins observed a trait they all had in common. The most effective leaders shared a "ferocious desire" to achieve sustained outstanding performance for their companies. They were, says Jim Collins, "fanatically driven, infected with an incurable need to produce *results*."[12] Effective change efforts are firmly rooted in that focused drive to achieve outstanding performance.[13]

Theory into Practice

Effective change efforts are built on a drive to achieve outstanding performance.

Building a Vocabulary of Change
Stretch goals clearly articulated and challenging performance expectations.

Jack Welch talked about **stretch goals** as a way of keeping employees focused on outstanding performance during a transformation. During his tenure as head of General Electric, Welch's emphasis was largely on financial goals. Welch's successor, Jeff Immelt, refocused expectations to emphasize innovation and customer responsiveness as GE's new stretch targets.

Establishing demanding performance goals supports change by focusing employee motivation and commitment on the goal of achieving outstanding performance.[14] It is that interconnection between achieving outstanding performance and employee commitment to change that makes this a core task of change leadership. It is the conviction that, given high performance goals—coupled with the requisite levels of autonomy and resources—employees will adopt the behaviors required to meet those goals.

Enable Upward Communication

Building a Vocabulary of Change
Upward communication the flow of information from lower to higher hierarchical levels in an organization

Effective leaders communicate *downward* to make sure employees at all levels understand in a clear and consistent way the purpose and direction of the firm. But effective organizations need **upward communication** as well. The simple fact is that employees further down the organizational hierarchy are well positioned to know things vital to the organization. Employees possess "local knowledge" about customers, competitors, and how the products and services of the organization meet the shifting needs of the marketplace that need to be communicated upward in an organization.

Through their everyday interaction with customers, suppliers, and peers, employees develop experience-based, tacit knowledge.[15] If that knowledge is not allowed to impact decision making in a direct and immediate way, organizations can find themselves in trouble. Employees can communicate upwardly both the need for change and the degree to which management's response is addressing that need. That is why a vital task of effective leadership is to enable upward communication.

Theory into Practice

Effective leadership involves listening, engaging, and learning as well as communicating.

Knowledge possessed by employees at lower hierarchical levels puts them in an excellent position to understand the degree to which the change goals articulated and pursued by upper management are both being implemented and achieving the desired results. The top management team that ran Asda, the U.K. grocery chain, learned the hard way that not enabling upward communication can lead to difficulties during a change process.

Theory into Practice

Particularly in situations of strategic renewal and change, formal leaders need to learn about how their effects are proceeding through a process of mutual engagement with employees at all organizational levels.

Asda's leaders formulated a new strategy for the chain, previously known as a discount store for working-class customers. They would move upmarket to capture highly profitable wealthy shoppers. As they directed that new strategy from above, however, store managers experienced a troubling reality: Old, loyal customers were discarded without being replenished from this new, desired niche. Upper management failed to create mechanisms to allow store managers to communicate upwardly that the chain's strategy was seriously flawed. Top management never learned—at least until the company faced bankruptcy—that their new strategy was not working.

To help ensure that knowledge lodged at lower hierarchical levels is captured, discussed, and acted upon, organizational leaders can enable upward communication by three steps:

1. Top executives can *acknowledge*, both to themselves and to the organization, that they do not know everything that needs to be known about the organization and its competitive environment. That acknowledgment needs to include the explicit recognition that they need to learn from lower-level employees.
2. Executives can *create channels* for information to flow upward in an uncluttered and unfiltered way. These channels often take the form of direct contact and communication between upper management and lower-level employees. Taken by themselves, such tactics—management-by-walking-around, internal comment and suggestion cards, "graffiti walls" where employees' comments are posted—may seem superficial and programmatic. They can and do become real when upper management seriously seeks and values such input.
3. Executives can also *push decision-making authority down* to lower levels, allowing employees to exert authority and take responsibility for the organizational-environmental interface. CEOs such as USAA's Robert McDermott and Komatsu's Tetsuya Katada expected employees at lower levels to make decisions on policies relating to customer service and even strategic opportunities for growth.

For implementation to stay on track, knowledge of whether interventions are working must be communicated upward and shared in a timely and candid way with top management.

Forge an Emotional Bond between Employees and the Organization

Building a Vocabulary of Change

Emotional bond a relationship between individuals and their organizations based on a deeply felt commitment to the organization's purpose and goals

Organizations consist of individuals who possess skills, competencies, and knowledge. Their connection to the organization is, in part, instrumental: They exchange those skills, competencies, and knowledge for the rewards provided by the organization. To transform an organization from a collection of individuals (even highly talented individuals) into a coordinated, interdependent unit requires a bond that transcends instrumentality. A deeper **emotional bond** provides a robust source of support for change when a company enters a transformational period.[16] One of the key tasks of change leadership, therefore, is to forge just such an emotional and personal attachment between employee and employer.

Organizational leaders can use their position to personify an emotional attachment among employees. Herb Kelleher, Southwest Airline's CEO for nearly three decades of profitability, helped create and sustain a bond that employees came to refer to explicitly as "love" (Love Field in Dallas, after all, served as Southwest's hub airport).[17] He involved himself in virtually every aspect of the business, from handing out onboard peanuts to dropping in on maintenance workers at 3 A.M. in Southwest hangars with coffee and doughnuts. That involvement had both a symbolic and operational aspect to it: providing employees with direct access to a CEO with whom they were on a first-name basis while simultaneously offering employees an up-close-and-personal opportunity to see and experience Kelleher as the human embodiment of the company's values and principles.

An emotional bond encourages employees to coordinate their efforts, communicate more honestly and freely, take the risks required of creativity, and manage conflicts in ways that benefit the organization. By locating a sense of purpose and meaning within the organization's mission and goals, employees are ready and willing to make sacrifices on behalf of the organization, to act in ways that are informed by the organization's core values and renewed strategies, and to alter behaviors in ways that enhance the company's performance.

The instrumental exchange of effort for reward cannot be overlooked in any organization. The drive to acquire—that is, the desire of individuals to boost their share of scarce resources—is fundamental to human nature. But it is not the *only* fundamental human drive. People also have a need to bond, to form networks, to be part of mutually reinforcing relationships.[18]

Leaders who fail to create the opportunity for emotional bonding will find it difficult to generate high levels of commitment to change. "It's hard to get excited about 15 percent return on equity," said a manager in a transforming organization.[19] Outstanding financial performance is a necessary, even appealing aim of change, but there needs to be more. Emotional bonds are much more than niceties of a pleasant business environment; they support outstanding performance and create a work context open to change.

Develop Future Leaders

Companies that retain market domination over long periods tend to develop leaders internally.[20] Paying attention to the development of leadership assures a strong pipeline of individuals capable of supporting transformation, both now and in the future. Jack Welch spent more of his time at the helm of General Electric on senior executive development than any other matter. GE, in fact, became so good at developing leaders that it was a major—probably *the* major—supplier of CEOs to other Fortune 100 companies. When the board of Ikon Office Solutions hired a new CEO from General Electric Lighting, the company's human resource director noted, "When a company needs a loan, it goes to a bank. When a company needs a CEO, it goes to General Electric."[21]

Some have argued that leadership is an inherent trait; that leads are "born, not made." Consultant Ron Morris observes, "Did you not pretty much know who the 'leader' of your Cub Scout pack was way back in 1955? He was the guy leading, was he not?" Nobody teaches leaders how to lead. While individuals may learn confidence and resourcefulness, "leadership is an art, and therefore it simply cannot be taught."[22] However, most observers accept the argument that leadership can be developed. "The truth is that leaders are made, not born," says consultant John Baldoni. "Leadership is developed by learning and refining a set of skills—skills that anyone, including you and me, can learn and develop."[23] Given a combination of experience, training, and circumstances, a wide array of individuals can be called upon to play leadership roles in an organization.

Failure to address the requirement for effective change leadership can prove disastrous. Paul Lawrence and Davis Dyer documented how the U.S. steel industry suffered from inadequate development of effective leadership.[24] Whether it was U.S. Steel, Bethlehem Steel, or the other companies that dominated the industry for decades, leadership development followed a common pattern. Future executives typically entered their organizations at a low level, worked their way up through a single function, then assumed top positions without the requisite skills to exercise effective leadership. Inadequate, poorly developed leadership drained the capacity of those companies to respond to the tide of global competition in the 1980s and 1990s. Nonadaptiveness in an organization or even an industry can be traced in no small part to the manner in which leaders are developed.

Theory into Practice

Inadequate attention to leadership development can ruin a company, even an industry.

With narrowly focused functional managers rather than broadly based leaders, organizations become nonresponsive. It is virtually impossible to mobilize adaptive behavior on the part of others when the individuals who sit atop the hierarchy are themselves engaging in nonadaptive behavior. The lack of time, resources, and attention paid to the development of future leaders can ultimately undermine a company's ability to maintain outstanding performance.

Even organizations committed to "making" future change leaders often find that the manner in which they are going about development fails to produce the desired results. In 2000, U.S. Army Chief of Staff General Eric Shinseki wondered why, despite all the attention paid to officer development, the military was still producing officers who lacked the ability to innovate and think creatively.[25]

A resulting study uncovered a pattern of leadership development that hampered the military's stated desire to transform itself into a more flexible organization. "Soldiers shuttle through units with dizzying rapidity," the report concluded. "Two-thirds of army personnel change stations every year, and the average officer spends only 18 months at each assignment over the course of a 25-year career."[26] Military personnel failed to develop key skills: an ability to create and sustain cohesiveness over time and a competency to implement organizational change effectively. The military's approach to leadership development was itself a barrier to the development of effective leadership.

Theory into Practice

Rapid upward movement of personnel through the hierarchy can work to hurt an organization's ability to develop effective leadership.

Rapid upward mobility is only one of the traditional development practices that can undermine the development of individuals capable of effective leadership (summarized in Exhibit 8-3).

Practice	Barrier
Rapid upward mobility	Prevents individuals from having to live with consequences of their actions and learning from their successes and failures.
Movement within a single function	Individuals never gain knowledge of total organization, particularly of how subunits fit together.
Short-term performance pressures	Individuals get better at tactical and operational management than at long-term strategic and visionary leadership.
Recruitment for specific technical skills	Internal employee pool is thin on individuals with real leadership potential.

EXHIBIT 8-3 Organizational Barriers to Effective Leadership Development.
Based on John P. Kotter, *The Leadership Factor* (New York: Free Press, 1988).

In order to learn how to lead change effectively, John Kotter suggests future leaders experience a number of situations:

- Work through coalitions rather than rely on hierarchical authority.
- Formulate visions and strategies rather than planning and managing budgets.
- Communicate purpose and build commitment rather than issuing reports and creating policies.
- Think in long-term time horizons rather than immediate results.
- Work with an organization's culture and not its formal structures.[27]

Approaching leadership development in a strategic manner while understanding that effective leaders can be "made" through experience, feedback, assessment, and training will provide a source of future leadership and support change.

BEYOND INDIVIDUAL LEADERSHIP

The exercise of change leadership is not limited to any one individual in an organization. Given the realities of today's business environment, the notion that any one individual can change an entire organization is inadequate. An increasingly dynamic competitive environment, especially when coupled with the growing complexity of organizations themselves, requires that effective change leadership be exercised by many people on multiple organizational levels.

Reliance on an individual decision maker, no matter how talented he might be, can actually undermine the effectiveness of a change effort. Think of the following potential consequences of a strong, individual leader:

- High levels of dependency can displace individual and group initiative.
- That dependency, in turn, can slow decision making.
- Providing the candid feedback required of learning and adaptation to any leader in possession of such singular power can become a risky, to-be-avoided venture.
- A dominant leader, particularly one who sees the exercise of leadership on the part of others as a direct threat, might be unable to build the sense of teamwork and shared responsibility required to sustain coordinated effort.

Dominant individual leaders such as Robert Horton at BP can create an internal dynamic that builds dependency while stifling initiative, innovation, teamwork, and change. Instead of being centralized within an individual, change leadership can be exercised both vertically and horizontally in the organization. Vertically means that organizations allow and encourage leadership to be exerted up and down the formal hierarchy. Horizontally means that leadership is exercised across the organization, in multiple divisions and units. Changing an organization—at multiple levels and across numerous units—is a challenge that requires distributed rather than individual leadership. Dominant individual leaders may allow—even inadvertently encourage—others to back away from the exercise of change leadership.

Theory into Practice

Dominating individual leaders can actually hurt an organization's ability to change.

Moving from individual leadership is desirable, but it is not easily achieved. The attitudes, decision-making style, and skill sets of top executives can all reinforce individual rather than shared leadership. Start with attitudes. Top executives often conceive their roles in independent rather than *inter*dependent terms, leading them away from the sense of shared responsibility so vital to teamwork. Especially when an organization has grown largely through acquisition, top executives can conceive their roles as highly autonomous individuals, resenting efforts to "impose" on them a sense of collective responsibility.

The management style of the chief executive can also influence the behaviors of other organizational leaders. The key variable here is the degree to which the chief executive insists on a tight hold over the reins of decision making. Shared leadership requires decentralized decision making. In a highly centralized situation, the chief executive controls the decision making, while other top executives engage in what is essentially political behavior aimed at preserving one's own position, turf, and power. Responsiveness to a highly dynamic environment requires that multiple leaders be involved in decision making, particularly around the question of how the organization's purpose and strategy are to be implemented.

Finally, top management teams often have a difficult time engaging in disagreement and debate over important strategic issues.[28] Executives often carry with them an assumption concerning disagreement and debate that also works against the desire to enhance employee influence. That view can be stated quite simply: Consensus is good, argument is bad. In what has been labeled the "unity view" of organizations,[29] managers often believe that diversity of opinions, debate, and conflict are best avoided.

The Challenge of "Walking the Talk"

Reflecting on his experience reversing the lagging fortunes of Nissan Motors, Carlos Ghosn talked about the importance of aligning leaders' actions with words. "Top management is highly visible," he noted. "What we think, what we say, and what we do must be the same." Discrepancies between words and actions, he warned, could "spell disaster."[30] The discrepancy between words and actions, as an example, undermined Robert Horton's attempt to transform British Petroleum by spreading suspicion and distrust among employees.

Ghosn addressed the requirement for leaders to align espoused values—the values of leadership that individuals profess to believe—with enacted values—the values that underlie their actual behaviors.*

Effective change implementation requires high levels of commitment among employees, a strong sense of shared purpose and partnership, and a climate of trust that supports candid communication, open inquiry, and joint problem solving.

During his first two years as president of Johnsonville Sausage, Ralph Stayer's effort focused on the behaviors of his direct reports. He hoped to instill a heightened sense of confidence, autonomy, initiative, and creativity among his top executives. Frustrated by his inability to achieve those goals, Stayer initially blamed *them*: They

---

*For a further discussion of espoused and enacted values, see Chapter 4.

were simply not rising to the challenge. It took Stayer two years to understand that the failure was *his*, not theirs—that is, his behaviors were inconsistent with his stated objectives:

> I didn't really *want* them [his direct reports] to make independent decisions. I wanted them to make the decisions I would have made. Deep down, I was still in love with my own control. I was just making people guess what I wanted instead of telling them.[31]

It was not until he aligned his actions with his goals and allowed real decision making on the part of his top executives that he was able to shape a real problem-solving team.

Conclusion

The intervention of leaders is critical in determining the effectiveness of an organization's change implementation. In order to mobilize adaptive behavior on the part of organizational members, leaders engage in six core tasks, starting with the articulation of a sense of purpose and direction for the organization coupled with demanding performance goals. Employees can then adapt to changing circumstances by finding new and innovative ways of meeting the performance expectations while aligned with the company's purpose and direction.

Communication channels, especially upward communication, support new behaviors and help ensure that leaders will learn from employees at all levels about the effectiveness of their efforts. Building employee commitment to the organization enhances the internalized motivation so critical in a change effort, which, in turn, helps energize learning and adaptation. Developing future leaders and creating effective teamwork at the top will greatly enhance an organization's ability to adapt, change, and maintain outstanding performance.

It is often said in organizations that if you are not leading change, you are not leading. That expression captures the central role of leadership to a change effort. It does not acknowledge, however, the difficulty in playing such a role. Just as a leader cannot run an organization on her own, no individual leader can change an organization. Effective change leadership requires that collaborative partnership among those individuals who hold positions of formal authority and employees at other organizational levels who can participate in the process of leading change. Entering into such a partnership involves formal leaders ceding their unilateral control and allowing for a kind of shared authority in which multiple parties participate. The goal, of course, is to enhance the likelihood that change will produce results that benefit the organization as a whole.

Discussion Questions

1. How would you account for Robert Horton's early exit as CEO of British Petroleum?
2. It is said that if you are not leading change, you are not leading. Do you agree or disagree with that statement? Explain.
3. Why is upward communication so difficult to achieve in organizations? Explain the barriers that exist and how leaders might overcome them.
4. Why is a strong emotional bond with the company especially important in times of change? What specific steps can leaders take to create such a bond?
5. Do you agree that traditional approaches to leadership development can hurt a company's effort to develop effective change leaders? Explain.

Case Discussion

Read "Leading Change—Carlos Ghosn at Renault and Nissan" and prepare answers to the following questions:

1. What are the strengths and weaknesses of Carlos Ghosn's approach to change leadership at Nissan? To what extent has he succeeded in mobilizing adaptive behavior on the part of employees?
2. Using the core tasks of leadership (Exhibit 8-1), evaluate Ghosn's change leadership at Nissan.
3. What are the beliefs and values of Ghosn concerning leadership and change? Show how those beliefs and values have been enacted at his various leadership positions.
4. Has Ghosn "walked the talk" on his leadership style, that is, aligned his actions with his words?

Leading Change—Carlos Ghosn at Renault and Nissan

"There is no business executive in the world I would rather see at the helm of Renault. Carlos has a golden touch. First at Michelin, then at Nissan—everywhere he has been he has turned disaster into success. He is very strong, very forceful, and very positive."

"Look, I cannot deny his past successes. But really, what has he done? He has relied almost exclusively on slash-and-burn techniques to cut costs and return these companies to profitability. But how long can that last? He has not brought any new ideas to the running of business: just cut costs. He is now returning to a profitable Renault. I'm unsure of what he can do now."

"I think you both are missing the point. Ghosn's past has been impressive, no doubt about it. But why is he trying to run two companies at the same time? Does he believe too much his own press? The way it is now, he cannot focus properly on either Nissan or Renault."

Three French executives offering contrasting reflections on Carlos Ghosn upon his return to Renault in April 2005.

Whatever qualms some executives may have felt about Carlos Ghosn (name is pronounced to rhyme with "phone"), senior management at France-based Renault harbored no such misgivings.[32] In April 2005, chairman Louis Schweitzer announced that Ghosn would return to Paris to assume control of Renault. Over the past five and a half years, Ghosn had engineered a remarkable turnaround at Nissan Motors, headquartered in the Ginza district of Tokyo. He had moved from Paris to Japan as part of the 1999 Renault-Nissan alliance. Ghosn's return to Paris, however, would not remove him from oversight of Nissan. He vowed to serve as a dual CEO—leading both Renault and Nissan, dividing his time evenly between the two.

Ghosn's career involved a number of remarkable leadership opportunities: Michelin Brazil, Michelin North America, Renault, Nissan, and now the Renault-Nissan alliance. But no story is more dramatic or exemplary of his approach to change management than his tenure at Nissan.

Nissan Motor Company

As part of a 74-firm Japanese *zaibatsu*—a powerful, interconnected industrial combination that included Hitachi, Nippon Mining, and Nissan Chemical—Nissan leveraged its considerable assets into becoming Japan's number-two automaker (behind Toyota).[33] Nissan began exporting their Datsun cars to the United States in 1958 and 17 years later became the top-selling import in the U.S. market. Their sporty Datsun 240Z, known as the Z car, gained an especially loyal following based on its reputation as "the ultimate thrill machine, an unbeatable combination of rakish lines, raw horsepower and affordability that young Japanese and American guys found impossible to resist."

A number of management missteps kicked off a debilitating and long-lasting decline starting in the 1980s. Executives changed the company's brand name in the United States from the popular Datsun to the completely unfamiliar Nissan. Additionally, they allowed their popular Z car to drift and decline with little infusion of innovative technology. Less obvious but even more troubling was Nissan's inability to find flexibility in its relationship with suppliers. Their cost of parts ranged from 15 percent to 20 percent above domestic competitors. Aggressive competition from Honda in the United States forced Nissan to take a $1,000 discount on their cars.

Sales declined, but costs did not. Despite several announced restructuring plans, Nissan executives achieved little real improvement. "Powerful trade unions, a societal taboo against layoffs and institutional inertia stalled any real changes." After the company borrowed money from the government-owned Japan Development Bank to stay afloat, executives decided to court potential partners. Talks with both DaimlerChrysler and Ford proved fruitless. France-based Renault agreed to an alliance. As a precondition of the alliance, Nissan executives agreed that Renault's second-in-command, Carlos Ghosn, would come to Japan as COO under CEO Yoshikazu Hanawa. The agreement was announced on April 15, 1999—and the Ghosn era at Nissan began.

Carlos Ghosn

Ghosn was born in Brazil in 1952 to a French mother and Lebanese father. He moved to Lebanon at the age of six to attend a French Jesuit school. He received his college education in Paris, first at the Ecole Polytechnique and then at the Ecole des Mines de Paris. Representatives from Michelin, a privately held French tire company, approached Ghosn in March 1978 while he was still a student. They were looking for French-educated engineers who could speak Portuguese (Ghosn's first language) to help them build a market in Brazil. Ghosn accepted their offer and worked his way through several manufacturing positions in France, South America, and the United States before joining Renault.

Ghosn at Renault

In October 1996 Ghosn joined Renault when CEO Louis Schweitzer offered him the number-two position (with potential succession to the top position). Ghosn had already developed a philosophy of change leadership at Michelin based on three premises:

- Assume nothing (find answers within the company).
- Work fast.
- Earn trust and respect with strong results.

At Renault, his formal assignment was to run engineering, manufacturing, and purchasing. However, Ghosn's main responsibility was to cut costs.

RENAULT.   Ghosn's early analysis of Renault's problems led him to conclude that the company culture emphasized narrow, functionally based thinking at the expense of a larger strategic view:

> The company was organized into completely separate departments, like silos. The heads of the departments often turned them into baronies or fiefdoms. This was an enormous problem, because I felt the road to recovery lay in implementing cross-functionality. And advocating crossfunctionality is tantamount to challenging certain practices that belong to certain functions. But I believed that cross-functionality was fundamental to our success . . . We had to break down some high walls and reorganize the company so that everyone worked together.

Relying on cross-functional teams, Ghosn came up with a plan to reduce costs by $4 billion in three years.

His plan, which included closing Renault's plant in Vilvoorde, Belgium, with its 3,500 jobs, earned him the lasting nickname: "le cost killer." Ghosn claimed to have no problem with his reputation:

> Businesses have always tried to reduce costs . . . I don't see how one can manage a business without keeping one eye glued to expenses. It's a fantasy to think otherwise. . . . There have been very few successful extravagant captains of industry.

Renault returned to profitability in 1997.

Within the company, Ghosn earned a reputation as a tough, demanding boss who set "brutally high standards." At the same time, executives considered him a consensus builder with a "knack for getting straight to the heart of tough problems and . . . an ability to motivate others by setting ambitious but realistic targets." Ghosn avoided personal confrontation. "To my knowledge," he said, reflecting on his entry into the Renault executive suite, "there were no personal conflicts, because by definition I'm not a confrontational man. I try to manage pressure where I find it. I don't make scenes or attack people. I'm firm, but not confrontational."

RENAULT-NISSAN ALLIANCE   Throughout the 1990s, Renault sought a partnership with another carmaker in order to expand its market reach. Early attempts had been disastrous. The company proved unable to close a potential deal for Volvo. Their purchase of U.S.-based AMC cost Renault billions of dollars before selling that unit off to Chrysler. Schweitzer and Ghosn, however, remained convinced that the company needed a partner to help it break out of the confining European market (85 percent of all company sales were in Europe) and seek robust sales in Asia and North America.

After Nissan's merger talks with DaimlerChrysler fell through, Ghosn pursued serious negotiations with the Japanese carmaker. As the companies engaged in talks, a difference in style and culture—Renault's highly legalistic style clashed with Nissan's preference for broad-based discussion—threatened to undermine potential agreement. Ghosn proposed cross-company teams to look at all opportunities for synergistic effort, creating 11 teams of members from similar jobs in the two companies. Once the companies approved the alliance, these teams allowed Ghosn to have a head start on what needed to be done at Nissan.

The 1999 alliance called for Renault to acquire a 36.8 percent stake in Nissan. "We are not merging," noted Renault's CEO Louis Schweitzer, "we are creating a bi-national company." At the time, Nissan had $19.9 billion in debt and losses of $250 million for the year. The company had posted losses seven out of the previous eight years. Their domestic market share had sunk from 34 percent in 1974 to under 19 percent in 1999, their global market share from 7 percent to under 5 percent.

Ghosn at Nissan

Upon his arrival in Japan, Ghosn announced that his goal was not to advance the interests of Renault but rather "to do everything in my power to bring Nissan back to profitability at the earliest date possible and revive it as a highly attractive company." He realized the delicate position in which he found himself:

> In corporate turnarounds, particularly those related to mergers or alliances, success is not simply a matter of making fundamental changes to a company's organization and operations. You also have to protect the company's identity and the self-esteem of its people. Those two goals—making changes and safeguarding identity—can easily come into conflict; pursuing them both entails a difficult and sometimes precarious balancing act. That was particularly true in this case. I was, after all, an outsider—non-Nissan, non-Japanese—and was initially met with skepticism by the company's managers and employees. I knew that if I tried to dictate changes from above, the effort would backfire, undermining morale and productivity. But if I was too passive, the company would simply continue its downward spiral.

The challenge, he said, was to save the business without losing the company.

While he was not the first Westerner to take the reins of a Japanese auto company (an American had led Mazda after Ford purchased the company), the local press still wondered how a Westerner would fit in and be able to adjust. Ghosn held no such concerns:

> By focusing on specific business objectives, people don't have time to worry about cultural differences or politicking (which is obviously a very dangerous thing in an alliance or merger). This focus on results instead of politics gives you a much greater opportunity to create a success in an alliance or merger if the turnaround works. Realistically, though, it can jeopardize the whole merger or alliance if it doesn't work.

He believed that by focusing on performance, he could bypass concerns for cultural differences.

By inclination, Ghosn avoided making sweeping changes in the makeup of his executive committee. He said he would make personnel changes only after giving people a "reasonable time" to change. "I do it, but only when necessary. I consider it a waste. It is more of a challenge to me to change people from within. It is more long-lasting and beneficial—more powerful—to change people than to change persons." Within two years of his arrival, however, Ghosn did remove a number of key executives for failure to meet performance targets. Accountability, he repeated over and over, *must* start at the top.

Ghosn insisted on consistency between the stated beliefs of top executives and their actions:

> Top management is highly visible. What we think, what we say, and what we do must be the same. We have to be impeccable in ensuring that our words correspond to our actions. If there are discrepancies between what we profess and how we behave, that will spell disaster. Included in this is our accountability. We must be committed to the responsibilities we've agreed to. When we don't deliver, we have to face the consequences. The Japanese culture is a very proud culture. Our workers and managers want to succeed. For that matter, so do the unions inside Nissan. They want to be proud of their company and their management. They need management to manage. And good management involves accountability.

Leaders, in his view, must do what they say and say what they do.

Early Diagnosis

Between April and late June 1999, Ghosn toured Nissan plants, subsidiaries, and dealerships in Japan, the United States, Europe, and Taiwan. He had learned from his experience at Michelin to start change without any preconceived ideas:

> This is extremely important in management. You must start with a clean sheet of paper because the worst thing that you can have is prefabricated solutions . . . you have to start with a zero base of thinking, cleaning everything out of your mind.

Performance numbers told him a great deal about Nissan but not the underlying causes of their problems. "You have to go out in the field to see what's going on." Ghosn engaged in a process he called "deep listening," speaking to over 5,000 people:

> I asked people what they thought was going right, what they thought was going wrong, and what they would suggest to make things better. I was trying to arrive at an analysis that wouldn't be static but would identify what we could do to improve the company's performance. It was a period of intensive, active listening. I took notes. I accumulated documents that contained very precise assessments of the different situations we had to deal with, and I drew up my own personal summaries of what I learned. In the course of those three months, I must have met more than a thousand people.

Ghosn's diagnostic tour built a good deal of hope and high expectations.

Almost immediately, Ghosn announced three changes based on decisions he had arrived at on his own:

1. The "official language" of Nissan would become English and all top management meetings would be held in English. Executives who did not learn English immediately would have to leave the company.

2. The Japanese press would be invited to attend Nissan shareholder meetings as a way of making Nissan's current problems and future plans transparent to the public.

3. The position of regional president for Europe and North America was replaced with four cross-functional management teams.

By early July, Ghosn reached some conclusions about Nissan. Perhaps the most surprising was the lack of urgency among Nissan executives: "For a company that has been losing money for seven years out of eight, there is not enough of a sense of urgency. People should be banging their heads on the walls everywhere." Increasing a sense of urgency was on his mind when he announced his diagnosis to the press and, more importantly, to employees within the company. In an "all-hands" presentation carried across the company via closed-circuit television, Ghosn listed strengths and weaknesses:

The fact that he spoke directly to employees was especially important to Ghosn:

Now, it's impossible to resurrect a failing company without first diagnosing its problems and then making sure everyone in the enterprise knows the results of your diagnosis. If there's a reticence about sharing the results, there can be no shared sense of urgency. . . . You have to identify the problem and circulate your diagnosis. When we pointed out in public that some of Nissan's products were not all that attractive, we got a lot of criticism. . . . But it was this very statement, the frank admission that some of the products in our line weren't appealing, that allowed us to straighten things out, even if what we said may have had a short-term negative effect.

Ghosn was enacting what he considered to be his primary role: "The only power that a CEO has is to motivate. The rest is nonsense."

Cross-Functional Teams

To enrich his diagnosis and specify action plans, Ghosn returned to cross-functional teams:

In my experience, executives in a company rarely reach across boundaries. Typically engineers prefer solving problems with other engineers, salespeople like to work with fellow salespeople, and Americans feel more comfortable with other Americans. The trouble is that people working in functional or regional teams tend not to ask themselves as many hard questions as they should. By contrast, working together in cross-functional teams helps managers to think in new ways and challenge existing practices. The teams also provide a mechanism for explaining the necessity for change and for projecting difficult messages across the entire company.

Ghosn pulled together nine cross-functional teams to examine all aspects of the business operation: from business development to manufacturing and logistics to supplier relationships to organizational structure. Each had ten members, all from middle management. Teams could also create subteams to help them collect data. In total, the effort involved about 500 people. Ghosn gave the teams three months to review the company's operations and make recommendations.

Only three explicit rules governed the activities of the teams. First: "Nothing is off limits to discuss and explore. Teams are not to be hindered by traditions or avoid sensitive corporate issues." Second: Teams had no decision-making power. That was left in the hands of the executive committee. And third: "Only one issue is non-negotiable: the return to profit."

Ghosn was tough and demanding on team members. When the purchasing team, for example, came back with a plan to reduce costs by 10 percent over three years, Ghosn's response devastated them. "Ghosn rejected our recommendations outright," recalled a team member. "He told us they were not aggressive enough. He told us to come back with recommendations that will yield 20 percent savings over the next three years." Far from being discouraged, the group went back to work. After what was recalled as "a wrenching two weeks of hard work and tough negotiations," the group met Ghosn's expectations with recommendations that, in retrospect, seemed obvious.

"Mr. Ghosn is always challenging us to make higher commitments and targets," said an executive. "We [constantly] talk about challenge and stretch." Added another executive, "I have never worked for anyone who is so demanding."

Nissan Revival Plan (NRP)

With the recommendations from the nine cross-functional teams Ghosn and the executive committee pulled together what became known as the Nissan Revival Plan. In October 1999, Ghosn announced that plan to the press, to employees, and to the public. He started his presentation by saying, "The key facts and figures about Nissan point to a reality: Nissan is in bad shape." The highlights of his action plan included:

- Reduce operating costs by $10 billion
- Cut the number of parts and material suppliers in half
- Create new product investment and rollout, including launch of 22 new models by 2002—capital investment increased from 3.5 percent in 1999 to 5.5 percent in 2002
- Reduce global head count by 21,000
- Reduce number of vehicle assembly plants in Japan from seven to four
- Reduce number of manufacturing platforms in Japan from 24 to 15

"The combination of growth and cost reduction will allow Nissan to achieve a consolidated operating profit of 4.5 percent or more of sales by FY 2002." Revival would depend on more than cost cutting, he emphasized. "While cost cutting will be the most dramatic and visible part of the plan, we cannot save our way to success."

In the question-and-answer period that followed his presentation, a reporter asked if Ghosn was prepared to take responsibility for the company's performance. If Nissan is not profitable in 2000, Ghosn responded, he and the entire executive committee would resign. Committee members had made that agreement privately but had not expected Ghosn to make it public. In hindsight, Ghosn thought it was an important statement. "To say Nissan will be profitable or I'll quit . . . this struck a chord. [Fellow] executive committee members were obviously surprised when they heard of my remark."

The Nissan Revival Plan contained several significant departures from traditional Japanese approaches to management. Nissan's relationship with suppliers, for example, represented the *keiretsu* system that linked large manufacturers, like Nissan, to its suppliers often through cross-held stock. "The *keiretsu* was like a big family," noted a reporter. "In the 1980s it was considered one of the key components of the success of Japanese manufacturing, as the cozy relationships ensured that manufacturers were delivered high quality parts, manufactured to specification, as they were needed." With suppliers now placing Nissan at a considerable cost disadvantage, Ghosn targeted the system. The number of suppliers would be cut in half, and they would be expected to cut costs by 20 percent by 2003.

Additionally, all purchasing would be centralized. Said Ghosn, "Purchasing represents 60 percent of our total costs, or a minimum of 58 percent of our net sales. Today, Nissan buys parts and materials on a regional basis, or even in certain areas on a country basis. This will stop immediately." From that point forward, purchasing would be centralized and globalized.

Traditional human resource policies would also be changed. Said Ghosn:

> Like other Japanese companies, Nissan paid and promoted its employees based on their tenure and age. The longer employees stuck around, the more power and money they received, regardless of their actual performance. Inevitably, that practice bred a certain degree of complacency, which undermined Nissan's competitiveness.

Nissan's seniority system would be abandoned, along with their approach to pay:

> In the traditional Japanese compensation system, managers receive no share options, and hardly any incentives are built into the manager's pay packet . . . We changed all that. High performers today can expect cash incentives that amount to more than a third of the annual pay packages, on top of which employees receive company stock options.

The revival plan sent shock waves not just through the company but through the entire nation. Japan's stock market reacted by dropping Nissan's price a full 20 percent. Ghosn was not alarmed:

> To be able to make changes, it is necessary to do some hard things. If you do those things, it does not mean that you do not value people. In my opinion, the reverse is true. People who do not tell the truth do not respect people. My concept of respect for people starts with telling the truth and establishing the facts of a situation.

Telling the truth and establishing the facts of a situation—those were to be the hallmarks of Ghosn's approach.

Results and More Plans

Nissan achieved the results promised in the Nissan Revival Plan a full year ahead of time. Ghosn became president of Nissan in 2000 and CEO in 2001. At that time, he announced a new plan, named NISSAN 180:

> Through NRP we transformed a struggling company into a good company; through NISSAN 180, we will transform a good company into a great company. The achievement of NISSAN 180 will rely on four pillars: more revenue, less costs, more quality and speed and a maximized alliance with Renault.

Once again, Nissan made good on its promises. "The story of Nissan's revival is now complete."

Moving Up

In April 2005, Ghosn officially returned to France to run Renault, announcing that he would continue to oversee Nissan. "I won't be a part-timer, but one CEO with two hats." Forty percent of his time, he said, would be spent in Japan (with Toshiyuki Shiga serving as Nissan COO), 40 percent in France, and the rest globally. In fact, Ghosn played a *third* role as well. The alliance board of directors—the body designated to oversee the strategy of the alliance as well as any and all activities undertaken jointly by Renault and Nissan**—had been headed jointly by the CEOs of Renault and Nissan, as well as five senior executives from each. With Ghosn now serving in both CEO roles, he became, in essence, the chairman of the joint board.

"It is very flattering," said Ghosn of his emergence as a kind of global superstar, "but at the same time you know that you are as good as your last quarter results or your last six-month results or your last year results. I know very well the rules. As long as you perform, you are good. Your management is as good as your performance."

Rough Seas at Renault

As he had done at Nissan, Ghosn set ambitious plans for Renault, emphasizing the introduction of 26 new models by 2009. As the market awaited the arrival of the redesigned compact Megane and other models, Renault sales slipped while competitors Fiat and Volkswagen grew. Profits at Nissan declined for three straight quarters and the Renault stock price took a beating. After selling off one-and-a-half million Renault shares, a fund manager expressed a concern. "The near term looks weak," he said, "and we remain concerned that Carlos Ghosn is still running both Renault and Nissan." Ghosn, however, reassured employees, customers, and the market. "My record," he said simply, "is to do what I said I was going to do."

**Joint activities included shared purchasing, shared research on fuel cell technology, shared factories in Mexico and Brazil, and shared car platforms.

Endnotes

1. The information in this case is based on Steven Butler, "Cutting Down and Reshaping the Core," *Financial Times*, March 20, 1990, p. 22; Horton's quotes are from Toni Mack, "Eager Lions and Reluctant Lions," *Forbes*, February 17, 1992, pp. 98–101; Christopher Lorenz, "Refining the Strategy," *Financial Times*, February 21, 1992, p. 16; Ian Hargreaves, "When Toughness is not Enough," *Financial Times*, June 26, 1992, p. 19; Manfred Kets de Vries and Elizabeth Florent-Treacy, *British Petroleum: Transformational Leadership in a Transnational Organization* (Fontainebleau: INSEAD, 1997).

2. *Forbes*, February 17, 1992, p. 101.

3. "Xerox Chief Aims to Bring Color to the World," *Boston Globe*, November 27, 2005, p. D3.

4. This definition of leadership as mobilizing adaptive behavior is offered by Ronald A. Heifetz, *Leadership Without Easy Answers* (Cambridge, MA: Belknap Press, 1994).

5. *Ibid.*, p. 20.

6. John P. Kotter, *The Leadership Factor* (New York: Free Press, 1988), p. 17.

7. See Bert Spector, "From Bogged Down to Fired Up: Inspiring Organizational Change," *Sloan Management Review* 30 (Summer 1989), pp. 29–34.

8. Jacques Steinberg, "They Know All the Stupid Sitcom Writer Tricks," *New York Times*, September 11, 2005, sec. 2, p. 90.

9. On Worldwide Pants, see Jacques Steinberg, "They Know All the Stupid Sitcom Writer Tricks," *New York Times*, September 11, 2005, Section 2, p. 90. On MySpace, see Patricia Sellers, "MySpace Cowboys," *Fortune*, September 4, 2006, pp. 66–74.

10. Sellers, "MySpace Cowboys," p. 74.

11. Christopher A. Bartlett and Sumantra Ghoshal, "Changing the Role of Top Management: Beyond Strategy to Purpose," *Harvard Business Review* (November–December 1994), p. 82.

12. Jim Collins, *Good to Great: Why Some Companies Make the Leap . . . and Others Don't* (New York: Harper Business, 2001), p. 30. Emphasis in the original.

13. See Michael Beer, Russell A. Eisenstat, and Bert Spector, *The Critical Path to Corporate Renewal* (Boston: Harvard Business School Press, 1990).

14. Edwin A. Locke and Gary P. Latham, *Goal Setting: A Motivational Technique That Works!* (New Jersey: Prentice-Hall, 1984).

15. Dvora Yanow, "Translating Local Knowledge at Organizational Peripheries," *British Journal of Management* 15 (2004), pp. 9–25.

16. Roderick D. Iverson and Parimal Roy, "A Casual Model of Behavioral Commitment: Evidence from a Study of Australian Blue-Collar Employees," *Journal of Management* 20 (1994), pp. 15–41; Roderick D. Iverson, "Employee Acceptance of Organizational Change: The Role of Organizational Commitment," *International Journal of Human Resource Management* 7 (February 1996), pp. 122–149; Jon R. Katzenbach and Jason A. Santamaria, "Firing Up the Front Line," *Harvard Business Review* (May–June 1999), pp. 107–117.

17. Information on Southwest Airlines is from Jody Hoffier, *The Southwest Airlines Way* (New York: McGraw-Hill, 2003), and James L. Heskett, *Southwest Airlines 2002: An Industry Under Siege* (Boston: Harvard Business School Publishing, 2003).

18. Paul R. Lawrence and Nitin Nohria, *Driven: How Human Nature Shapes Organizations* (San Francisco: Jossey-Bass, 2001).

19. Quoted in Beer, Eisenstat, and Spector, *The Critical Path to Corporate Renewal*, p. 85.

20. James C. Collins and Jerry I. Porras, *Built to Last: Successful Habits of Visionary Companies* (New York: Harper Business, 1994).

21. Quoted in Ellen Florian Kratz and Doris Burke, "Get Me a CEO from GE!" *Fortune*, April 18, 2005, p. 148.

22. Ron Morris, "Great Leaders Are Born; Great Managers Are Made," *Techyvent Pittsburg*, November 7, 2005.

23. John Baldoni quoted at *www.johnbaldoni.com*.

24. Paul R. Lawrence and Davis Dyer, *Renewing American Industry* (New York: Free Press, 1983).

25. Dan Baum, "Battle Lessons," *New Yorker*, January 17, 2005, p. 42.

26. Max Boot, "The Struggle to Transform the Military," *Foreign Affairs* 84 (March–April 2005), p. 109.

27. John Kotter, *Leading Change* (Boston: Harvard Business School Press, 1996).

28. See Kathleen M. Eisenhardt, Jean L. Kahwajy, and L. J. Bourgeois III, "How Top Management Teams Can Have a Good Fight," *Harvard Business Review* (July–August 1997), pp. 77–86.

29. Gibson Burrell and Gareth Morgan, *Sociological Paradigms and Organizational Analysis* (London: Heinemann, 1979).

30. Victoria Emerson, "An Interview with Carlos Ghosn," *Journal of World Business* 36 (Spring 2001), p. 9.

31. Ralph Stayer, "How I Learned to Let My Workers Lead," *Harvard Business Review* (November–December 1990), p. 66.

32. This case is based on the following publications: Michael A. Cusumano, *The Japanese Automobile Industry: Technology and Management at Nissan and Toyota* (Cambridge, MA: Council on East Asian Studies, 1985); Emily Thornton, "Remaking Nissan," *Business Week*, November 15, 1999, p. 70; Stephane Farhi, "Ghosn Sees Fast Start at Nissan," *Automotive News* 73 (April 5, 1999), p. 1; S. Strom, "In a Change, Nissan Opens Annual Meeting to Press," *New York Times*, June 26, 1999, p. C2; Chester Dawson, "The Zen of Nissan," *Business Week*, July 22, 2002, p. 142; Carlos Ghosn, "Saving the Business without Losing the Company," *Harvard Business Review* (January 2002), Michael Yoshino and Masako Egawa, *Nissan Motor Co., Ltd., 2002* (Boston: Harvard Business School Publishing, 2002); Michael Yoshino and Perry L. Fagan, *The Renault-Nissan Alliance* (Boston: Harvard Business School Publishing, 2002); David Furlonger, "Back from the Brink of Failure," *Financial Mail*, June 28, 2002, p. 102; Carlos Ghosn, speech at INSEAD Global Leader Series, September 24, 2002; Tim Larimer, "Japan, Nissan and the Ghosn Revolution," *Chazen Web Journal of International Business* (Spring 2003), p. 5; David Magee, *Turnaround: How Carlos Ghosn Rescued Nissan* (New York: HarperCollins, 2003); Brian Bremmer, "Nissan's Boss," *Business Week*, October 4, 2004, p. 50; Carlos Ghosn and Philippe Ries, *Shift: Inside Nissan's Historical Revival* (New York: Currency, 2005); "Nissan Reports Record Results for FY04," *Japan's Corporate News*, May 25, 2005, p. 1 (*www.japancorp.net/Article.Asp?Art ID=9931*) James Brooke, "Nissan's Mr. Fix-It Is the Talk of Detroit," *New York Times*, November 19, 2005, p. C4; Laurence Frost, "Renault's Chief Losing Support as Share Price Drops," *International Herald Tribune*, September 8–9, 2007, p. 13.

33. For background on Nissan, see Michael A. Cusumano, *The Japanese Automobile Industry: Technology and Management at Nissan and Toyota* (Cambridge, MA: Council on East Asian Studies, 1985).

INDEX